2

BLIND GLORY

BLIND GLORY

Colonel Bo's Middle East
Spy Assignment

Col. Heath Bottomly, USAF (Ret.)

VANTAGE PRESS
New York

Published by Vantage Press, Inc.
419 Park Ave. South, New York, NY 10016

Manufactured in the United States of America
ISBN: 978-0-533-15829-4

Library of Congress Catalog Card No.: 2007904291

0 9 8 7 6 5 4 3 2 1

Author's Note

That which you are about to read will sound like a story—a Cold War story. But really, it's more than a story. It's a patch of world history. For half a century this tiny patch on the complex Cold War quilt has been cloaked in secrecy. Why? Because this is a spy story. And like every serious spy assignment, if it goes bust, no one ever knows about it. This one was particularly dicey because if the truth had surfaced earlier, the war in Iraq would have come fifty years earlier and would have involved Israel and the U.S. against all the desert and oil nations of Asia Minor. Moreover, in this one, I was the spy, and I was sworn to secrecy. And even though I got caught red-handed, I escaped—so no one was ever to know.

I'm eighty-eight years old now. When I die, this story dies with me. But this is history and it happened to me, an American fighting man, so I'm telling it before it's too late. I am fully aware this is a personal honor violation, but so is silence. And the man to whom I swore secrecy, William Colby, masterspy, is now dead and the Cold War is over and the war in Iraq and Afghanistan has turned the Arabs against us anyway; so, to hell with it, I'm telling the story.

My credentials—for 33 years, I flew and fought for my country through four wars in every major theater in the world. I began with the old Army Air Corps in WWII. We flew Aussie Spitfires off the Fijis and Henderson Field, Guadalcanal, until our Lightnings arrived. We covered MacArthur's return to the Philippines, then finally, we checked out in the Mustang on Okinawa and destroyed the Flying Sun. Then following VJ-Day, we flew the first Jets in Japan and Korea out of Yakota, then K-28 in Korea. Next came a tour in the Middle East as graduate student, peacekeeper and spy. On a tour in Europe, we stood nuclear alert with the F-101 at Royal Air Force Station Bentwaters in East Anglia. Next, I went to Vietnam as commander of a task force of A-37s and then on to Thailand commanding a wing of F-105 Thuds. In between combat assignments, I served with the NSC in the White House and as Secretary of the Joint Chiefs of Staff in the Pentagon. I went out with the Twentieth Century, but every time things get hot in the Middle East, I get recalled to active duty. Why? Because some of my graduate school classmates at the American University in Beirut now own the gulf and desert oil. Others lever the powerful mullahs. Still others drive OPEC. The most nationalistic Arab leaders today are old classmates of mine. I know which side they're on—which will join us and which will twist our tail?

BLIND GLORY

One

The trouble with William Egan Colby as a spy was that he looked like a spy. Cecil B. DeMille, the classic film director, stopped him on the street in New York—didn't know him from Adam—and asked him if he'd ever read Baroness Orczy's book. They walked and talked. DeMille said that he had always wanted to film *The Scarlet Pimpernel.* He offered Colby the lead right there on a bench in Central Park. No dice.

Jack Kennedy knew Bill Colby. He knew that for half a century, this iceman had been the most productive and the least exciting undercover agent in the world. Both Malenkov and Khrushchev had offered him a million bucks and a dacha on the Black Sea to come over. No dice.

Kennedy wanted to reward Colby with the top job at Langley. He called him in from a very productive position in Berlin in 1973 and made him head of the Central Intelligence Agency—made him important. This was a mistake. Colby didn't want to be important. He was satisfied, and his countrymen were happy, with his just being the best.

In 1976, Nixon fired him, and I thought at the time, *A very compassionate move, Richard—and very brave. You'll be roundly criticized, but you've saved his life.* Nixon knew something about secrets. He suspected that once surfaced, Colby wouldn't live a year. He was wrong. Colby was good. It took the KGB's Joseph Bizanski twenty-three years. On Wednesday, 14 May 1996, in a season especially unsuited for solemnizing the despairs of heroic sacrifice, Colby's body bobbed

1

to the surface of a swollen tributary of the Potomac. The soldier-priest, as his colleagues called him, had paid the price—paid-in-full for quietly and carefully serving his country for half a century as his nation's spymaster. It took President Reagan to say it right: "Bill Colby may have had more to do with our victory in the Cold War than any other single soul."

Well, this story does not focus on William Egan Colby, masterspy. But like a thousand stories involving America's interlocking relationship with her allies in NATO, her third world little brothers in democracy and with former archenemy, Soviet Union, William Egan Colby opens and closes this story. And you will find his uncanny, electric presence connects the twelve separate vignettes that make up this story.

First, the setting—a lone cypress tree a thousand years old stands guard at the northeast corner of the American University campus in Beirut, Lebanon. This gnarled but proud relic of a tree hangs on the edge of a steep, limestone cliff. To the west, the Mediterranean Sea paints its epic blue, eight thousand miles west—a third of the way around the globe—to the Rock of Gibraltar.

A mile up the coast to the north lies the harbor and action center of the bustling crossroads city of Beirut. Directly below this tree falls the student path-of-steps. These steps cut in the stone, zigzag a thousand feet down the cliff to the university swimming beach. Harbor Boulevard starts there at the swimming beach and follows the waterfront north, around the busy port, to the world-famous St. George Hotel.

The St. George was once the watering hole and crossroads of caravan routes connecting India, Persia and the ancient silk road from China to Turkey, Greece and western Europe. But by mid-20th century it had become the elegant, wealthy tourist rest stop to anywhere "out east." It served the best cuisine beyond Karpages in Ankara. And it served it in the most sumptuous and exciting out-over-the-water dining facility on earth. Still, with all its upscale, European elegance, what put Beirut on the world map was St. George's jazzy, Kit Kat Klub downstairs. There, in a strange world of smoke, loud music and laughter, it hosted—and still does on certain days, I'm told—the largest and most intricate spy rendezvous on Earth.

More important to us grad students in the 1950s, the hotel's front to the city of Beirut is a lush, green park. It was huge—perhaps three acres—complete with age-old, gum arabic trees, picnic tables, and live music in the evening—a cool place for students to hang out on Friday nights.

Najua stood beside the cypress tree sort of collecting herself before we started down. "A thousand steps, they say, to the bottom. Do you believe that?" Her coal black hair caught the sea's twilight whisper. It danced a swirl, then fell soft across her face and throat.

"Of course," I laughed. "Who's going to count?" I stepped past her and started down the sandy path. But Najua caught my arm and turned me to face the sunset.

"Holy Smoke!" I exhaled it. It was exactly that time of day! It was that moment of Technicolor majesty that has struck man speechless through the ages. Looking west across the sea from the cliff path, we watched the dying sun laying half in, half out of the sea at the farthest reach of its golden path.

Together, frozen in breathless wonder, we watched it slide quickly down. It was gone. Only the scarf of burnished gold hung there on the surface of the sea. Then it turned scarlet, bled to violet, deepened to purple. Finally, it just vanished.

We stood there hand-in-hand sort of glorying in God's breathtaking beauty. Then, bonded by the magic of the moment, Najua turned against me, and I took her in my arms. We held each other perhaps a minute, warm and close. And, though the events of this night would tear us forever apart, neither of us would ever forget this moment of sweet, gentle, passion at sunset.

The cliff path down from the ancient cypress tree is guarded only by the west wind. There is no rail. The path and steps are cut into the native limestone plate that rises sharply out of the water—and upon whose peak, two thousand feet straight up, the university campus is sited. It is truly a glorious park-like place for a college campus, and it is an awesome cliff in its own right. The path must measure a quarter of a mile zigzagging down to the beach and to the street that connects to the city-center downtown.

The students find it an exciting, breathtaking route used by many undergrads to escape to the city. The more mature, the parents and the faculty take the civilized route via Le Boulevard St. Charles that winds down the hill from the opposite end of the campus. Needless to say, though exciting going down, the cliff route is a very athletic journey up. Equally needless is the observation that with no guardrail and unpredictable, onshore wind puffs, either up or down, this route is a legitimate terror by night.

I held Najua's hand most of the descent. It was safer that way, and too, we were very much in love. Perhaps halfway down, laughing, chattering and enjoying the warm, summer twilight, we were stopped by a shout from above. "Major! . . . Najua! . . . Wait up!" It was my roommate, Shukri, charging headlong down the path to catch up.

Najua and I sat down on a step, side-by-side, to catch our breaths and to await Shukri's arrival. Several small clutches of friends passed us on their way down and other

4

couples were further down while still others were above us, coming. It was going to be another lively Friday night at the St. George park.

I should introduce myself. I'm the storyteller. In 1951 I was a thirty-year-old, United States Air Force Major. After graduation from West Point early in WWII, I was assigned to fighters and sent to the Southwest Pacific. I fought up the island chain with General Kenny's 35th Fighter Group of Fifth Air Force. When the Korean War broke, I was commanding the only jet squadron in the Orient, the 82d Tactical Reconnaissance Squadron at Yakota, Japan. We moved it to K-28 near Seoul and along with a dozen or so other fighter and bomber units, fought our way to a major, air-war victory. The ground war, as you will recall, went back and forth and ended pretty much where it began.

You may remember the controversy in strategy between General MacArthur, the Supreme Commander Allied Powers, and President Truman and his Secretary of State Dean Acheson. This disputed strategic leadership, plus Mao Zedong's Chinese Army of a million, twisted the allied victory into a long, drawn-out, stalemate—a stalemate still holding today, more than half a century later.

I returned from Korea to the U.S. in 1951 like all jet-fighter pilots then, sort of a hero. I expected to be assigned to command a squadron in one of the Z.I. fighter wings. Nyet! As often happens in the service, when heroes return from war, back home they are not nearly the heroes they thought they were. I was assigned to a non-flying graduate school billet at a place I could not even find on the map, The American University of Beirut in Lebanon, the troubled Eastern Mediterranean republic. I was devastated. In fact I was fit-to-be-tied, and I raised enough dust to find myself in the Pentagon office of the Air Force Chief of Staff.

As I walked into the Chief's outer office, I noticed the motto on his E-ring Door: *The mission of the United States Air Force is to fly and fight, and don't you ever forget that!* Inside I found cool, erudite, strategic organizing genius, General Hoyt S. Vandenberg. I explained that I was a career fighter pilot just back from the war, and I hoped to have his job one day. To get there I needed more command experience, not more school.

General Vandenberg heard me out, and when I was out, he smiled, took a drink from a bottle of coke and said, "Son, we are the new Air Force. You are an officer in the out-in-front arm of the new world power. We will need to man bases and command units of air power all over the world. As of now, most of my senior officers don't know the geography nor the culture nor the leaders of any of the nations beyond their narrow combat zone. I intend to change that."

This Middle East graduate program was on the cutting edge of this new era. General Van told me I had been chosen because of my potential for very high rank. I listened to him paint this broad, world-view; then I repeated that I was a fighter pilot, I needed to stay in the cockpit or I would be left behind.

The Chief responded as follows: This is a direct quote from my journal, "Son, you are first of all a major in the U.S. Air Force. You go where you are told to go and you do what you're told to do. And you will do this even when you have my job. I picked you for graduate school in the Middle East. You will go get your Masters degree, and if you're as smart as I hope you are, you'll find a way to enjoy every minute of it. Good afternoon, son." His eyes dropped back to his desk full of papers.

Somewhere east of Gibraltar I decided that I could either grouse and complain and write letters to Mike Mansfield, majority leader in the Senate and my old mentor at

Montana U, or I could decide I was going to make a fine student and enjoy this new adventure as General Vandenberg had directed. In other words, I could drag my feet in bitterness or I could run with the wind and enjoy. I decided to go-for-it. As a result I soon found I enjoyed school, and I became a good and quite popular graduate student.

The American University is a collection of serious young men and women from all over the Arab world. Most students come to Beirut on national scholarships. The University goal is to build each nation's bank of professional talent in Science, Medicine, Law, Business, Engineering and Education. The faculty is about half Arab scholars educated in America or Europe and half volunteer American professors from all over the United States.

I should say the one aspect of our Masters program that really caught my spirit: We changed roommates every two months. And virtually every weekend we went home with our roommates from Friday noon 'til Monday noon. My faculty advisor, Dr. Kurani, was very strong on this cross-cultural aspect. He enthusiastically encouraged my getting to really know my fellow students and their families—learn Arabic, study the Koran, get the feel of the social forces at play across the Arab world—and get immersed in the culture. Become an Arab.

I took him at his word and got to sort of "live with" a handful of Arab scholars over a wide spectrum of geography. For instance, an early roommate was a lad whose family ran a shop on the Street-Called-Straight in Damascus. Later, I got to live with a craft-family in Baghdad. While I visited their riverbank home, we gathered reeds, wove mats, tooled leather and pounded brass. And we spent several exciting days peddling our wares in the dusty bazaar. I joined another family's camel caravan from Bahrain on the Persian Gulf to Riyadh, the capital of Saudi Arabia. Again, I worshiped in

Jerusalem with a Muslim roomy who took me to prayers at the magnificent Mosque of Omar, the third holiest place in Islam.

But by far the most pleasant part of this unusual, growth adventure was falling in love with Najua Shaheen, the pretty, dark-eyed daughter of the university physics professor. Najua and I sat side-by-side on a stone step half way down the zigzag student path that led from the university campus to the harbor below. We could hear my roomy Shukri's puffing approach above. Still, we enjoyed a love-glow all our own, watching dusk's deep, blue, curtain slide down the Lebanese Alps and creep out across the sea.

"Look. We're under attack." Najua pointed to the northwest. With dusk came the normal evening scud, a gray roll of mist. Almost immediately warm summer spit began to blow about us; and at the same time, the harbor lights came on below and off to the northeast. There we could hear the park mix of locals and students already generating music and laughter.

"Sorry," Shukri, an outgoing Palestinian from the old city of Jerusalem, puffed in upon us. "I was detained . . . puff, puff . . . Dr. Freehan wanted to discuss my Cyprus paper." Najua reached out and touched Shukri's hand in greeting. "I'm sorry we left without you, Shuk. I wasn't sure where you were or if you were coming down." We hurried on down together. It was Friday evening and we were on our way.

Most every Friday when we were on campus rather than traveling around the area, many of the graduate students left the campus after class and drifted down to the huge, open, acacia-shaded park on the waterfront. Remember in the 1950s there was little air conditioning anywhere in the Middle East. Thus, townsfolk also gathered by the dozens at the picnic tables under the ancient trees. You see here a continuation of an age-old Levant tradition with roots in the Bible—gathering at the city gates at eventide.

The city of Beirut has encouraged the tradition. Riviera-type, colored light-lines have been strung among the acacia trees. It's a wonderful, relaxed atmosphere. People gather in clutches to picnic, talk, listen to popular, American swing music. Often the young join in singing the lyrics. When I was recalled for the Gulf War, I stopped by to remember. It's still the same—or was sixteen years ago.

Beirut was an Open City. That is, no duty or customs were levied on imports, exports or purchases. Moreover, it was traditionally a city where all nationalities, races and religions were welcome and could expect to be treated warmly. It was the timeless crossroads of the Middle East, so there were always crowds of tourists from everywhere. You could stand on any corner and hear a dozen languages. The St. George, noted for superior French cuisine and classic service, was always packed. Its spy center reputation insured lots of intrigue and drama. If it happened, it was said, it probably happened on Friday evening within earshot of St. George's in Beirut.

You can see why the grad students, young men and women from all over the world but mainly, erudite and affluent Arab youth from around the Middle East, would find this place a draw. For me, it had all the ingredients for carrying on a storybook romance. Taken all together, the St. George and its park had become over the years, not only the AUB student collecting point on Friday evenings, but also in summer especially, a Friday night collecting place for locals as well as hotel guests from far and near.

The mist and Shukri's dramatic appearance brought us to our feet, and together hand-in-hand, all three of us jogged along Harbor Boulevard toward the growing symphony of music, laughter and chatter. One of Najua's nursing school friends came running to meet us. "Najua! Najua! Come dance with us."

Shukri and I joined the crowd of students pulling tables together. Najua was a captive. She was almost dragged by a cluster of mostly girls who were moving through the tables to an open patch of grass. I could see from where we settled amidst a crowd of law students that my girl was in good hands. The dance-bunch was trying with some success to hop and skip their way through a sort of Bedouin version of the hokey-pokey.

You may have noticed that law students the world over gather like bees. Where one is at leisure, you'll normally find a couple dozen. I had gotten to know a few, so I dove into their circle hugging and shaking hands, greeting, meeting and laughing. Being an American, wherever I went where Arab students gathered, I was surrounded. Everyone wanted to practice his English on me. Sometimes, lacking confidence, they would gather in a circle and just listen, repeating phrases out loud now and then. The warmth of these Arab friends was amazing. They would take tons of time helping me with my Arabic. Repeating phrases over and over to make sure I got the sound exactly right.

Perhaps a half-an-hour later I decided the dancers needed help. I had started out to join them and was about halfway to Najua when I noticed walking directly toward me from the opposite direction was a man I knew. Not a student. Then I saw the black embassy Buick parked along the circle perhaps fifty yards distant.

The man approaching was the U.S. Air Attaché from Damascus, Colonel Butch Barber. He waved and called, "Hey Ace, I'm sorry to bother your fun, but duty calls." He pointed toward the car. "Someone over here badly needs your help." Butch only called me "Ace" when he needed a favor or wanted me to pay for the drinks. But what's a man to do? After all, he was a colonel, I, a major.

I need to pause here in the story to add a little context. Butch Barber was assigned to the embassy in Damascus because there was no embassy in Beirut. Lebanon was a very peaceful, predictable little country in the 1950s, and very friendly to the U.S. Syrian capital, Damascus, was their next-door neighbor, and while quite America-friendly in those days, was more actively involved in Middle East and world affairs and particularly in the endless hostilities with Israel. The State of Israel was barely four years old in 1951. Israel and its Arab neighbors were still at war, softened by periodic UN-imposed armistices. Syria, Saudi Arabia, and Egypt could not believe they could not push the Jews into the sea and be gone with it. With this conflict unsettled, Damascus was more important to the U.S. as a diplomatic and intelligence center. For this reason we maintained a full embassy in Damascus while holding only a consulate in Beirut.

I turned to Shukri who was following me out. "Shuk, keep an eye on Najua. I'll only be a minute." Then I stepped into the dance group and, pointing to the sedan, I whispered to Najua, "Pssst, Duty. I'll only be a minute." I returned to Colonel Barber with whom I had developed a close friendship through our flying. "What's the problem, Butch?" I was curious. The diplomatic set rarely connected with me except for flying.

"You'll see." Butch was taking very long strides as though he wanted to get me there suddenly. As we approached, I saw a man in uniform sitting in back. Butch jumped in beside him. The man in front driving, I recognized as university staff, but I couldn't place exactly who he was. He reached across and threw the passenger front door open. I met a hand to shake and a strong whiff of Old Spice to sniff. "Bill Colby, Major. Thank you for coming." I slid

11

in beside him, and we were immediately underway up the long hill toward the university. The man in back leaned over the seat. "My name is Ryan. I'm from SAC in the states." We shook hands.

I was caught by surprise at our moving. "Where are we going? I thought I was needed back there. I have a dinner date, Guys." I pointed back. At that point Colby turned the Buick up an alley to the back of the consulate. The rear of the American consulate in Beirut was a famous garden. It consisted simply of a patch of groomed green shaded by a cluster of ancient sycamore trees. A thin, winding, walkway with scattered wrought-iron benches led from the curb to the building's rear entrance. Its fame arose from its parties. Some of the finest international barbeques and New Year's Day parties in the area were held there.

Colby drew up and parked. No one got out. "Go ahead, Ryan." Colby half turned indicating the man in the back seat. The man from Strategic Air Command and Barber both leaned forward over the seat. Ryan spoke, "Major, what I say here is the essence of National Security Council, Top Secret Operation Sandstorm." He paused a moment and pulled back to light a cigarette. Then: "We need to know which of the old WWII runways in the desert are long enough and strong enough to hold the SAC bomber fleet. In case we strike the Soviets, we may need to refuel and rearm out here. Our home bases will likely be gone."

Now Colby turned to face me directly and while Ryan was shirt-pocketing his package, pushed on, "There are an even dozen old WWII British, French and U.S. bases around the desert on friendly real estate. We need to know which, if any of these oldies, are still strong enough and long enough for our B-47s and B-50s."

"And the new B-52," Barber interjected.

Although a career ambitious flying officer, I had been totally out of communication with America and its security problems for six months. I had literally forgotten about the Cold War in my enthusiasm with my new culture. I had totally focused on the Middle East, its people, its religion, its way of life. I was a good student. SAC, Deterrence, WWIII, and the Soviet Union were far from my mind. Moreover, I had heavily and warmly invested in a dozen fascinating new Arab friends and their families, and I had fallen in love with the university physics professor's daughter.

I spoke to Colby, but I looked out the windshield at the consulate building trying to estimate how long it would take me to walk back to the St. George park. "So?—Look 'em up in the library. You're at the university, right? Now, if you'll excuse me . . ."

At this point everyone piled out of the car except me. "Come on, Ace. We need to talk." Colonel Barber opened my door and grabbed my arm. We headed toward the building. About halfway along the walk, Colby pulled me down onto one of the wrought-iron benches. Barber and Ryan stood facing.

"Major, I'm at the college. You and I have passed each other on the campus. I am the visiting professor of Economics up there." Colby's voice was low and remarkably gentle. Still I noticed a granite quality of ultimate authority that caused me to look directly at his eyes when he spoke. His eyes were light gray and gripping. I guessed mid-forties, executive-tough, sharp suit, expensive tie and unruly pile of gray hair. I liked this man, but I was totally disinterested in his project.

He continued, "That's cover. To be brutally quick, I'm the *Agency-Man-in-the-Sand*. The President asked me to come out here and see how we could use all these friends and all this territory." He paused, lit a Chesterfield and blew a small cloud between very tall Ryan and very fat Barber. These two had planted themselves closely in front of and facing us. I thought, *These guys are guards. I am to stay put.*

William Colby continued. "I am terribly sorry to interrupt your social activity out there, Major, but this airfields thing has come up. Top national priority. And you're a pilot and you have friends here. We need your help." He smiled with surprisingly casual warmth.

I now looked up directly at this SAC bomber man Ryan and remembered: Months ago, I had landed an F-84 jet fighter at Offutt's, SAC Headquarters, low on fuel. I was told by a bomber refueling sergeant (who was illegally wearing a flying suit on refueling duty) that Offutt fuel was for bombers only, and I better keep moving as General LeMay lit his cigars with hot-shot, pea-shooters like me. Without a word, I taxied back out, flew over to McConnell at Topeka for fuel. I just made it—flamed-out on roll-out. For approximately two years I had managed to avoid contact with SAC. I now felt a deep, slow burn developing.

I spoke out of the corner of my mouth like Humphery Bogart, "Well, Mr. Ryan . . ."

"General Ryan," the tall man corrected me.

"Well, Mr. General Ryan, you can tell your Mr. General Curt LeMay that he can kiss my ass. I'm a fighter pilot. And no fighter I know takes orders or jet fuel from Mr. General LeMay or any other bomber bozo."

My fat colonel friend jumped in. "Hey Ace! Don't! Don't! Listen!" He was standing close in front, leaning over me and speaking directly in my face. "Look, pal! You are foremost a Major in the United States Air Force and . . ." Butch could see that as a student I had forgotten who I was. He smelled trouble. He wanted to head it off.

Ryan ground out his Kool on the walkway, blew out some smoke with, "Not for long he isn't. I see no one has knocked you on your butt recently. Let me take care of that, right now." He shucked his blue Ike jacket and began rolling up his sleeves. I ignored the brevet-brigadier, middleweight. "I ain't inspecting no runways for no bombers. It's Friday night at the college, and I have a dinner date." I started to get up.

Cool William Colby had been looking without emotion from one of us to the other and back again. Now he cleared his throat and reaching over, he took a firm grip on my shoulder. I resumed my seat and looked directly at him. His gray eyes caught mine, and held me. "Major, cut the bullshit. This is not a crappy, bomber-fighter squabble. This next hour may be the most important hour you have spent in the service. We don't have time for games."

With this brief statement, the rules of the meeting changed. William Colby's quiet intensity outwilled my rebellious attitude. Something inside me relaxed. Colby saw this and moved on. He looked from Barber to Ryan. "Who's got the list?"

"Wait a minute!" I broke in. "Don't you attachés do this kind of stuff?"

Colby touched my arm again. "Washington wants a *friend* to do this—an *Arab friend*. No attachés or other known spooks. Major, you are always moving around visiting with people who love and trust you. You are almost one of them. General Vandenberg has asked for you by name."

Colby squeezed my arm like an old friend. This clever, subtle, big brother move did it. I wondered where I could get some Old Spice cologne.

He continued. "Major, we want you to measure these runways. The going wisdom is that you know combat aviation, and you can do the job better and quicker than probably anyone around. And no one need ever know." Colby leaned away and with both hands he illustrated. "We need

15

the length, the width and the depth of concrete. No notes. You call in the numbers only, to the VOA Vienna as 'Sandstorm Numbers.' "

We both stood up. Colby again put his hand on my shoulder. "Major, President Eisenhower's son John was your classmate at the Point. Ike suggested you." There was a pause. He reached out and took my right hand. "Your country needs you, Major. This is huge! It may well be the most important thing you will ever do."

The other two, seeing the task completed, started toward the car. Colby stood looking directly into my eyes and gripping my right hand. "Now, security! I don't have to tell you of the paramount sensitivity of this project to the host nations. No one must know what you are doing or why. These people trust us. If any one of them ever got an inkling that we were in any way putting them in jeopardy, the oil would dry up, the real estate would vanish, the UN support would suck. Walter Winchell or Edward R. Murrow—The Evening News would yell, 'Perfidy' and, well . . ."

I was looking directly into Colby's eyes and thinking, *Brother Colby, you are a cold-blooded spy. These people love me. They trust me. Contrarily, to you they are an area and a population useful to national security. To me they are friends and families of classmates and their countries. But Butch is right—when all is said and done, I'm a Major in the United States Air Force.* I closed my eyes for a moment. Then, I spoke, "All right, Mr. Colby, I'll do it."

At these words, Butch stopped his withdrawal. He fingered in his left shirt pocket a minute, then returned and handed me a twice-folded, five-inch square of paper. I opened it onto a numbered list and a telephone number neatly penned on half an embassy envelope. I read it, and I knew at once I was holding the list of twelve airfields that comprised *"Sandstorm."* The number was the Voice of

America in Vienna. I recognized all the bases but one. With the three men whispering two steps away, I memorized the list and the contact phone number in Vienna and ate the paper.

Nine o'clock tolled from somewhere off in the city just as the Buick paused at the park curb once again. The ambience was still colored lights and music, but no people. I tossed a salute at the two in back. I looked directly at Colby. He grabbed my hand and squeezed it. "Major, remember—no one—ever." He was pressing his left index finger against his lips. The car door clunked shut. The Buick engine growled. I stood a moment on the curb and watched the single taillight recede up Le Boulevard Saint Charles and finally disappear.

The tables in the park were all but vacant. Najua and Shukri sat alone talking quietly, earnestly in Arabic. Our crowd had long since gone into the hotel to eat or had just drifted away. It was late. I told my friends that I was very sorry, but the president had needed my help. Shukri, a buoyant Palestinian, had not missed me. Najua was hungry.

The three of us walked across to the St. George, climbed the wide, elegant stairway to the busy, over-the-water dining deck and ordered a bottle of Chateauneuf-du-Pape and a candle. The Pieta-fish was delicious.

By midnight Shukri and I were in pajamas talking Arab-Israel politics. When silence finally fell, I lay on my back on my school-issue, sky-blue, quilt and strangely enough, my thoughts wandered back six years to another "spy assignment." This one involving General MacArthur, my WWII inspiration. My War Journal tells the story well.

Two

The Supreme Commander had been out visiting units. On his way back to Tokyo he ran low on gas. I found his black Packard pulling in to our front parking lot just at dinnertime. I went out to meet him. I invited the Five Star to join us while his driver refueled. Surprisingly, he accepted. We had a little room off the big mess hall where the officers ate, but the general wanted to go through the line and talk to and eat with the GIs. As soon as his plate was clear, I nudged my adjutant to have his driver bring the car up to the front. But instead of leaving, the old gent walked across the hall into the pilot's ready room—sort of curiously looking around.

He lit his famous pipe and with a squadron mug of coffee in his hand, he stood before the fireplace chatting with the pilots. He shook hands with each fighter pilot, and I noticed he looked directly eye-to-eye with each pilot and thanked him for his part in the victory. I could hear my kids answering the old man who asked each where he was from. Then most explained that they were in the service for the duration and were eager to go home and get out.

At length the old man put his cup on the mantel and held up his pipe to ask for quiet. "Gentlemen," he called out. "Let me give you some advice. Don't be in such a hurry to get out of uniform. Next to serving God, I have found serving country the noblest pursuit of man." He looked from one young face to another and spoke deliberately as though he were dictating an important letter. "Whether you serve for a moment as in casting your vote, or for a lifetime

18

as I have, this serving your fellow man is essentially what separates us from the beast. Because we are so poorly paid, meanly treated, and quickly forgotten, the profession of arms must be the most unselfish work in the world. Yet in what other role can a man spend his life with his heart so filled with satisfaction—guarding his country in order that happiness might be pursued by neighbors he doesn't even know. In what other profession could an ordinary lad like me have been able to serve my countrymen, and yet thrill to the challenge of the call to the most exciting tasks man can be assigned: to explore, to teach, to minister, to doctor, to judge, to spy, to lead, to fight, to conquer, even to rule in the name of God and the United States of America."

The guys all clapped as if they had been listening to a guest speaker. One of my sharp pilots handed the general his legendary tan cap. Another threw his brown cape over his shoulders as he strode from the front entrance. For me—a memorable grip, a piercing look, a smile of thanks and he was gone.

Now six years later in graduate school, and myself enlisted as an agent, I thought back through the years. How often I had pulled up that brief speech about *service*. When a lieutenant gets to shake hands with and host a legendary five-star general like Douglas MacArthur, the entire hour is forever, indelibly imprinted on his mind. I especially clearly recalled his crisp listing of the tasks one can expect to be assigned in the service. And I always paused to wonder where MacArthur had explored? Where had he taught? Where ministered? Where doctored? But most intriguing, where spied? And I would always follow that wonder, by another wonder: Where do you suppose I will be assigned to spy?—Now I knew. I turned over and dropped deep into sleep.

My Daily Journal over the next month, August in Beirut, was mainly about people. I tell stories about Najua, Shukri and Ben, Lila and Ali, plus a character sketch of our faculty advisor, Professor Kurani. Besides listening to the area's intellectual giants speak on the Arab-Israeli problem, the gulf oil phenomenon, the crossroads syndrome, Bible history and the fundamentals of Islam, besides reading everything saved from the historic Library of Alexandria, the currently-being-discovered Dead Sea Scrolls, plus original Phoenician papyrus scrolls about the life of Abraham, we played soccer. We went swimming. We read half the local university library, and we listened to lectures from both scholars and celebrities including Anwar Sadat, then a rising Egyptian freedom fighter; J. William Robertson, CEO of the Arabian-American Oil Company; Nuri Said, Prime Minister of Iraq; and King Abdullah of Jordan's American wife. This was a super graduate course.

Najua and I also cruised around Lebanon, Syria and Palestine with my Jerusalem roomy. Ali ben Adam, who came to the university driving a 1940 Chevrolet roadster. It held five passengers, counting three in front plus two in the rumble seat. We drove to the ski resort in the Lebanese Alps, out to Balbec in the desert, north to the Crac de Chavalier, a classic Crusader fortress castle and across the desert to Damascus.

I got in my flight time by flying as co-pilot for the neighboring U.S. Air Attachés: Colonel Barber in Damascus, Colonel Watkins in Baghdad and Tony Martinelli in Cairo. Every weekend I tried to get the attaché with whom I was flying to visit the city near one of the airfields on my list.

I had long wanted to visit Mosul. Not only was my twelfth runway there, but it was Najua's hometown. Her mother still resided there. I had heard a ton of stories about Mosul and the Kurds. Najua had lobbied me strongly about Mosul's incredible place in history. She had grown up, gone to school there and wanted to take me home and show me her town. Actually it is an historic and geographically fascinating city. Ancient, biblical, Nineveh is directly across the river from Mosul. Also, Gaugamela, where Alexander the Great won his greatest battle against Darius the Great of Persia, is almost due east of Mosul. The battlefield lies in an indenture in the rugged Zagros mountain wall. Nimrud, the arguable location of the Tower of Babel, is just down river a stretch, named for Nimrod the biblical hunter son of Cush who became, the Bible tells us, the very first king, ever.

So, all things considered, the third week of September, I made plans to visit Najua's mom, take her some things and pick up some items and measure the runway. The partially active, Royal Iraqi Airbase Mosul was in reality ex-RAF Station *Courage*. I had intentionally chosen the date when Najua was on an exchange visit to the University of Cairo and could not accompany me. Further, I had scheduled myself to just ride along as a passenger, not fly co-pilot as I usually did when getting in my flying time. The pilot was scheduled to be Cairo's attaché, Colonel Tony Martinelli who had told me on the phone that his official destination was Karachi in Pakistan. But he could let me off at Mosul, then pick me up at Baghdad on my way back.

A few days before this Mosul adventure, my journal notes that as the visit-date approached, I began to get increasingly nervous. I was having more serious guilt problems than usual. I suppose because it was Najua's hometown. My patriotism and other rationalizing worked in other cases, but betraying Najua and her family—setting up her town as a nuclear target—was more than I had bargained for. This relational aspect evidenced itself in poor sleep, daydreaming, upset stomach, and finally, a kind of mystic foreboding.

Each *measurement-trip*, as I planned it and executed it, was in my conscience what we would call at West Point an "honor violation." Thus, each trip stands out, even today, indelibly in that rotten, special secret vault of my memory, down that long dark stairs, along that shadowy, echoing corridor and down in that moldy, damp pit where I have lifelong dumped my *Dishonors*—the skates I stole from Tom Burns in fourth grade, the dollar I took from the counter where I worked as delivery boy at Victory Grocery in eighth grade, a couple dozen lies over the years, cheating on a physics test at the university, a major promise broken and these dozen betrayals of faithful, Arab friends.

For example, I paced off the Beirut International Airport first. It was the only commercial airport on my list. I chose to measure Beirut International on a day when Najua and I were sunning and swimming at that popular student beach just west of the International Airport runway. We were with a gang of friends. I remember getting excused from the beach soccer game claiming that I didn't know how to play soccer. Which was a lie as I played varsity soccer at West Point. In this way, each measure-visit involved creating a *cover-story*. And each demanded a totally dishonest explanation.

I remember pacing off and digging under one end of the Baghdad West airfield with my Sunni Moslem roommate, Sayad. I remember because we got permission from the authorities by convincing both Sayad and the locals that I needed a bucket of that particular sand as a soil sample for a paper I was doing on Historic Assyrian Agriculture back at the college. I paced the runway length and width without being noticed and found the depth of concrete while filling a bucket with sand. Even Sayad was deceived. I was ashamed. I wondered how Douglas MacArthur, who to me was the epitome of honor, handled the intrinsic dishonor in espionage.

When the day arrived for Mosul, the nine of us culture adventurers gathered at Beirut International Operations, and awaited the arrival of the Cairo airplane. I was accompanied by two of my classmates from Amman, Jordan; a couple from Damascus; two from Baghdad; and two from Tehran. I was very nervous, and I had this heavy shadow that kept me from joining in the excited chatter of the student group. I sat apart as Martinelli filled out the clearance form. I had pulled my journal from my daypack to make an entry concerning this odd but very clear foreboding. I decided for some reason to start a new set, and I entitled this day as "Day One" and made that my heading:

The Mosul Gig, Day One

It's the morning of 22 September, 1951. As I climbed into the Cairo Embassy C-47 in front of Base Operations at Beirut International Airport, I have an overpowering sense of shadow—a foreboding—an expectancy of approaching, looming disaster. My Methodist friends would say I feel like Satan is following in my footsteps waiting for me to relax my attention. Honestly, I feel a clear physical, as well as an intuitive, mental feeling of dark clouds. There is no question in my mind, it is going to *rain* today!

I climbed into the aluminum cigar with its American flag painted on the tail and yelled at Colonel Martinelli, "Okay, Chief, what are we waiting for?" I wanted him to appreciate that although we were merely grad students, we lived a very busy life, and we had been waiting for half an hour. The pilot, Colonel Tony Martinelli, who claimed to be an ex-Thunderbird, turned in his seat and yelled a laughing greeting back to me. Tony earlier had told me he was a fellow, frustrated fighter pilot (frustrated by having to fly the demeaning Cairo embassy C-47 transport rather than a hot, new jet fighter. Like me, he saw himself as a Korean War hero).

We had made immediate friends months before when he had stopped by to pick up several of us to fly to Kuwait on the Persian Gulf for another weekend of visiting roommates' homes. I flew as his co-pilot. We were still in the process of trying to remember what battle in what war we had fought together and where. Fighter pilots do that a lot—normally over a beer at Happy Hour.

I waved, shouted back some banter and then joined the flight engineer who was helping the Arab students adjust their shoulder harness in their bucket seats along the side walls. The shiny silver Gooneybird vibrated with the increase in power as the colonel taxied us out onto the two-miles of north-south runway for final checks and takeoff. The flight across the desert was uneventful. We dropped off a couple of kids at the new International United Nations Airport at Amman in Jordan. The hot desert dust of midmorning swirled in at the cargo door.

He then flew on to Damascus and let off my former roomy, Amad Ghazi, and his new roomy. Amad's family lived on the Street-Called-Straight. I had gone home with him in early June. During that visit, I had measured the abandon RAF field northwest of Damascus. By the time we touched down in Baghdad it was noon. I had taken a brief sitting nap and although I still felt dark and heavy, the foreboding was still only a heavy feeling. The lightning, thunder and heavy rain was still out there somewhere.

I had a strong urge to get off the plane there in the dusty capital of Iraq. It was only when I stood in the cargo door ready to jump down that I remembered my visit this weekend involved looking in on Najua's mom in Mosul, a half-hour further north. I had in my pack a nicely wrapped package from Najua to deliver. A birthday gift, I seemed to remember. I buckled back in.

At the sand-drifted, rundown, former British fighter base, Mosul, I was alone among the bucket seats except for the two Iranian kids. I walked forward to say "Good-Bye" to Tony and remind him to not forget me on Tuesday. I had a clear urge to tell him I had changed my mind and would stay on 'til the next stop at Tehran. Nonetheless, I threw out my daypack and jumped to the ground. That funny feeling was in my stomach—the challenging excitement—the before-the-battle expectancy, the fear-edged-with-joy. I could taste the rain. Trouble was out there somewhere, and like cocaine, I knew it was dangerous, so I wanted some of it.

Najua's mom lived in the northern suburbs. I had glimpsed her upscale, wall-guarded, palm-scaped, blue-pooled, whitewashed home from the tiny window at my side as we banked onto final approach. Martinelli had not cut the engines. The prop-wash pushed and swirled around me. I grabbed my leather pack and scurried around the wing. The flight engineer slammed the side door. I waved to my friend in the cockpit and stood clear as he cracked the throttle. Blowing dust, he swung the silver bird around to taxi back out for takeoff. I avoided Mosul Base Operations. I waved casually to the Ground Crewman driving the Follow-Me jeep. I intended to indicate I would need no further assistance.

Because of, or perhaps along with, the lurking dramatis foreshadow, I began now to move under a strange compulsion. I had earlier planned to walk directly into Ops, as pilots called the operations office, and place a phone call to Leah Shaheen, Najua's mom. Within fifteen minutes she would pick me up or send a driver. Instead, I deliberately avoided the office and walked around the flight-line operations building to the parking lot. I stood behind a dusty, old Iraqi Air Force delivery van and surveyed the runway area out beyond. The ramp and taxiway complex were vacant of activity except two Arabs in fatigues securing the Follow-Me jeep near an equipment shed under the tower.

The echoing roar of takeoff-power led my eyes to follow Martinelli's Cairo embassy plane lift-off, wheels tuck up then bank and disappear in a sweeping turn to the southeast. "I will do it now!" This sudden decision was accompanied by a surge of ice-cold adrenaline and a full-body, spastic shake. My eyes made one final sweep of the flight line. All routine, I walked casually down the paved driveway leading toward the guarded, off-base gate. The parking lot behind Base Ops showed two parked cars. As I crossed it, I stopped a moment to view the main gate perhaps a hundred yards south. This gate, I noticed, opened directly onto the northwest termination of al Mawsil, the city's main thoroughfare.

The airport is a former British Royal Air Force base from the days of the mandate, which Prime Minister Churchill dubbed RAF Station *Desert Hawk*. If you have ever been to Mosul, you have noticed how this airdrome is almost embedded in the city. The main runway 220 (northeast-southwest) lies along the prevailing off-desert wind. It fits into a notch in the northwestern Mosul suburb. And it fits so snugly the boundary fence borders the backyard gardens of dozens of nearby city dwellers. In the modern jet age, this closeness would not be considered safe—especially for a military base. The British were concerned about their RAF Spitfires being raided by the Nazi-friendly Kurdish bands. They wanted them "in-close."

Some history. You will recall Iraq had been mandated to Great Britain following WWI. Under the steady hand of

King Faisal I, she had won independent statehood in 1932 with military base rights accruing to the British. When in 1940 a convey of Iraqi leaders and army officers secretly sought an alliance with the Axis powers, Churchill upgraded the airbase with a mile long concrete runway, modern hangars and a squadron of Spitfires. After a flurry of desert dust-ups, the Axis-friendly leaders were driven from the country. Their poorly equipped tribal militia was driven back into the badlands of Kurdistan. King Faisal returned from Switzerland and Iraq joined the Allies.

With the allied victory in 1945, Air Marshal Tedder flew out with the first jets—a squadron of *Swifts*—and broke a bottle of champagne over the propeller of the last Spit; and in the name of the crown, dubbed the base RAF Station *Courage*. It was the first overseas flight station where the Royal Air Force based jet aircraft. And this was before jets were really deemed totally safe-for-flight. RAF *Courage* was originally manned by a remnant of the gin-drinking Battle of Britain heroes. At the turn of the fifties, economic pressures caused the British to pull the squadron of Swifts back to NATO Europe. Now, in 1952, Iraqi Prime Minister Nuri Said was negotiating for MIGs from Russia against F-86s from the US. Neither was in residence yet.

Back to the story. When I arrived at the privet hedge that separated the parking lot from the guard-gate road, I stepped through a break in the bushes—a workers' shortcut. There I crouched watching. I noticed that my heart was beating faster than normal. I reminded myself that I needed to relax, stay cool. Although I was on my eleventh airfield measurement, each time, the psychology of the spy-mission as a capital crime—and the prey-tension—was putting me instinctively on an epinephrine alert. I felt hunted, when in fact, no one was even aware of me.

I eased along the hedge. At the corner, I turned to square the east edge of the parking lot. Next, I strolled casually across a vacant lot to the deep blue shadow behind the hangar next to the control tower. From the shadow of the hangar, I shaded my eyes with my hand and examined the darkened glass of the tower, fifty feet above. One Arab technician with binocs was watching the U.S. embassy C-47 departing. He now dropped his glass and made a note in his log. He seemed to be alone which I noted as aberrant. By international agreement, commercial control towers are manned by a pair of observers or controllers. Military towers are normally manned the same, with an officer often in attendance.

I slid quietly and nonchalantly onto the concrete ramp leading to the taxiway. A rusty shovel leaned against a post. As I passed, I swung it onto my shoulder and, thrusting my free hand in my pocket, kaffiyeh blowing in the wind, I ambled lazily out toward the runway. My thought: *I look like any normal, bored Arab worker performing a routine duty on the airfield grounds.* I was wearing GI khakis, a worn, university T-shirt, dirty sneakers and a raggedy tan kaffiyeh held on by a dirty agal. To add to my authentic look, I wore a half-full daypack holding my survival kit from Korea, my journal and a few personal items. Now I swiped a long stem of timothy from the grassy edging and poked it in. Chewing the stem, I fished from my daypack a piece of folded paper. I held it in my free hand. As I walked toward the end of the long runway, I periodically inspected the pavement edging, dug a bit with my shovel and made a note on the paper as to the depth of concrete. I reasoned the man in the tower would see me and would view me as one of a base engineer crew on routine assignment.

If I could convince him that I was on legitimate business, he would check me off without further inquiry. Knowing the military and knowing Arabs, I ventured that the guy up there would find it too much effort to make a phone call to check with Base Maintenance or if he checked, the GI on the maintenance desk would not wish to divulge that he was not knowledgeable of the crew-schedule, and thus would affirm my presence out here as legitimate. This bold approach had worked before. I had to risk it. Waiting until dark complicated all my plans for the weekend. I kept walking and digging and noting and walking and digging—never glancing at the tower.

During one of these digs, I pulled away sufficient sand to find the base of the concrete. I had the depth I needed. I would double-check it at the end. I paused at the run-up area where the concrete widens about 25 yards near the northeast end. Here I shaded my eyes and looked toward the far end. It was not visible, only heat waves. The sun was nearly setting and the desert haze made visibility impossible to the southwest. I would have to estimate the length.

Here are my thoughts as I moved through this estimating process: Martinelli graduated from Harvard, so he is very predictable. The reason I can't remember him is because he is really not a career fighter pilot. He is more of a career diplomat. I could tell that from the way he launched and landed the C-47. Still, I had made note of the fact he was airborne as he departed Mosul a thousand feet before midfield. The Goonybird, empty, takes off in fifteen hundred feet at sea level. The conservative British normally operate the *Swift* with Rolls Royce engines off 7500 feet. I made a mental note. *This runway is 7000 feet long.* That's why Tedder billeted the Battle of Britain heroes out here. Those blokes were honored by the risk of a new aircraft and a slightly short runway.

Right now I stepped off the width of the overrun at the very end. I made another mental note—*fifty feet.* Next, I paced the length of this asphalt overrun, and I noticed that the distance from the end of the blacktop to the boundary fence was only thirty feet. One hour bled into another. As I turned back to the southwest to pace off the width of the active runway, I noticed two things: My heavy anxiety was gone, and dusk was settling fast. The far end of the runway glowed with a mystic pink-gold. The sun was in the sand, and the calm of evening was settling down. There wasn't a breath of air moving. There was hardly a sound except the endless, low pulsing of the city behind me.

Wait! Something more!—Way down the runway something was moving. In the very center of the runway were two bright lights. At first I thought an airplane must be landing—probably a small, private craft as there seemed to be no accompanying sound and the lights were close together. I stood arrested, curious, staring. Suddenly, I heard the double-crack of two rifle shots! I put two-and-two together and came up with a jeep on the runway—probably the Follow-Me vehicle. It was barreling hell-bent to my end of the runway. More alarming, as it approached to about a quarter of a mile, I could discern that it was full of soldiers. The soldier beside the driver appeared to be standing up, and it was he who was firing the rifle—apparently into the air. I could see in silhouette that the jeep was kicking up a fair cloud of dust, so I surmised it was traveling at high speed.

Instantly, the prey feeling that had been lurking around the shadows of my activities all day returned. I dropped the shovel I had been using as a kind of walking stick in between diggings. Crouching low, I cut immediately across the asphalt to where I had seen a large draining culvert pass under the concrete of the main runway. It was perhaps 25 yards from the very end. I found the entrance was perhaps four feet in diameter and clogged with huge, dried Russian thistles, some old newspaper clumps and drifted sand.

I made an emergency decision, I glanced one last time at the fast approaching vehicle now heading onto the hundred yards of asphalt overrun. The soldiers had apparently not noticed my movement—if, indeed, they ever had seen me at all or were even interested in me. I was not in a mood to risk. My thoughts focused totally on one notion: *They are after me!* Friend or foe, I knew I was essentially on an espionage mission. I did not desire to be interviewed about what I was doing. The casual stories I had prepared in case I was ever asked, that I was a curious tourist interested in aviation or an American military pilot wondering if I could land my F-86 on this strip—neither seemed appropriate. I put my notepaper in my mouth and began to chew.

Careful not to move any of the debris nor make a track in the sand, I slid out of my daypack, clipped it onto the back of my belt and crawled into the culvert. It had been fast-drawing twilight outside. It was gray-dark inside. The size of the tunnel varied as I scrambled deeper into the darkness. Clog after clog of dry stalks and weeds and torn, wedged newspaper and broken cardboard boxes slowed my progress. I was panic-stricken and irrational. I could hear Arab voices now approaching the tunnel entrance. Then silence. I stopped to listen and rest. I was exhausted, but energized by terror.

I was breathing very hard, and it was extremely dusty. It was impossible to see the air in the dark, but I could taste the grit. I desperately fought coughing or in any way relieving my dry, irritated throat and nose. I just lay there gagging and silently choking.

Perhaps thirty minutes passed. I was making plans. I would sit tight until I was sure the airport posse had vamoosed. Then I would ease out toward the entrance and take a listen and a look. If all was clear, I would split the area—go under or over the boundary fence, take a taxi to

31

Shaheens and later make a call to my contact at Voice of America and pass the figures while they were still fresh in my memory. I was convinced that this whole thing would be over and life would be back to normal by dark.

Suddenly, right then, all planning collapsed—DOGS! The savage growling of numerous attack dogs brought me into totally focused alert! I could see that I was not being ignored or forgotten by the Arab Legion outside. Now, even worse!

POW! . . . POW!

Two spaced rifle shots! The percussion left my ears screaming. Instantly, my mind flashed. *How could the guy miss killing me? I'm down a straight tube with no shielding in between? The goon doesn't even have to aim. On the other hand, I'm an American. An Arab airman cannot just shoot an unarmed American officer in cold blood. I need to back out of here and confront these guys.* The culvert kept the rounds from straying off target. One bullet whined past me. How it missed my bulk only God knows. The other hit into the ribbed wall, ricocheted and thunked into my butt with the impact of a sharp kick, but no pain. I decided I would be a dead duck backing out. I pulled off the impossible. I stayed quiet. Down the long tube came the hollow voice of an excited soldier shouting in Arabic, apparently making a radio report to a superior.

"That got him!—Right, Lieutenant! Yes Sir, Jasus Israeli! Kharraba! Israeli spy saboteur! Yes Sir, I'm sending in the dogs. They'll chew up what's left."

I tried to flatten out—to leave some room for misses above me. The firing ceased and the sound of snuffing, clawing, drooling attack dogs filled the culvert back beyond my feet and daypack. All thoughts that I was going to mosey out and grab a cab for a mansion in the city were fading fast.

I needed more than anything else to get deeper into the tunnel, or I was going to be late lunch for the Siberian

Rottweilers. At least two and perhaps three vicious animals were now growling, biting, snarling, clawing and digging into the culvert sand and debris, my daypack and each other. I thanked God the posse had no flashlight. My daypack alone guarded my feet and legs from claws and fangs. They knew, and through their vicious aggressive demeanor, they were transmitting the info to their handlers, an unauthorized something or someone was hiding in this tunnel, and with persistence they could dig him out.

Mosul Gig, Day Two

I do not remember how long I dug and skootched, dug and skootched, dug and skootched. It seems like all that night and well into the next day, I crawled. Time lost all meaning as it was pitch dark, the air was dusty—gritty in my mouth—and my mind was desperate and frantic. I would meet a stoppage and dig with my clawed fingers. Sometimes it took an hour or more to break through, but I knew I could not go back.

I would break through one clog and crawl on only to meet another clog of weeds, sand and miscellaneous rotten-smelling debris. The dusty blackness and the general idiocy of the situation was terrifying and dragging me into a deep depression.

Still I would claw free and skootch on. Can you imagine my mental condition, a thirty-year-old, Major in the U.S. Air Force, an international graduate student, hero of the Korean War—an hour ago planning to visit my sweetheart's mom nearby, now squeezed in a black, painful, probable coffin? My major adversity was the fight to ignore the insanity of the moment and concentrate on the unbelievable effort of somehow crawling out to freedom.

For the first few hours I seemed to be making some progress. But as time passed, deep in my soul a dark ogre was born and began to grow—a dark ogre named "Hopelessness."

My daypack, tied around my waist and dragging behind, had earlier saved my life, but as the hours wore on, it became a major pain. Though only partly full of personal stuff, it was a serious impediment. Besides, it got stuck on things and had to be laboriously worked free. Once I lost my temper and snapped to a decision to cut it loose. You will certainly understand my frame of mind was continually just barely off insanity—panic. I had to constantly fight back the thought that I had made a stupid, suicidal, snap decision to enter this culvert in the first place. Now I was compounding the error by a worse decision to keep crawling.

For God knows what reason, I sobered long enough on this daypack issue to convince myself that the stuff in my pack was the stuff that could save my life again. There was likely to be a lot of evading and escaping across the countryside if I ever got out of this coffin. I might well have to lay low and get far away from RAF Station *Courage* before I surfaced.

After an eternity of digging and skootching, I came upon a "Y" in the culvert! I felt along each passage. Same size, same blackness, same gritty air. Ho Man! Here was a possible life-or-death dilemma. I tried to visualize the outside directions—where would each passage take me? I could only visualize a culvert opening on the opposite side of the main airport runway similar to the one I had entered. Still, this sort of exit hole should have appeared long ago. Then, as an indication of my para-insanity, I was gripped suddenly and totally by this thought: *Am I sure I want out? Would out mean dogs and soldiers waiting? At least I am alive and free in here.*

So far I had been driving myself with fear-energy and escape-adrenalin. My main effort was to stay sane, with calm reasoning. Now because I needed to pause to make a choice, I felt total exhaustion, a lack of air, and a sense that the size of the tube was diminishing. Also, I noticed for the first time that I hurt all over, and I could barely move. As I fought to face the dilemma coolly, I convinced myself the tube was getting tighter and tighter.

Now for the first time the killing claws of panic began to rule. How could I tell which way I should go? And how long could I keep up this squeezing, skootching? My fingertips were wet with a stickiness I could smell—blood—from digging the sand and gravel. My eyes, normally closed, were full of burning grit. Now with a needed decision, I just lay there defeated. I began to sob and pant in the dark.

This is absolutely hopeless, I thought. *I'm doomed to die in here. Should I turn around and go back and take my chances with the dogs and guards? Could I stay alive long enough to get back to the entrance? But that's an irrational thought. Turning is not an option. I can't physically turn around in here. I've just got to cool down, settle down and keep on digging. But, which way? Either way, you idiot, just go, it probably doesn't matter which way.*

I fought to regain control of my sanity. I tried to figure out why there would be a split in the culvert here, and I tried to decide where each of these tunnels emptied. I reasoned that the right one might go on out under the city for miles to the Tigris River. That dictated the left fork. As I squeezed into it, I made the mistake of reconsidering. This fork must drain the entire length of the runway, then on to the river up north. That could be even more miles. I needed to go the other way!

From somewhere out there in the pitch black of nowhere came the thought, *Boy, you're losing it! You better pray.* I spoke out loud, "God! Help Me! If you don't intercede,

I'm going to die in here for sure. Please! Help Me!'' With that little speech said, I began to cry again. I wept and wept, and that led to yelling, then screaming. I just totally lost it. I screamed some profanity and some just noise. This violent noise brought dense dust making breathing impossible. This led to gagging and coughing and wild claustrophobia. My whole being screamed to act-out violently, but I could just barely move.

In my thirty years, including more than ten in the service covering two wars and imprisonment, I had never before experienced such wild, violent, deadly despair. I totally lost emotional control. The truth swept over me like an icy bath. I was a coward. And because I was afraid to face a jeep full of Arab soldiers and tell my story, I had crawled myself into a sure grave.

If you have ever experienced arriving at the very edge of where life falters. If you've ever found yourself in a corner so tight that you were convinced you would never get out alive. If you have ever been so terrified and in such exhaustion and pain that you are not sure whether you are conscious or beyond—and the screen of your mind is filled with a swirling whirlpool of changing colored lights—and I mean totally out beyond.

I need to note here—I was not yet a "Born Again Christian.'' This mighty spiritual transformation would come to me eighteen years later through my eldest son during the Vietnam War. Nonetheless, along with my six brothers, I was raised by a Presbyterian mother. All through our youth, she put us to bed with Bible stories and prayer. I knew the saving power of God, and how He loved me, and how I could call on Him for help when my back was to the wall. And I usually did.

"God! Oh, God! Help Me!'' I'm not sure whether I once again shouted or whispered or merely thought this simple, last-ditch plea. This time, almost instantly, the swirling lights slowed and stopped. A thought flashed onto the screen of my mind, *That was a passage! We passed it. We're going to live, not die.* And there in that hopeless, sucking nothingness, a reservoir of soul-strength—the non-material essence of life arose like a phoenix from the ashes.

Very slowly, though buried, almost immobile, terrified and claustrophobic, I somehow quieted. I don't know how or why, but I sublimated the awfulness of the situation. I could feel strength surge through me. I began again to dig and scrunch along. Now, as you can imagine, progress is a relative thing. I was in pitch dark. I had no room on either side, but a little above my face, stomach and knees. Each scrunch meant I moved at most a foot forward—if *forward* it was.

For several hours now following my decision at the fork, I lay on my back, scrunching along foot-by-foot. I found this easier than crawling on my stomach where I had to push-up each move. Beside the physical effort of pushing my weight up, each time I moved, my butt or my head would scrape the top ribbing and my elbows would rub against the sides. Contrarily, on my back, I could pry up with my hands at my sides, push along with my heels. This took less energy. But in this position it was more difficult to dig out a stoppage. I could reach over my head, but I could not get any dig leverage, and I had to pass the debris over my face to dump it beside my chest or stomach. Equally exasperating, on my back, stuff kept falling in my face. As you can visualize, because of the tight quarters, it was almost impossible now to roll over from back down to belly down. Fortunately, the thick, packaged stoppages were now becoming fewer.

As often seems to happen when one hits an encouraging break in overcoming adversity. I made here a serious careless mistake. I had been digging and skootching along with my eyes jammed tightly shut. However, every so often, I would pause a moment and blink my eyes to check the grit. Here, for no particular reason, after blinking to check the grit, I inexplicably left my eyes open. Actually, the total absence of light, made it difficult to know whether my eyes were open or closed. However, on the very next dig, I inadvertently hit the ribbed metal above my face. My eyes were instantly filled with rusty metal dust. When I squeezed them shut, this dust burned so badly that even crying like a child did not wash away the pain. I could only scream, "Ooooooh! Ooooooh!" I needed to put my face down so the grit and tears would run off, but I was wedged too tightly on my back to even turn my head part way. So the tears flowed and the rusty dust burned, and I howled in the lonely dark.

Exhausted and in agony I could not escape, I was vulnerable to fear. I thought, *Even if I get out now, I'll be permanently blind.* Between screams, again I called out loud, "God! Oh, God! Help me!" Again, prayer worked. The crushing weight of the hopelessness coupled with the cutting edge of panic's power that before had ruled, now gave way before pure God-power. I sobbed softly. I forced my head far to the side. This allowed my eyes to slowly wash free of grit. The pain slowly ebbed. The swirling vortex faded, and I consciously rolled my now-closed eyes round and round. I thought, *Come on, Bozo, dig! You don't need eyes to dig.*

From somewhere deep in my exhaustion, I felt a strange, calm buoyancy—a warm energy in my stomach. During this stretch of my trip underground, the shape and sequence of my mental imagery had a predictable design. If I prayed and asked God for help, I would work a stretch of strength and encouraging buoyancy. Then for no apparent reason, this positive resilience would fade into a dark despair. Utter exhaustion would accompany. "God!" And a

glimmer of virtual light would turn my stream of consciousness back upward, and hope would return. But this stretch
would ultimately fade again. The mood swings were cyclical.

Some training tools helped in this psychological war-
fare. I remembered in survival school we had been told that
when you were in deep trouble and things seemed to be
slipping away, you should bite down on our bottom lip, hold
our breath and push hard on our stomach muscles. Whenever I felt hope slipping or my mind fraying out, I tried this
when calling out. It worked. God used this gut-power to turn
things back from the edge.

What happens here physiologically makes sense. This
effort forces blood into one's brain and clears one's
thoughts. It's really an old fighter pilot trick. We are taught
in fighter training when you have a MIG on your tail and
you are scared to death or you are blacked out from a High-
G turn or you lose control of your airplane in the violent
currents of a massive thunderstorm, you must lock your
throat, press down hard with your stomach muscles. Extra
blood is forced into your brain. Clear thoughts make good
things happen.

Mosul Gig, Day Three

As the hours passed, one thought kept nagging me in
spasms: *I took the wrong fork at the Y. I must be crawling the
entire length of the main runway and out across north Iraq toward
Turkey.* I found that I needed not let that "enemy thought"
rule. I could force it out with the strong and friendly notion
that I had seized command of this hole and freedom was
just ahead.

In reviewing this experience in detail a half century
following its occurrence, I have discovered this positive:

"There is apparently an inner power in a man that when backed into the final corner—when the grapes of wrath have all been smashed—when there is nothing left to guard the edge, and even a skeptic is driven to prayer, there is yet a deep, inner, *vis vitae* or *life-force* that won't budge if you don't let it. It flat won't go there, if you don't give in." This moral fiber, or whatever it is, rallied my frenetics and marshaled my scattered energy to feeble, but steadfast action. Of course, there was a price. This deep-bank of mystic energy would not last forever. With each passing hour, I had to stop and rest more frequently.

Still, hour after hour, I crawled on, digging and crawling. There was no longer any threat of dogs or gunfire. That had been left far behind. On the other hand, I could not help but notice that the further I crept, the smaller the space seemed to be. Or was this just a depressing figment? It was just enough to cause the question, "Is the metal ribbing of the culvert narrowing in diameter?" Of course, there was no sight in the pitch black. More, there was little sound when I wasn't whispering to myself, or grunting, only the constant scrunch of my shoulders and hips against the ribbed walls or along the gravelly sand. The air, as you would expect in an underground pipe, was fetid with necroses, sewage and mold. Worse, here and there, I would crawl upon the decaying bony remains of a dead animal.

Finally, finally, finally I came to an exhausted halt. My body now barely seemed to clear the ribbed sides. I ached all over. This apparent narrowing down of the crawl-space—coupled with the total lack of any sense of "getting somewhere" and my deep, aching fatigue—resulted in a serious psychological as well as physical choke. No matter how gutsy-tough, no matter how much testosterone I dug up, my "blessed assurance" slowly leaked away. I found myself totally overwhelmed by despair and an accompanying urge to "just quit."

I did. I just quit. I dropped flat on my back and mentally I dropped into a bottomless pit. Down, down, down I fell and kept on falling. The screen-of-my-mind was filled with a swirl of pastel panels. I tried to concentrate so that I could control the falling—slow down the color swirl. I fought to think rationally—to struggle on again. Nothing worked. I just kept on falling.

Mosul Gig, Day Four

Hours must have passed. I awakened suddenly out of this complex falling, flashing-color dream. I use the term *awaken* loosely because of the incredible seamlessness of my entombed world. Everything was pitch black. Yet in this total absence of light, I thought I could see things—objects and colors. Yet I wasn't sure whether the images I saw were real or virtual or dream. The pastel panels of a moment ago were very real to me. The falling was a "real dropping down in space." I could see and feel the whirr of falling. I wondered: "What is reality anyway? Is a *thought* real? Is an *idea* real? Or must something have physical size, shape, form, weight to be real?"

My mind slowed its circular, downward spiral and leveled off for a landing. My arms, I was again aware, were locked down at my sides. I could not breathe deeply because of the narrowness of the culvert. *Aha!* I thought. *That is a reality for sure! I cannot reach my eyes to see whether they are open or closed.* I tried blinking my eyelids. They blinked. Still there was absolutely no change in the sensory picture. Whether my eyes felt open or closed, I could see the metal cylinder roof right there inches above my face. But I was not sure I actually saw it. Perhaps I visualized it because I knew it was there. I had felt it rough and ribbed during my endless digging and skootching. I had seen it earlier in the half-light of my crawl-in. Moreover, I could feel it with the backs of my pinned-down hands.

I lifted up my head and shoulders and touched the ceiling with my forehead. I now reasoned that the texture in what I seemed to see here was illusionary. Although in retrospect it seems almost irrational, I next set about carefully exploring whether I was really awake or asleep. I felt fully conscious, but I knew from experience that often when one is fast asleep dreaming, the sense of reality is so complete, one never questions his consciousness. Nonetheless, I found myself reasoning that when I am asleep, the question of whether I am awake or asleep never arises. I always assume I am awake. All things considered, I was here coming up out of a weird dream, *questioning*. I decided: I must be awake.

Right there and then, I made a clear, rational decision to shake off the mystic—the dreamy, the dead. I literally whispered myself into action. "We will advance even if it can only be an inch at a scrunch. We will not let our negative, disheartened lower-self regain control of our thoughts and fears. We will fight down any evidence of anxiety and doom. Now, let's roll!"

I pulled up my legs a few inches, dug in my heels, lifted my butt slightly until my knees just touched the ceiling ribs, and pushed hard—TTHHRRUUNNKK. "Alleluia! I moved!" I shouted it out. Of course, the dust raised by my push, plus that stirred from my shout, choked me. A violent spasm of coughing raised more. I could not see it, but I could chew the muddy grit. Still coughing to get my breath, I whispered defiantly, "To Hell with ya—I'm alive, awake, alert, enthusiastic!" For some irrational reason, the old scout-camp wake-up chant hit me.

I drew up my knees, and I shoved again—TTHHRRU-UNNKK. I drew up my knees, and I shoved again—TTHHRRUUNNKK. I drew up my knees, and I shoved again—TTHHRRUUNNKK. My spirit rebounded. I shouted the whisper, "Hot Damn! This works! We're moving!" Now, I discovered that by holding my breath while pushing, I could rest, count to ten and then breathe. Ha! No grit. It apparently took the count of ten for the dust to swirl from the effort, then settle.

Soon I had myself a rhythm that was showing progress even in the squeeze. I cannot explain or describe the change in buoyancy-of-spirit that seemed to take charge of me now. I had somehow simply and completely turned my back on the unhinged hysteria of the long night past. I simply refused now to go there. Whenever my mind ducked back toward that dark agony of defeat, I would consciously block its imagery. Some part of me now would stand at the edge of the pit and hold up a forbidding hand like a traffic cop.

Now and then, along here, I would visualize a cloudy, grim, "God-face" out there. Then, a mighty wind would swirl down out of the clouds and clear out the shadows of defeat. These, taken together, gave me a real assurance that God was on my side. I simply kept it up. I dug in my heels until my knees hit the ribs above, gave it a painful, but mighty shove—TTHHRRUUNNKK.

My head now was getting scrubbed raw by the friction of the jagged metal ribbing and the coarse sand in the bottom of the culvert. I needed to incorporate, a "lift" move into my rhythm. I came up with: If I pulled up my knees, then lifted up my head then TTHHRRUUNNKK—this not only would ease the wear-n-tear on my head and neck, but it would also allow me to keep sort of glancing ahead. Because my "head-lift" would automatically tip my head back so I could at least try to see ahead.

Of course, in the blackness, I could see nothing but fine dust which I only thought I could see because I could feel it against my closed eyelids, and I knew the dust was there. Still the fact that I thought I could see it—see ahead—gave me a sense of expectancy, and the positive hope of the expectancy was real even if the sight of the dust up ahead was illusionary.

Notice the level of minutia as well as the mix of fact and fiction that was working for me here? Notice also how this vague, gauzy, ethereal supposition that I was able to glance ahead could only be a very tiny input toward my ascending morale. Still, when one is where I was, every tiny bit counts. And any tiny bit may ultimately prove to be the decisive factor. Notice also how the positive aspect or *God-quality* of my soul's essence was arising slowly through this segment of my adversity. But also notice this positive, will-power soar was my first glimpse of victory here—out of this bleak hopelessness of an endless and unknown nowhere.

Strange as it may seem, right along in here in my mole journey, although time had lost its meaning, I gradually became aware, between my TTHHRRUUNNKKs, as I kept glancing ahead as I skootched along, of a visible change in ambient illumination. At first I denied it. I kept saying to myself, "Nothing has changed. Let's don't start that wild, psycho thing again. I'm not a dumb monkey swinging from high hope to deadly despair and back." Still, I thought I noticed a dim haze of *moving dust* following one especially strenuous push. It started so ephemerally that I mentally recorded it as the same old "taste" instead of a visual sensation. Another push. "There it is again!"—Just the slightest visual awareness of the blackness, graying and moving.

Can you empathize with what that tiny hint does to the heart of a man on the sharp edge of despair? Can you feel what I now felt lying at the very bottom? Can you sense what was beginning to enter here in the soul of a man who has fought with the devil on the precipice of hell, and only by the Grace-of-God did not quite fall in? It was huge! Awesome! Here I was just beginning to experience. No. Here I was just beginning to become aware of the faint, first film of the fuzzy fabric called, "Hope." It brushed by me as I worked at the lowest possible level. Nonetheless, it spoke, "Hope!"

"Calm down, now." I was whispering admonitions again. "Just keep the rhythm. Draw up knees. Dig in heels. Lift up head"—TTHHRRUUNNKK!—"Count. Breathe. Now, draw up knees. Dig in heels. Lift up head"—TTHHR-RUUNNKK! "Calmly now, just the rhythm, man." I was out loud again, but very softly. "Just the rhythm. Don't imagine things. Just the rhythm. Draw up . . ."

Here I became aware that my shoulders were fitting into the culvert more easily. I was no longer scraping the sides with my shoulders and wrists as I skootched along. I was now sliding freely. "No! Don't let your mind screw you up. Just maintain the rhythm, man. Draw up knees. Dig in heels. Lift up head"—TTHHRRUUNNKK! "And count."

Soon there was no possible way to deny that the illumination in the tunnel was improving. I had to stop and focus on this. I went over the *rods* and the *cones* thing with my eyes. I tested the sensitivity of different portions of my eye's seeing-center. The rods around the periphery proved definitely more sensitive to low levels of illumination, and there was definitely a blind-spot in the cone-zone.

Pull up knees. Dig in heels. I suddenly found myself physically exhausted. I had to pause for rest. As I allowed myself to feel around and roll my eyes around and try to see, I found that there was getting to be quite a bit of room in my cave. I tipped back my head to see if I could see some kind of hole ahead. Nope, no opening, but definitely a crepsucule out there!

An hour passed. Then another. As the dim light ahead grew to a glow, my spirits rose proportionately. I began to feel a difficulty controlling my surge-of-hope. I began thanking God out loud. I started a continuous, soft but earnest chat with my God, "Thank you, Lord. We've licked him! We are winning this thing!"

I found myself encouraging myself like an athletic coach: "Go! Go! Go!" I began chanting the words in rhythm with my skootches. I was clearly making progress. Foot-by-foot, I was advancing toward the light. Now I had much more room. I was alternately pushing with my heels, then my butt and simultaneously swimming with my elbows. Even though the backs of my arms, my shoulders and my bottom were raw from friction and persistent use, I kept at it. I knew I was getting to an end—a way out of some sort, somewhere.

Conditions and circumstances had bottomed out back there during the night. Now, I could actually see and feel the tide turning. The diameter of the cylinder was definitely increasing. The air quality was definitely improving. The faint gray illumination ahead was definitely brightening. And with these pulses, all aspects of life joined in the rally.

This role reversal was such a morale breakthrough that I found it necessary to pause my "Go's" periodically and remind myself, "Easy, easy—keep the rhythm. No celebration yet. One-foot-at-a-time."

Mosul Gig, Day Five

Almost suddenly, I am there! I rolled over onto my stomach in the grassy, weedy opening. I pushed up onto my elbows and looked out. Unexpectedly I found myself unable to handle the dazzling light. Although it was just breaking dawn, the intensity of this soft, gauzy, green-gray illumination, compared to the blackness of the tunnel, coupled with the recent total despair of my soul, was too much. I was momentarily blinded. I shook my head to clear my eyes.

Again, I peered out. I was lying on my belly, elbow-propped, trying to see where I was—where I had surfaced in relation to Mosul and the Tigris River—and spot something familiar. I hurt all over, but my spirit had taken control of my body, and the victory over death and despair was so totally engaging, once I got my eyes adjusted, I spontaneously shouted out into the gauzy dawn; "WHOOOOAAAAH!"

Then I heard it—another sound—the musical chatter of women out and below. I thought momentarily how odd it was that my sight was impaired by the long darkness, but not my hearing by the long silence. Then I realized, the experience had not been nearly as *silent* as *dark*. Drifting across the morning calm came what sounded like a clutch of women chattering and laughing in Persian. I dropped flat and pulled back in. Then I thought, *What am I afraid of? I'm not a fugitive. I'm among friends. I was only fleeing the guards and dogs of the airfield police. I am here on the threshold of freedom. No one here could possibly know I am an international fugitive.*

But still cautious, I peeked out again. I wondered why the women I heard were talking Persian, not Arabic. Then I remembered: Mosul—Kurds. My thoughts tumbled on: *This whole scene here, the mouth of an escape tunnel, sudden, apparent victory after thirty-six hours of squeezed, exhausted, painful, dark, hopelessness—insane claustrophobia and near-death psychosis—now rather sudden freedom! Wow!*

Here, facing a different life in a different place under different circumstances—free, but somehow flawed, ordinary people should pose no threat. Still the shouted words of the dog-handler into his walkie-talkie spoke to the lingering flaw in the freedom: "It's an Israeli spy sabotaging our runway. Yes, Sir! Dynamite, Sir.'' Then, too recent to either ignore or forget—the vicious, snarling growl of the attack dogs at the culvert entrance straining against their leashes.

Three

The dawn's early light was growing. And as my eyes adjusted to it, I focused out upon a strange scene. Nothing was familiar nor helpful in orienting where I had emerged, or which way I should go. I was indeed totally disoriented. I was overlooking a wide river. Below and all up and down the bank cattail reeds. Down near the river, a muddy bank slid out to water's edge. There I could see a pattern of yellow or tan sticks embedded in the mud near the water's edge—sticks with colorful bundles tied above, connecting the sticks. Some baskets seemed to be bobbling between these stick-bundles.

A massive masonry bridge blocked my long-range view up to the right. A more modern suspension bridge limited my view to the left, upstream. Carts, a few automobiles with lights and a multitude of black silhouettes—people—moved along a road or street on the far bank of the river. Contrarily, on my side, no street. I was directly above the muddy riverbank and a bank of reeds that sloped gradually down to the water.

Wait! One of the colorful bundles moved! Oh, oh. These bundles were actually the sources of the voices. The bundles and sticks were actually women's ample bottoms with bare legs protruding down into the water—local washerwomen, facing away toward the river, bending over their work.

My mind now grasped the picture of the little clutch of women splashing their clothes in the muddy shallows. These were Kurdish women, not Arabs—no chadors. Now as I watched, the brightening dawn cleared the scene. Two of the younger girls were teasing each other in a friendly water-fight. A mother was gently admonishing.

I decided to slide out of my tomb and drop down. My plan was to ease along the riverbank to the ancient bridge. Once there, I should find familiar landmarks. I had studied the entire Mosul area both from the air earlier and via map with Najua, anticipating visiting home with her.

I slid out carefully grasping the heavy, ribbed metal in my hands. Then, rolling my feet down first, I let out to arms length and immediately let go. KERSWISH! I landed in deep reeds with hardly a sound. The girls' laughing chatter and horseplay continued without interruption. I avoided the women and worked my way carefully through the tall reeds. When perhaps fifty yards downstream from my original drop point, I pushed down to the water's edge. Here, a couple of yards of packed mud provided a reasonable walkway.

I headed for the bridge with positive thoughts surfacing quickly now: *I'll bet I know where this is. There are three major bridges across the Tigris River connecting the city of Mosul to the busy street on the east bank. I'll bet that street over there is the road south to Al Kuweir, the Kurdish fishing village on the Zab River.*

My immediate goal was to blend in with the locals I could see beginning to populate the streets. I needed to quiet my twisted psyche—get over this guilt syndrome and become one of the folk—and pick up a cab to Najua's folks' huge residence in the northern suburb. There I could prop-erly cleanse my scraped limbs, get medical attention if neces-sary and a ride to Baghdad where Martinelli could well be waiting to return me to school. The thought of needing some kind of cover story loomed but did not focus. Marti-nelli had buddies in Baghdad. He would hardly notice if I happened to be a day late.

As I approached the open market under and in the shadow of the massive bridge, I identified this crossover as the middle bridge. Najua had shown me this crossing as the one direct to the digs of ancient Nineveh and the highway to Irbil, half way between the Mosul oil fields and the Iranian border. Irbil is actually near the site of the historic Battle of Gaugamela. Alexander the Great, in one of the great battles of all time, with only about 30,000 Greek troops, cleverly drew Persian King Darius, with about two million soldiers, into a trap against the granite wall at Gaugamela. The year was 331 B.C.

I was getting very hungry about now and thought about picking up some fruit or a croissant at one of the little, shaded canvas stalls. I stopped and leaned a moment against a flat, wooden fishing dhow—locally called a mu-helah—drawn up here on the mud in the shade of the bridge. I hesitated. I still felt quite tense—hunted—and was also trying to solve the no-money problem. My eyes darted about as though I were concerned someone would recognize me. Then I saw a ground cloth covered with fruit, vegetables, a dead chicken and a dead cat. No one was tending this tiny market. I moved quickly toward it. I would steal a carrot or something. Not adjusting well to the sudden shadow under the bridge, I tripped over the dhow's bow-rope and sprawled flat on the mud bank. This sudden, embarrassing falter brought me what I wanted least, a half dozen little Arab boys. These kids had come to the bridge market with their mothers, but found little of interest. One carried a soccer ball. The others, just looking for some action, circled around me and laughed at my predicament.

There happened to be, near where I sprawled, a portion of abandoned newspaper. It had apparently been picked up from a newsstand by the river breeze, blown under the bridge and caught between the frayed rope and its securing

peg. For whatever reason, the youngest of the urchins secured the paper and handed it to me. I was in the process
of flinging off hunks of mud that my arms and pants had
collected in my fall. I presumed the kid had reasoned the
paper might be helpful.

I thanked him, stood up and leaning against the teth-
ered boat, I dipped a wedge of newspaper into the water. I
needed to squish-off some of the mud and blood that had
scabbed on my arms, elbows and the back of my head.

The wet newspaper sponging was major soothing, and
two of the little boys joined in helping with my ablution.
The others pointed out scab marks and dirt that needed
attention. In the course of this team effort, I got to peek
inside my pants. The bullet bruise on my left hip had become
quite painful. I discovered why. Although it was not bleeding,
the spot was a badly discolored scrape or tear that had been
exacerbated by the long culvert crawl. I obviously could not
cleanse or treat the wound here in public at the river's edge,
but it would need medical attention or the oozing blood
and crusted serum promised sure infection.

I now noticed that our first aid activity had drawn a
small crowd. Arab kids can smell an American. Above all, I
did not want to attract adult attention as a foreigner. Unfortunately my university T-shirt was not traditional Arab garb.
Still . . . suddenly a radio in a nearby food stall stopped its
Vincent Lopez American music. An emergency announcement burst forth. I was frozen by a Baghdad "Revolutionary
Command Council" special alert announcement!

Everyone stopped to listen. A small cluster of shoppers
gathered around the nearby Philco radio. The citizens were
being warned: "Watch out for an Israeli terrorist who might
be an American. This man, dressed in Western garb, escaped
capture at the Mosul Airbase day-before-yesterday. He is still
at large in spite of a wide and vigorous manhunt. He was

apprehended briefly by the alert and valorous Iraqi Airbase Police. He was caught in the very act of sabotaging the Mosul Airbase runway with dynamite but escaped."

This warning was followed by a rundown on the Revolutionary Command Council, its recent successful coup, the names and its current heroic function. I glanced at the remaining pages of legible newsprint, thinking, *What is this Revolutionary Council stuff?* I found I had a Friday, *Baghdad Evening Press.* That meant I had been out of circulation three days during which an impending coup everyone had been expecting, had apparently succeeded.

The radio spokesman continued, "The foreign agent managed to elude the airport police. He disappeared right before their eyes employing some radical new technology. That is why Israel or America is suspected. The Israelis test these new systems for the Zionist British and Americans. The man is considered armed and dangerous and probably lurking in the vicinity of Mosul to renew his efforts to blow up the Iraqi Air Base runway." I was totally shocked. Still I could not help but smile to hear the exorbitant reward offered for my capture dead or alive. Finally, the report noted that all border crossings had been sealed until further notice.

I flattened up against the hull of the muhelah and tried to look like an ordinary Arab. My mind raced: *What is this Revolutionary Council? This cannot possibly be the predictably friendly Iraq I left, what, three days ago? Dependable American ally, Nuri Said is PM. Nothing this serious could go wrong over a weekend.*

I had expected to briefly visit the airfield, pace off some measurements and walk out the gate to Najua's mother's. There delivery a tiny package from her daughter (held in my daypack), pick up a Monday flight to Baghdad and fly back to school. Now where do I go? If I go out onto Al

Mawsil to catch a cab, I'll be arrested. These Kurds can tell an American a mile away.

Suddenly I was looking down at a wrinkled, crumbled page of this newspaper this lad had recently liberated from its catch on the frayed rope tether. I had used most of it in sponging my wounds. Now I was viewing the front page and looking at the pictures of two men everyone in the Middle East knew: popular King Faisal and his pro-West Prime Minister, Nuri Said. The Arab text verified the headlines: Friends of the West, the popular King and Nuri had been driven from power by a military coup, midnight Thursday. Both are in custody at Revolutionary Command Headquarters awaiting trial by military court-martial.

"Unbelievable!" My reaction was one of total shock. My thoughts careened: *Power in Baghdad has changed hands while I was inching along that dirty, dark, dismal drain to freedom. This paper was Friday's. What day was this? It had to be either Saturday or Sunday. But regardless, apparently Iraq was no longer America-friendly. That changes the name of my game completely.*

Until now I had been leaning on a plan to slip unobtrusively back into the city. I would cover up my bruises as much as possible. I would walk or catch a cab northeast on Al Mawsil, the broad street leading from the bridge into the great square. From the square, I would hike west to the Shaheens' home. Later today or tomorrow Mom Shaheen would drive me to Baghdad. Martinelli would be doing embassy work waiting for me. On the return trip I would work on a respectable, believable story I would tell back at the university explaining my rather beat-up condition to my friends and professors.

Now, however, I was not only on a different page. I was in a different book. I had become a fugitive—worse, a capital fugitive. Worse yet, I had become a capital fugitive of the

Jihadist Arabs, the fundamentalist, terrorist Mujahedin. This group of insurgents had been discussed again and again at university, but each discussion had ultimately discounted their coming to power. I couldn't believe this was happening.

I reasoned that I now needed to move into some form of survival mode. As I learned against the boat and stared out at the slowly drifting river, my mind fled back to that October meeting behind the consulate in Beirut. I could hear that SAC man, Ryan, tell me this was a simple routine, "pacing-and-digging" duty. I had nothing to fear. "All the countries are dear friends, Major. You only need to say, if you are clumsy enough to get caught. 'I'm an American pilot friend. We're planning on selling you some jet fighters. I need to know how long . . .' " My mind flashed in anger, *Damn! How stupid can a fighter pilot get? I had shaken Colby's hand and said "Okay, I'll do it. A fighter pilot can do anything." Damn! Dumb pride!*

At that moment a young Kurdish girl jumped off the bow of the muhelah from the deck above and landed right beside me there in the sand. "Murhuba!" She laughingly shouted this common Arab greeting and, smiling warmly, she untied the worn old bow-rope. Caught by surprise, I pushed away from the boat and just stood there admiring her tan, healthy, good looks.

"Okaayyee!" She called the American term musically to someone above on the boat deck. I started to move away into the crowd. The rising sun through Rawanduz Pass told me it was about eight o'clock. And by now literally hundreds of men, women and children had gathered under the bridge bartering their fish or corn or baby ducks for needed veggies, sugar or flour.

The girl jumped directly in front of me, blocking my way. This caught my attention. She was maybe fifteen, dressed more Kurdish than Arab—no veil or chador—with a flashy scarlet scarf binding long, coal black hair. She had brown, bare legs, bare feet and a bold, very attractive smile. She took my hand and in very slow, broken English, "You-are-English-scientist?" She was somehow connecting me to the digs that the London Museum was currently doing at ancient Nineveh across the river.

"No, I'm American student." My response was defensive-instinctive. I was totally caught by surprise by this girl's sudden, fresh, attractive boldness.

"Come-help-push!" She pulled me back to the dhow, and together we put our shoulders against the bow and gun-wales. The heavy boat slipped silently down the slippery mud into the river. "Come! Need you help." The girl, laughing, took my wrist, and before I could gracefully pull free, boosted me onto the deck and in a flash stood beside me. For the first time I could see the full deck of the muhelah and that we were drifting slowly downstream. Our flat-decked riverboat was being turned as we drifted, by a lone, brown, thirtyish Arab athlete with a splendid beard, facing us from the distant stern. He shouted and waved.

The man was muscling a sizeable, polished wooden til-ler. He grunted out some kind of orders to the girl who had moved along the deck toward him. Now she bounced for-ward again and, grabbing my arm, pointed to a complex of hemp lines that dangled in the water. "Work!" She laughed, proud that she could come up with an appropriate English word. Following her example, I grabbed some rope and we both began retrieving and coiling. In a few moments we were out from the shade of the bridge into a gorgeous sun rising. The sudden brilliance brought into sharp silhouette the spectacular 15,000-foot Zardeh Kuh on the eastern horizon. Our captain at the tiller had been carrying on an intermit-tent shouting conversation with a man on a neighboring muhelah. Now apparently he sighted friends on the bridge above. He switched his river voice upward. Although I was getting pretty good at Arabic, this Kurd-Persian-Arabic mix was beyond me.

Slowly, amid several between-boat and boat-to-bridge conversations, our fleet of various types of riverboats slid south away from the noise and activity of the city. Soon we were floating near the middle of the quarter-mile-wide Tigris through the quiet countryside. The river was dotted with an assortment of water craft—flat rafts up on inflated goat skins, a few log barges, a round boat and a couple of muhelahs like ours and, sort of together, two long, thin sailboats. This scattered fleet was floating south with the awesome current.

The girl now took me by the hand, and helped me along the canted deck, past a low hut covering the hatch, on back toward the man. "Papa! Papa!" She shouted the universal word against the mild, desert wind. I moved instinctively to help with the tiller that appeared to be a real strength-test. "Papa" was holding the rudder-bar against the current to maintain a safe separation from nearby craft. The powerful Tigris seemed to be fighting to push everything into one another or ashore.

I shouted in Arabic, "My name is Major Bo. I am American student. Your daughter shanghaied me." His shouted laugh was a ton of sunshine. "Shanghai! My Benji shanghai you?" He howled. I laughed. We all laughed. It was an unbelievably warm first meeting of total strangers.

"Mahmoud Abu"—the wind caught a long, classic Arab family name that I recognized as Shiite probably from Basra or the south. I was surprised the family was not Kurd. Abu reached for my hand, but the river called him back to his tiller. I grabbed his arm in a friendly gesture and put my weight against the heavy, polished lever to help steady the dhow. Abu grinned and nodded, affirming my help. "Call me Abu. I'll call you Bo. Keep it simple, right?"

As I got the rhythm of the craft and the current, the team pressure needed on the tiller lessened. We relaxed and began to chat. Abu's normal conversation was a river-shout. I discovered that came with the territory. Casual talk was impossible because of the diurnal river wind, and not only the wind, there were a dozen boat noises—the water, the creaks of the wood, the birds following, and Abu kept shouting bits of conversation to friends on other boats.

He began right away telling me about this boat of his. He got it in a trade from his father-in-law. While he was narrating, his wife, whom he called Sofia, emerged from the hut-hatch near the center of the deck. She and the girl, who seemed to be called Benji, each with an armful of assorted reeds, sat down lotus fashion on the forward deck. From where I stood beside Abu, the women appeared to be weaving then painting reed baskets and mats.

Now in midstream, the dhow floated easily and seemed to maintain separation and follow the current naturally. Abu just kind of rode along, the tiller tucked under his arm. We began to chat. Fortunately, he understood my Palestinian Arabic. I asked him how long he had been at this, and he laugh-shouted, "Since I could walk. My grandfather brought us boys up on the river after my Daddy drowned in the flood of 1916."

This led to a "how-to" boating interchange. Abu took an hour shouting me "up-to-speed" as a riverboat pilot. He needed me to pull my watch at the tiller. He first began talking about "piloting" in general. Then he pulled me to his side and gave the polished steering shaft over to me while standing with his left hand on my shoulder, ready. He talked about steering, about avoiding other craft, docking and launching. He told stories about the Tigris River's idiosyncrasies and storms on the river. Through it all, he emphasized that the key is staying awake and staying in the center-third of the ever-widening river.

I was surprised at how many of the other boatmen Abu knew and with whom he carried on hundred-yard conversations. Most of his friends were shipping merchandise or farm goods to markets in the south, usually Baghdad. Some men floated in pairs of round boats. These I noticed were skillfully guided with one long oar. These round boats didn't seem to be going anywhere very far. Once in a while a boat or raft would pull along side our craft and almost touch for hours as the women exchanged materials, shared food or, as happened once, just changed boats to talk and examine one another's crafting.

I noticed that all the traffic moved with the current and relative positions changed little. There was almost no upstream traffic. After an hour or so, Abu let me steer alone. It was, for a non-boater, actually fun. It was a perfect weather day, and my fighter pilot's eyes seemed to have recovered from my long darkness and grinding grit. I gazed and guided, visualizing myself as an ancient Old Testament river captain plying between Nineveh and Babylon—keeping an eye out for a big fish that may contain Jonah.

Benji brought us a local version of "fish tacos" for lunch. I was beginning to feel warm and good and useful, and I found my hunted, guilty syndrome was fading. I whispered a thanks on-high.

Abu, in our early conversation, had told me how the deckhand hiring normally went. He explained there was no pay connected with this deck job, only food and travel. Benji normally enlisted a deckhand for the trip north at Abadan or Basra in the far south. She chose from the young men she knew visiting or working in the delta who lived up north and wanted to return home. On the southward voyage, as this, the reverse.

The most recent deckhand, Ahmad, lived in Tall Kyaf, a town upriver. He had failed to show after spending last night in Mosul. Yesterday was his first day, and Abu was not surprised when Ahmad deserted. He apparently didn't take to life on a boat. He got seasick, so Abu had not expected him to show up. He explained that his daughter should have enquired about this problem before hiring. Her oversight meant she would perform the deckhand work. Benji was lucky to find me. She would much rather craft with her mother. Abu suspected she chose me because of my apparent availability, plus she had a burning desire to learn English and go to school in the West some day. "Besides," he laughed, "you are big, handsome American. Girls marry young on the river, Ho, ho, ho, ho."

The two women spent the day busily chattering and weaving mats and baskets. About an hour after lunch, Abu disappeared inside the hut and returned with a pottery mug of Turkish coffee. It was predictably hot and sweet and thick. We both drank from the mug.

I must say, Abu was large for an Arab—well-muscled and bare to the waist. As I say, he normally talked loud and fast in a mixed laugh and shout of Kurdish Persian and southern Arabic. I could get about half of it and guess at the rest. He was pleasant and encouraging to be around. In all the time we were together, I never heard him put anyone down or speak harshly about anyone or cuss, criticize or show anger. He appeared to me to be happily married, in a profession he knew well and loved. It was uplifting to be this suddenly associated with a human who just found life and the people on this planet felicitous.

Abu knew nothing about the politics of Iraq. When I cautiously asked him about the coup in Baghdad, he indicated total disinterest. Likewise, he was totally ignorant of world affairs. Contrarily, Abu would talk all day about the river and his life on it. He explained to me that he towed this dhow up from Al Amerah, way south in the Tigris-Euphrates delta where many of the drift-boats end up in the spring. He explained to me how there is a pathway or roadway along the east riverbank down south, but at Baghdad it is necessary to cross a bridge. This is because the tow-road goes on the west side of the river from Baghdad to Mosul. At Mosul, once again the built-up area of the city, particularly the industrial sprawl near the river, makes it necessary to cross over and tow on the east or northeast side as the Tigris River bends around the city and turns northwest toward Turkey.

During the summer, he and his family had towed their muhelah north with a second-hand John Deere tractor all the way up to Mushorah near the rapids that fall out of Turkey in the north. This towing normally took all summer. By September each year, they arrived in Mushorah, a primitive Kurd village on the edge of the Taurus mountains. Then, while he sold the tractor, repaired and painted the dhow, Sophia and Benji collected craft materials and visited with friends and relatives.

I asked him why he didn't rig his dhow with a sail. I saw no dhows using wind power. This I thought would allow him to sail up the river in the summertime instead of towing. Moreover, sailing would have allowed him to stop and trade along the way going north, as he did going south. He patiently explained to me that it would take him nearly a year to sail up against the current. Also he noted that there were many treacherous sandbars and mud banks just below the surface—worse, the bars and banks were constantly moving. He claimed he could tow up in a couple of months. Also, as far as trading en route, he currently stopped where the trading was good on his way up just as when floating down.

61

In mid-afternoon there came a long silent spell. I decided to try again on the coup. I asked Abu if the new government would be better or worse for his river business. A classic Arab, Abu gave me a French salute and the common Bedouin disclaimer, "Malesh." Here on Abu's muhelah I verified a notion that I had picked up at the university. Ordinary, country Arabs and Kurds respond similarly to bends in the journey-of-life—even huge changes—triumph or disaster. They come up with the same shrug, the same two-palms up, the same word, "malesh," which loosely translated says, "Whatever Allah wills."

After another several minutes of silence, he loosely repeated the broadcast news. The military had not harmed the king, but had dissolved the parliament and were ruling by decree. A popular general who had recently chased the Iranians out seemed to be in charge. Army units were taking over the larger cities. The Kurds were to be moved back into the mountains. The enemies of the state were to be dealt with summarily. All Israeli and other foreign spies were being rounded up.

I now found myself modifying my earlier plans of return to school. I had given up all hope of visiting the Shaheens or even returning to Mosul, or now, even Baghdad. I found myself thanking God for giving me this respite on this riverboat and with it, a time to plan a less frenetic solution to my problem.

I was toying with the notion of jumping ship at a village near the Iranian border and hiking across. I knew it would be a long trip no matter where I chose to cross over. But I also knew, from a recent visit to Iran, that the American military mission there was very strong and nicely scattered. I knew the Shah was firmly in power and the Iranian people were friendly to us. I could report in to any of the numerous U.S. military detachments training the Iranian units along the border. As an Air Force Major I would be provided all amenities, transport and much respect. I could plan to be back in the university by late October at the latest.

I could make my report to Keystone in Vienna. I knew the depth of concrete and the runway width at Mosul and 7000 feet was a close estimate of its length. No one would ever know of my narrow squeak with the guards and dogs or my humiliating and painful crawl to escape. I surely would not need that news to get back to my fighter pilot friends in America. I would be called "The Mole" for the remainder of my career. Worse, I might even have to face a court-martial for carelessness—nearly blowing a critical U.S. WWIII strategy-of-deployment.

Four

Through the hot, desert-windy afternoon we slid south on the historic, flat, yellow flood. We took turns at the tiller. The heat from the inescapable sun, both direct and reflected, was debilitating. The girl's main duty, which she knew without instruction, was drawing yellow soup up from the river with a rope and wooden bucket, then splashing the duty-tiller cool. Both shores here were distant—barely visible, no distant mountains now—only the flat desert, with no clear horizon. Sky and water melded. This slow, cooking, bleed south through the endless desert must have given the early Assyrians their notion of hell as a "lake-of-fire." By late afternoon we had drifted thirty miles. Here just before sundown we were treated to the most impressive scene of the trip so far: the river Zab al Kabir plunging into the Tigris from the northeast. Hundreds of mountain rivers cascaded down the western slopes of the Zagros, across the border from Iran and into the mighty Tigris. Of these many, by far the most dramatic is Zab al Kabir—aka the Great Zab.

All jabber and play on passing boats stopped. All eyes turned. All passengers and crews noticed how the Tigris widened here, steadied and became a really Great River.

This was September, I saw a fairly tame but very picturesque mountain stream. The Great Zab has been described by the Persian poet, Bandar Shalone as "a bundle of crystaline capillaries plunging down from the high Zagros of Kurdistan to wash in mist the sloping plateau and the flocks thereon, then having cooled the brow, slips quietly as a huge tear onto the face of the frowning desert and the shouting excitement and awesome terror is done.'' Bandar apparently was not thus impressed with the poetry of the mighty Tigris River and its expressive, even dramatic, sweep down across the storied desert to the sea.

This Great Zab of Iraq is indeed a river of character itself. It rises in the near glacial snows of the high Zagros mountains of Kurdistan, the unsurveyed, pathless and rarely even footprinted wilderness corner where Turkey, Iran and Iraq almost meet. The tangled, tortuous, mountainous area has never been surveyed. It is locally identified as the Armenian Knot. For hundreds of thousands of years—since man first stood up on his hind legs and began to move across the earth in search of better food and more room—whether alone, or with his family or leading a tribe or marauding as a nation-on-horseback (the Mongol Khans thousands of years later), all man has avoided this desolate corner of Kurdistan. It is just too high and wild, too gnarled and snarled, the canyons too steep and, including the prevalence of vicious, wild animals, too dangerous.

Of course, the character of any river is defined by its context. Through its higher reaches, Zab is a savage mountain lion. She becomes a civilized though spirited lady where she plunges into Iraq near the famous and terrifying Khan Chasm Bridge. This fantastic bridge was named for one of the great Khans who legend says chased Alexander the Great out of Tabriz and Kermanshah and the greater Caspian Sea basin after Guagamela.

Local Kurdistan legend tells a different story of Alexander's Arabella campaign than we read in Western history. On the muhelah deck and around later mountain campfires, I heard tell that the real victor and hero here was Kubla

Khan's great, great grandson, Ali Khan, who with a thousand, tough tribal warriors made a decisive stand at this same chasm bridge. A very stubborn fight here a month following Gaugamela, forced impatient, thirty-year-old Alexander to turn south, and cross the Zagros into the Azerbaijan by way of the traditional, herd-migration route, Rawanduz Pass.

As I stood my watch at the tiller, my mind followed Alexander across into the Azerbaijan and relative safety in Iran—then Persia. I could do that. The current at the confluence was strong. The distance was perhaps 400 yards. I could easily swim it. I would never see this family again, so there was no need to explain my priorities. In fact, I could go now—just step to the rail and fffffttt, I would be gone. But, for reasons known but to God, I stood my watch at the tiller. Actually I lingered a few moments at the point-of-decision (leaning against the port rail), realizing that I probably must go on east soon. Then I heard a very clear inner voice say to me, "No Bo, I want you to go south with this family now."

It would be three more days before circumstances would free me—in fact, inspire me to turn my face east toward safety and freedom, and with an inner voice of encouragement. The decision to *go* rather than to *stay*, portended an unbelievable journey a dozen times longer, a hundred times more difficult and a thousand times more edifying than I had anticipated. In truth, the journey would prove more wildly violent than any evasion and escape adventure I had ever experienced before or would experience again—including my Vietnam ten-mile crawl-to-freedom after being shot down over Dac To. The journey would nonetheless also prove more meaningful than any other of my life hikes.

As the September sun sank among the palms and willows and a huge full moon peaked over the Zardeh Kuh,

Abu took the watch and bent our clumsy craft in toward a cluster of small fishing boats at a break in the rushes on the eastern shore.

The taupe current fought hard. Abu shouted for me to stand by. Together we swung the tiller pole and slid our muhelah into the opening. As we approached shore, we found, up ahead, a crowd of Arabs—mainly children—fishing on a long quay. "Dinner providers." Abu puffed on a cigarette and gestured me to jump ashore with the line.

"Take a quick belay on that middle stump, Major! Girls, get ready!" He called separate instructions to each of us in one breath. I jumped—snagged the flying line and wrapped. The heavy dhow's bow was caught. The stern swung with the current and bumped the old car tires that guarded the dock's riverside.

Abu showed me the tie-up and check-in procedures. We were ashore at an ancient fishing village, now called Kalhu—pronounced "K-y-oo"—near the famous archaeological ruins at Calab Nimrud. If my memory serves me right, this is the Old Testament, *Nimrod*—great grandson of Noah, spoken of in Genesis 10:8–10.

Grab your Bible, let's look: "Cush begot Nimrod; he began to be a mighty one upon the earth. He was a mighty hunter before the Lord; therefore it is said, 'Like Nimrod the mighty hunter before the Lord.' And the beginning of his kingdom was Babel, Erech, Accad and Calneh, in the land of Shinar."

Mosul Gig, Day Six

During this stretch of the journey, the days get mixed up in my memory. So, to keep the story true and moving correctly, I am taking this segment of the adventure directly from my journal with very little memory-editing. You will notice that I sometimes relate a dashing or exciting stretch in the "present tense." I journalled it that way in 1951, and the rules of the IJS say that you are not to amend your journal in retro. Most all the inconsistencies in history or Holy Scripture can be traced to retro-amended journaling.

Dawn breaks in a world of white. Fog-on-the-river. I am rostered to help lay out our rugs and arrange our wares in the marketplace. Then I am to watch Abu and learn how to hawk the craft items. The two girls sit quietly holding up various pieces of our craftwork as Abu describes each in glowing terms. Only Abu calls out. As one would expect from his river speech, he has a classic county fair voice and employs it like a circus barker.

This marketplace is a standard Middle East suq, pronounced "sook," or open air bazaar. The shopping crowd starts small, early. It grows until about mid-morning. We market people, both buyers and sellers, are a colorful mob of many costumes and languages from everywhere. Our market-spot is beside the mosque, so my new experience is watching the tiny door high on the minaret open. Then out on the balcony the muezzin steps to call us to prayer. Everyone goes down flat to pray five times each day. I go too.

I pick up quickly on the barking, and Abu lets me join him. Shouting is apparently a "men only" thing in the desert lands. I'm apparently good. Before noon, I am drawing a crowd. I'm worried about Abu becoming jealous of my crowds, but when I tell him I'm sorry, he laughs. He says my major value is "I'm a foreigner." He says any good-looking foreigner draws the curious, not so much to buy as to gawk. Then he quickly adds: "Nonetheless, my friend, with a crowd of gawkers, there are always some buyers. Plus a crowd draws more crowd, ya know, to see what's going on—what the bargains are. So you're earning your rice and blanket." He gives me a bear hug for encouragement.

The wares: We have baskets of various sizes, shapes and materials; neat reed mats; hand-dyed cotton fabrics; quilted coverlets, and some toys for children—plus a box of baked goods. Our girls are very crafty, but they are not alone as suppliers. Abu Mahmoud brings ashore a box of his leatherwork and woodcarvings, and Abu made the toys by hand. Even I am learning to braid the reeds. I'm four feet into a colorful rope, working when the crowds are slack. I find here in the market I must concentrate my shouting on superlatives: "World's finest!" "Made by a precious Bedouin's hands!" "Nowhere else on this planet!" etc. I'm not really that good at Arabic or Persian. I throw in a little English and a few words of Farsi. I hear the passing Bedouins, especially the kids, repeating the English words to each other, then they laugh with total glee.

The day is busy and exciting. I am impressed with the flow of cash and barter. We pick up in trade enough food for lunch. After lunch I take a break to visit some shops in the suq. My most interesting find is a British archeologist named Dr. Max Mallowan. He is here on a *National Geographic* grant to find the building stones of the Tower of Babel. He has a personal goal of defining the first culture to occupy the site.

Some scholars hold that biblical Nimrod built, or at least engineered, the Babel Tower on this site. Actually the archeological tell of the magnificent, ancient Assyrian city of Nimrud lies a couple of miles east. The Tigris flowed directly beside the great palace and along the fortress wall of the city 10,000 years ago. Dr. Mallowan tells me that the savage Tartar warlord, Tamerlane, sacked the city and destroyed the irrigation system. Moreover, he says with a wink, his words so frightened the river it fled two miles to the west where it flows today.

I like this unusual British scholar. Max is totally capable of explaining the unexplainable with New Yorker style humor. He came out from Cambridge two years ago with a small team of students to continue the work begun by the famous adventurer, Pasha Layard, of the British Museum. Dr. Layard dug here trying to find Nineveh. He later moved north and is mainly responsible for outsmarting the Louvre-backed French and finding the great treasures of Nineveh for the British Museum. Dr. Mallowan promises me a beginner's, pointy-talky tour tomorrow.

Mosul Gig, Day Seven

It was a long night. These open markets or suqs never really go quiet. We sort of piled up our merchandise and slept in a row on the rug. It was warm and reasonably comfortable. Every so often an Arab customer would shake Abu. He would roll to his knees and make the sale, then drop back to sleep.

For some reason the constantly moving people made me nervous. My mind went into a dozen different vignettes. All ended with me in cuffs before a firing squad. Then, whenever I opened my eyes, I found Benji there just a few inches away, eyes wide-open, staring at me. This was a little disconcerting. Then, a town crier moved around the various corners of the village shouting out the hours. "Nine o'clock and all's well!" The British convinced all these colonial countries that "shouting-the-hours" like they once did in London, improved security.

When I heard *five*, I eased away and sauntered down to the waterfront. I just stood on the dock for a long time gazing out to the west across a mile of brownish-yellow water scarfed here and there with clean white mist. My thought-flow, without any effort or guidance on my part, washed into an "appreciation mode." I found myself calling into memory earlier experiences and reaffirming the soul-deep sense of how the really great rivers like the Tigris carry a strange, mystic, almost hypnotic power. This is completely separate from a river's horsepower or hydraulic, electric or other physical power.

I was once again beside a *Great River* and my spirit was trying to describe or comprehend a notion too abstract and too sublime for the mind of man. You may have sensed this epiphanal conceit standing beside the Mississippi, the Columbia, the Ganges, the Nile, the Indus, the Brahmaputra, the Rhine or the Yangtze. The river totally abducts one. Even in the gray gauze of dawn, the Tigris is a boundless, flat, chartreuse sea, imperceptibly moving, carrying with it a vast-ness, a majesty, a mystic expectancy. I stand there with my legs apart, arms folded, just looking, but not staring. You've done this. It's an almost worship-like looking—an appreciation of a holy essence or personality beyond comprehension. Moreover, it's an expectant-looking. It's as though instinctively I have a premonition that something significant is coming down here from up above. You know? This mighty motion, without any apparent control—it has got to lead to something or mean something more than just river eternally flowing by.

As the sun burns away at the light mist enveloping Kalhu, I think of the Rhine River at Dusseldorf. A majesty poised to split, forming in the west the delta that is Holland and in the east, three major German rivers that power, irrigate and quench the thirst of north Germany. My mind's eye moves to the Indus, looking west from the busy dock at Hyderabad. The southern Indus is a much deeper green in color, just before it explodes into eight mouths, including one called, for some strange reason, Kori Creek, where it forms the border with India.

I breathe again, now in deep sigh-like sucks and my eyes turn north, upstream. I'm fascinated by the villages of floating craft. This sweeps my mind far east to the mighty Ganges and its Siamese twin, the Brahmaputra. The two, then one, birth on the same glacier, Nanda Dvi, in the central Himalayas. Then, just born, the plunging icy waterfalls strikes a white granite wall and splits! One half plunges southwest to wander-drain northwest India. The twin cuts east a thousand miles across south China, around Nepal and turns south, almost touching Burma then rejoins its glacial twin near the Bay of Bengal. Now one again, they form a massive, common delta east of Calcutta. Fascinating! Are you an amateur geographer?

Probably the most spine-tingling experience in all the world's river scenes is floating the Ganges in a muhelah and arriving at the confluence with the Brahmaputra ten miles west of Dacca. The delta mud is so flat, the mighty water of the rivers, now joined, moves upstream half of the day. Then it suddenly turns with the tide and drifts downstream becoming the Bay of Bengal when the tide goes out.

Anyone from our own Mississippi Valley will have stood somewhere at some time on a bank of "The Big Muddy" and just looked, frozen by its vastness and by its slowness, but relentless and alive with traffic, inexorably flowing south toward New Orleans. Historians, remember? It was at Civil War Vicksburg, early one morning, in the midst of the siege that led to its surrender in 1863. General Grant's deputy found him standing motionless and transfixed. Historian William Mansfield relates that young Brigadier Armstrong Custer had to touch Grant's arm to shatter the trance. He jumped, startled, then quietly expressed his awe: "Hmmm, yes, good morning, son. I was looking at the river. Have you seen it?"

I was to discover the same mystic fascination when abducted by the mystic Mekong on the delta of IV Corps south of Saigon in 1969. I was standing watch one delta dawn in 1969 aboard a Navy jet-boat. It was partly the unique orange light of sunrise at Vinh Long. But it was mainly this whole river-mystic of vastness and power and the awesome calm of God's Presence. Whole families—even whole villages—spend their entire lives out there afloat on that mighty river, busy and contented.

Back to Iraq, I am fascinated by this Tigris River scene. It's not yet fully daylight. It's almost religiously quiet. Yet water-craft of every sort—rafts, round boats, log barges and flat boats like our muhelah—drift slowly south; ghosts in the gray, eerie silence. And on the various decks as they pass, frozen statues watch the dawn gather in reverential quiet. I, too, just stand there on the pier, together with perhaps a dozen sleepy Arabs of all ages, in this meditative, anticipative stillness.

A Brief Geographic Sidebar

My river reverie pulls out of the confused milieu of past and present and into focus the Old Testament story of Jonah and his encounter with the whale. Remember, it ended not at sea where a whale might normally be found, but hundreds of miles up the Tigris River at Nineveh, near present-day Mosul. Nonetheless, standing there on the edge of the very same river, in the pre-dawn, bluish wash, watching this incredible mass of xanthic-green, water slide silently south, I can easily handle the Jonah story. The terrain here is so flat, and the river has followed so many different visible courses over the millennia, you can visualize this whole country of Iraq as delta. The entire surface of this plate of the earth's crust is made of silt—silt sifted down from the two great rivers, Tigris and Euphrates, plunging out of their steep, craggy, granite fortresses in the curved, highland, continental heartland of Kurdistan (Turkey, Armenia, Azerbaijan, Persia).

Look at a topographical map of the Middle East. A million years ago yesterday, an observer afloat on the Mediterranean Sea would sail east past Lebanon, Syria and Iraq to the sharp Zagros bluffs. Paleontologists tell me that sailor would find water covering much of Egypt, the Sinai, Jordan and Saudi Arabia. Moreover, he would probably also stand in awe of hundreds of mile-wide, sheet-like waterfalls from the Taurus Cliffs of Turkey in the north, dumping down out of the Armenian Knot and the Caspian Sea from the northeast all the way south along the Zagros front to the point where the Persian Gulf then joined the Arabian Sea. When a later cold snap hit Earth, macro-tons of this water froze to ice and was spun, by Coriolis effect, north and south to form the high ice mountains of the Arctics. The desert lands Egypt, Palestine, Jordan, Syria and Iraq emerged much as we see them today. Sunrise, sunset, swiftly flow the eons.

Now, I stand there on the bank of the historic Tigris in the year of our Lord 1951. I stand in my quiet reverie feeling the power of the river, the closeness of Biblical history and the clear sense of advent. Suddenly, out of the lavender, misty river ambiance, the day bursts open! The sun jumps up from its purpose, eastern shadows, ka-boom! Then first the boats, then the dock, finally the village springs to life. Silent, ghostly forms now begin to laugh and chatter and dance. The stream of merchants, workers and fishermen, heretofore milling in shadowed silence between the village and the pier, begin now to chatter and laugh. Boats begin to splash down into the water. Somewhere a child screams. A mother calls frantically. An old man swears. And from high on a nearby minaret, the haunting voice of the muezzin calls the faithful to prayer. Perhaps two minutes of facedown worship and the people are up and the action is again in high, noisy gear.

Almost immediately from behind me, up the roadway toward the village comes a British accent shouting my name. My half-hour package of quiet-time for the 28th of September is over. I toss my daypack onto the deck of our muhelah and turning, I find Dr. Max leaping from his mud-colored Chevy roadster. He dashes down the sandy roadway, out onto the pier. He doffs his straw fedora and grabs my hand in an enthusiastic greeting. "I say, going for a swim? Ho, ho, ho!" He belly laughs at his tease. "Bloody big drink of water, wouldn't you say, old chap? Ho, ho, ho." I know right away this is going to be a fine day. Max is more Bavarian than British in shape and demeanor and has a California sense of humor.

Notice: The entire thoughts, impressions and activities of "Day Seven." I recorded in my journal after returning from my "show-and-tell" day with this amazing limey scholar, Dr. Max Mallowan. I learned later that my new friend Dr. Mallowan was an eminent British archeologist. He has published several books on digs in the Middle East, one of which, tells of our day together here at Nimrud beside the Tigris. I have borrowed from it, with permission, in my telling here.

Dr. Max said he knew a coffeehouse. In a trice we were humming across the edge of the village to what looked like a New Mexican adobe. Uuuugg! The coffee was black and thick and sweet. Still, I knew it was the right stuff to start a day in the digs.

For half an hour we bumped due east along a non-road—two car tracks through the sand. The sun rose briskly, and the misty cool of dawn turned mean. By nine o'clock, though beginning autumn, we were living Kipling's "Somewhere east of Suez, where the best is like the worst; Where there ain't no Ten Commandments; And a man can raise a thirst!"

We could see the digs before we could see anyone digging. The line of tells (research mounds) runs north and south along the clear mark of the ancient east bank of the Tigris River. The present east bank now runs ten miles to the west. Max chatted along—super interesting stuff—the historic and archeological preface to my tour:

"This site at Nimrud—" he pointed up ahead—"was first explored by a young and inexperienced Oxford grad, Austin Henry Layard. He was looking for biblical Nineveh and instant fame. It was mid 19th century, and both the British Museum and the French Louvre were eager to get *objects d'art* from the ancient Assyrian culture."

Max drew up in a cloud of dust alongside nothing—several mounds of sand, but no building or tent or such. We piled out. Max pointed, "Young Layard liked the earlier-piled mounds here. He hired a team of Arab workers. They just tunneled into these hills, one after another, until they found something ancient. It was awful!" Dr. Max took out a worn old meerschaum, loaded it with tobacco, lit it with a stick match and puffing, continued, "Soon the whole site was moonscape. But he found Nimrud, the ancient city, here on the edge of the river. You see the Tigris was then here, way farther east."

Trailing smoke like a destroyer on patrol, Dr. Max lit out pointing, describing and explaining. I followed at a trot and tried hard not only to keep up, but to show a keen enthusiasm in sand. Mallowan was in heaven. While he knew exactly where he was going, I could see nothing but sand dunes and diggings. Still, Max carried on like I was a cluster of fascinated Cambridge undergraduates, "Young Layard was no idiot, you see. He soon recognized his major find was the palace-capitol of a notable Assyrian King."

Max kicked something, stooped and picked out of the sand a chard of ancient pottery. "Pffft!" He blew the sand away and handing me this *special gift*, continued, "Young Henry grew to fame collecting for the British museum a wealth of booty—carved statues, ivory and gold ornaments, cuneiform tablets plus huge, wall-size friezes of bas-relief. Still, the whole thing here as well as concurrent digs up north had no deep cultural meaning . . ."

Max turned now and we circled back through the rows of tells. "That is, no meaning until another British scholar named Henry Creswicke Rawlinson, working at the Behistun Holy Rock, across the mountains in Persia." Max pointed high to the east. "Broke the cuneiform code. That was a hundred years ago. Rawlinson unlocked the secrets of the three major archeological explorations." Max now pointed north. "Nimrud, Nineveh, east of Mosul and Khorsabad, still further north."

We were now back beside the Chev. We jumped in, drove north a mile, winding in and out among the long, narrow tells which I now noticed were ugly, piled scars on the otherwise legendary Iraqi desert sand. Sir Max parked his roadster beside the mud-brick house built by Layard a hundred years ago. It still served as residence and office for this adventure. Max ducked in, issued some instructions, then he took my arm, and we headed on foot for a rock-strewn tunnel—apparently once a royal burial mound.

I was immediately transported back a quarter century to my first childhood visit underground. I suppose I was nine or ten. It was during the Great Depression and Pop had decided we could save a buck by going for a load of coal ourselves. We had a utility trailer pulled by our reliable, old Dodge. I remember Pop loaded up five boys—we didn't take Mom. This was to be men's work and as much education as labor. We drove out into the hilly country north of Chinook and found this mine largely by following the spilled coal along the road. I remembered five of us brothers followed Pop. We wallked cautiously down into this walk-in, slanting coal mine. It was darkish, lit by some of Thomas Edison's original, bare light bulbs hung along strings of equally primitive, frayed cord strung from pegs stuck in the dirt walls. It was one of those starkly threatening, early memories you can never really escape. It got worse as we descended.

I was kind of hanging on to Max. It was that same underground dark that made me shudder, remembering the coalmine. Suddenly we came upon a cluster of workers huddled around an ancient kerosene railroad signal lantern on the floor. The workers were intently examining a flat rectangle of stone, broken off at one end. In the dim, flickering lamplight, it looked to me like a piece of ancient stone tablet.

To my utter surprise, a flashy blonde girl smiled out of the group to meet Dr. Max and me. Shawnell Reese, a Rhodes Scholar at Cambridge in her early twenties, was in charge of this team. Hearing our approach, she looked up, then stepped over the lantern and seeing me, she let out a scream, "An American! An American!" We all laughed as she gave me a huge hug of greeting. She was a UC Davis, California graduate student whose Davis days were interrupted by the scholarship.

Shawnell now took over escorting me and narrating this section. Max excused himself temporarily to go see to a problem at the loading platform. This tunnel, I discovered, was Shawnell's study, so she was the authority on "what" and "why." She told me how this very tunnel was where Layard had found Rawlinson asleep in the only cool room he could find after a long, hot, dusty camel ride from Baghdad. Together they translated a wall-size frieze of cuneiform and discovered whose palace and whose tomb they were desecrating. Since then and including the present, many workers, as well as Shawnell herself, had slept in the cool tunnel for comfort. And this liberated American had set up a small office in one corner of her royal chamber down under. Her books, writing desk, sleeping bag and pile of belongings were casually arranged in a California heap. In the 1950s, air conditioning was still not widely available to archeologists anywhere.

I was fascinated to hear Shawn tell of the ancient, royal need for recording historic events for posterity. And being that Shawnell's kings were recording events a thousand years before papyrus had been discovered, the writing was done on stone slabs. The innovation of papyrus by the Egyptians and brought to the Mediterranean world by the Phoenicians was to prove as huge a jump for mankind as the printing press and the first step on the moon.

The ancient kings wanted their family and kingdom size, their travel exploits, victories in battle, together with the spiritual glory of their watch to last. The only medium they knew was stone. The only tools that would work stone were hammer and chisel. They got craftsmen to cut their life-stories into huge plates of stone. Then, here at Nimrud at least, the kings piled these huge tablets in pits. The ubiquitous sandstorms of course covered over these pits securing the presence of tablets for posterity.

Shawn showed me where the Assyrian kings had chiseled their stories on wall-sized friezes that had then been carefully piled in pit libraries near the royal palace. The sheer volume of these chiseled records was shocking. Each Frieze was ten-feet high by twenty-feet wide. This came to more than a mile of Nimrud friezes laid end-to-end for the edification of later generations.

Early in the afternoon, Max intercepted us and took me with him to his current deep dig. We walked about a quarter mile north. A platoon of Arab workers was bringing deep sand and mud from a cave-like entrance. Inside we found a primitively lighted, zigzag path that led down to a railed overlook. Far below in the flickering torchlight, another team of workers dug and sorted. Max explained that he had not reached the base of the earliest civilization that had once occupied this site. He explained that the work was very slow because of his need for care in sifting the ambient dirt as they dug. The clues to the culture, once on the surface, were now imbedded in the deep, long-packed sand.

I asked him about Rawlinson. I was fascinated by the thought of a man with the patience to decode an early culture's writing and thus open up to us, thousands of years down the line, how those people lived, what they ate, what the people did for a living, what they thought about and talked about, what they believed and why and what their priorities were, everything about them. Dr. Max was so pleased that I was interested in his work that he took me back to his car, and we sped out onto the desert a half a mile east of his main operation. As we drove he explained the fascinating back-story of Rawlinson.

British, and of course a graduate of Oxford, Rawlinson came out to Iraq with the sole goal of translating the cuneiform language or code that his professors and friends in England said locked in the secrets of the ancient Assyrian-Babylonian-Chaldean culture. The whole book of Genesis in our Bible was based solely on legends passed down from generation to generation for literally millennia at the desert firesides of nomadic, herding Bedouins. The sole, written documentation was there on these wall-size slabs, but in cuneiform code that no one could read and buried under centuries of sandstorms.

Dr. Max told me that Rawlinson spent a couple of years in Baghdad and wasn't getting very far. He decided to take a trip to Isfahan across the mountains in Persia where the French scholar, Louis Sanchette, was doing a digging project for the Louvre in Paris. Rawlinson's mini caravan chose to camp at the historic ruins of Behistun.

Behistun was an ancient caravan spring and campsite in the time of Darius the Great when the caravan route from Karachi in India to Babylon on the Euphrates was the southern trade thoroughfare across Persia. It was the southern caravan highway equivalent of the "Silk Road" across China, Tibet to Tashkent and on into Europe. Rawlinson had heard about and wanted to examine an historic cuneiform-covered, "holy rock" that marked this particular spring oasis. The "Behistun Holy Rock" is really a flat limestone cliff that rises suddenly hundreds of feet out of the desert on the eastern foothills of the Zagros mountains. It's still there if you would like to visit. The legend familiar to Rawlinson held that Persian Emperor, Darius the Great, knowing the strategic location of the spring—everyone passed or camped there—and desiring that everyone in his empire know who he was, declared the cliff-face a holy monument. He directed slave craftsmen to cut, in cuneiform across the cliff-face, his family tree, his religious beliefs and his heroic conquests. To make certain everyone would know, the cuneiform was cut in all three languages common to the Persian Empire.

Rawlinson had hired a half dozen camels and some supplies plus a Kurdish guide for this trip. It took two days from Baghdad, but he found the huge slab of limestone protruding out of the earth several hundred feet into the sky. Only a primitive road now passed the site. Rawlinson studied and studied the stone cliff. In fact, as days slid into weeks, he had to send an assistant back for more supplies. The Frenchman in Isfahan was forgotten. Rawlinson discovered that the engravings were in three parts. One part was in Old Persian, which he could read. A second section was in Babylonian he could not decipher. The final section he could not even reach. It was on a sheer part of the wall too far out in space.

Now my new friend, Max, parked his roadster beside his protruding slab and used his slab to demonstrate the Rawlinson story. Apparently Rawlinson was familiar with the way the hieroglyphic code in Egypt had been cracked because British scholar, Byron Rhodes, found a tablet, the Rosetta Stone. On this stone, the message had been recorded in hieroglyphics in two translations on two separate sections so that different peoples could read it. One section was in Egyptian. No dice for Rhodes. But a second section was in Greek. Rhodes could read Greek. The hieroglyphic code was broken and ancient Egyptian history came to life.

Rawlinson could see the possibility here because Darius wanted to be sure the Babylonians read of his glory as well as the Persians. He also wanted anyone else who in significant numbers traveled this route to hear his story. Someone else did—who was it? To solve this mystery, he had to first get access to the far out section.

One day a curious, twelve-year-old Kurdish boy whose family was drifting south with their herd, stopped to camp at the spring. The lad came out to where Rawlinson was trying to build a scaffold to reach the far sector. He was not having much success. The lad showed the British scholar that, in his bare feet for a few piasters, he could scramble all over the huge monument like a fly. Dr. Rawlinson got him to take paper and chalk and climb out and exactly copy the "far-out" cuneiform designs. Knowing Old Persian, and reasoning that the three stories were the same, Rawlinson found that the third section was in Scythian. Darius, of course, would want the well-traveled Elamites who spoke Scythian, to read of his heroics.

Rawlinson cracked the cuneiform code on Darius' holy Behistun Monument. That September he came to Nimrud with his camels and slept in Shawnelle's tunnel and the next day went to work on Layard's tablets. The tablets of Genesis and, slowly, the Old Testament began to come alive.

Dr. Max showed me the cuneiform on his desert slab that had been unearthed by Layard a hundred years ago. Patient Max must have spent an hour carefully teaching me how even I could write in this strange code that used black, chiseled, golf-tee-shaped indentures to form whole ideas—ideas, rather than words, as we normally write today.

When I finally graduated in archeology and Max deposited me back with my crafty family, it was late afternoon. I was surprised that almost nothing was at our selling site. Then I found Abu and Benji returning from the Muhelah. Abu and Sophia had earlier decided that business had fallen off, and we would do better moving on to the next site this evening, so that we could be set up before the Moslem sabbath.

I set about helping to close out our shop in the suq. The sun was still about fifteen degrees off the western horizon when I stood with Benji on the pier, and we loosed the lines and jumped aboard.

I made a note in my journal that evening that I looked back as Abu muscled us out into the powerful Tigris current. I froze. There on the sandy main street leading from the village to the pier was a clutch of soldiers or police in uniform. They were talking earnestly with the dock boss who was pointing out to our dhow. I quickly got involved in busy-work to appear ordinary to any observer on the water or on shore.

Almost immediately we came under the influence of the Little Zab River. This powerful stream is much less dramatic than the Big Zab. Still it comes tumbling out of the Zagros and throws a wedge of clear water into the mighty Tigris. Also the current's power, coming from the east, changes the course of the whole river and causes the boatmen to hustle and watch their clearances carefully. This problem was exacerbated for us by the drawing dusk. Visibility was cut by the evening mist now settling in over the wide, flat hydraulic. I really came to appreciate the strength and river-smarts of my friend Abu. He was a jump ahead of every trouble, and did a world-class job of piloting.

I noticed, as Benji and I got everything shipshape on the deck, Sophia was neither crafting on deck as she often did when we floated, nor was she cooking supper, although it was suppertime. Then I saw why. Abu was closing on the west bank. Very carefully, he was moving us into the right-hand lane, so to speak. At first, I wasn't sure why. Then I saw why. Through the fast-falling twilight, a huge cloud of smoke hung like a stratus cloud ahead and off to the west. Then I could smell the smoke. Soon I could see the light in the sky. You know how the light of a city reflects off the underside of a flat cloud or smoke? We floated south along the west bank, and soon, there on the flat desert, burned hundreds of little campfires beside hundreds of grayish, tan tents.

Abu shouted and pointed. Up a quarter of a mile ahead, a pier reached out into the water. Abu was guiding us toward the pier. I ran forward to starboard, but for some reason, he called on Benji to jump ashore with the heavy line. I looked directly at him to make sure I didn't misunderstand. Nope. Then Abu called out an order I didn't hear.

There was a lot of noise and activity on the dock. Dozens of people seemed to be unloading meat and fish and vegetables from small local boats. Women were loading them into baskets carried on their heads. Loaded, they moved off west down an incline and disappeared into the tent village. Now Abu shouted my name, pointing. I snatched up the stern line and jumped. The moving boat and the rising and falling pier coupled with smooth, wet planks were too much. I hit the slippery dock and went down.

Benji was also in trouble. She just wasn't strong enough to throw her bowline around any of the passing pilings and belay. I dropped my line and jumped to help her. Our muhelah was drifting fast. Abu was shouting. Others were shouting—some on the dock, some on boats like us trying to dock. It was evening traffic just like anywhere in the world. Bodies were everywhere. Benji and I, working together, threw a hitch around a piling. The bow of the Muhelah caught, but the stern now swung wide and hit.

BAMB! Or rather, CRUNCH! would better describe the sound. We smacked heavily into another dhow already moored. The impact sent the shouting man on board to the deck. I heard Abu erupt with an Arabic obscenity, but I was too busy recovering the stern line, which I had dropped, to worry much. Now others of the family of the neighboring dhow which we had hit, came running out on deck. They had apparently been eating dinner inside. The man, a muscled Kurd, jumped back to his feet and checked his railing. Fortunately he found only cosmetic damage. Abu was immediately at the scene. He made a strong apology and pointing toward me, told the man that I was inexperienced and totally at fault. This apparently mollified the boatman who glared at me from under enormous black brows. The family disappeared back into their on-board hut.

Abu took me aside and explained to me that the trouble had been his fault for not putting me ashore first as the current was too strong and the boat too heavy for Benji to catch. He put his arm around my shoulder and asked me to please understand, that he knew what was required to bring peace. He confided that hitting into already moored shipping was a worldwide, major no-no. It caused innumerable fights on waterfronts everywhere. He turned me to him, held me at arms length, his hands on each of my shoulders. "Sir, I made a mistake. Forgive me?"

We hugged. I patted his back. "Abu, I forgive you. But I don't mind taking the heat. I'm in the service. I'm used to it. I fell on the pier and lost precious seconds when seconds were gold." Abu was laughing now and waving his arms about as he relaxed the tension by reenacting our blooper. Even Benji and Sonia were laughing as we each took a line and secured our boat to the pier. I knew we were still bonded so I relaxed. While we went about finishing the work of tying off and unloading our stuff, I was preoccupied in thought. *What's happening here? It is profoundly important to me that Abu likes me and is not angry with me. Odd, while we have only known each other a few days, already we are bonded. Our caring links are very strong. I would be seriously hurt right now if Abu had not put his hand on my shoulder a moment ago. And apparently it's the same with Abu. Abu knew it was important to me. It was important to him, also.*

My eyes swept east out across the mile of still busy river bluing in the dusk. I noticed that almost none of the major shipping that accompanied us downstream seemed to be interested in stopping here. "Fishing Village?" I asked Abu. He turned me to face the west. He swung his arm in a wide arc covering the whole western desert. "Major, this is Ash Shar-qat, the largest refugee camp on earth." He continued his narration as we walked to the shed-office and checked in. This time I noticed there was no charge.

Outside again, Abu pointed west and swept his arm from south to north across this vast, moving, mumbling anthill on the desert. "Here are Palestinian refugees, Shiites from the

86

delta, Gypsies from Azerbaijan, Pakistanis fleeing India, Kofis from Afghan, Zereh Depression, even, ho, ho, ho! Even some hippies from California." We both laughed at that.

"Mustafa al Barzani. You've heard of him? One of the classic Middle East tribal warlords. He runs this place. The UN and various interests supply it by air to Baghdad." He pointed to a Boeing transport in the distant sky. "Baghdad-to-camp by truck. Everyone here—everyone is waiting for something. And everyone is poor. We may not make a piaster, but, as you'll find, it's too interesting to pass up. Plus, we may find friends. Ha, ha, ha." Abu laughed, hands palm up in a French salute, one of his favorite gestures.

Abu hired three scruffy, hashish-smoking youths squatting by the pier-shed. They followed us back to our boat. Sophia had set out a pile of stuff. We all loaded up and followed Abu down the incline west, out across a reedy drain toward the campfires.

Suddenly we were in the city. The rows of tents came almost down to water's edge. I noticed they were surplus WWII squad tents, all stamped with a huge, white UN on the roof, then a sun-faded U.S. ARMY underneath. We trudged along for what seemed like a mile. Outside nearly every tent sat a family around a small campfire, eating. Here and there a tent had been modified into an outdoor café or coffee shop. One space was not a tent, but rather an open area perhaps twenty yards a side. At the back, a worn, old sheet hung stretched from two poles. Obviously, this was a movie theater with no chairs. Patrons were gathering already, sitting on the sand. One large tent had a shingle posted: MEDIC and in Arabic script under. Other tents were open-sided, apparently craft or food shops. One was only a tarp stretched to cover an arrangement of tools and a work area. My thought was: A repair facility. Still I saw no automobiles at all.

Abu was headed for a favorite spot apparently quite deep into the city. As we trudged along the sandy street between the rows of tents, the piles of supplies and belongings, smoking stacks of burning refuse and general refugee camp environs, my mind floated back to an encampment of Japanese on the edge of my airbase at Fuchu in war-torn Japan. The sweat and flies of Ash Shar Gat, this Tigris River desert camp, gave way to a moment's reflection on the bitter cold winter of 1945.

Defeated Japanese families, hungry and aching with cold, lined up behind my mess hall for leftover food scraps. I had gotten into trouble because I had issued a warehouse of Japanese flying equipment to help the freezing citizens survive. My memory flashed to a few years later, a 1950s refugee camp on Tsu Shima, an island in the Korean Straits. There were no tents. Everyone crowded onto boats seeking refuge from the war that had pinned them on the Pusan perimeter until it overflowed with Korean soldiers and American GIs. I thought, *Refugee camps come in all shapes and sizes, but one thing is common: Expectancy! In every camp I have visited there is a sense—a feeling of expectancy. Something good is about to happen. Something better is on the way.*

Then, *How lucky we are in America. Almost no American has ever lived in a refugee camp.* Then I thought of the WWII west coast Japanese and Niseis, then on to the current flood of Latin American immigrants. I tried to think of where on earth there were no refugees.

Suddenly a shout went up from Benji. "HIIEEE!" She dropped her load and rushed forward. A Kurdish girl about her age—barefoot and in a colorful folded headscarf, scarlet blouse and khaki shorts—came running and shout-laughing toward us. I ducked behind a water-point sign. Then following the girl came an older woman, running. Sophia dashed forward. Abu started to shout and laugh. He dropped his gear on the sandy street. His arms went wide. "See, Major, I said, friends!" I came out of hiding and witnessed a major love reunion. These two craft families went a long way back. They had often set up next to each other at villages. They had not been together for almost a year, and were in emotion overload from the good luck. The man appeared. Abu was beside himself. Everyone was hugging and chattering and laughing. We actually drew a crowd there in the sandy street.

Total joy and happiness were rare here. Ours spread among the resident refugees all round. Lots of curious, lots of bored, lots of generally depressed humans. And, Abu, with that laugh, and that river-voice, we should have had a merchandise display up. We literally drew a crowd, mainly kids. Of course, some of these kids recognized that I was an American. While the old friends hugged and reminisced, I was swamped by little beggars who thought I would be the source of chocolates. One teenage girl knew I was a movie star and wanted my autograph. Trying to maintain a minimal profile until I could vamoose, I had a major attack of paranoia.

The joy-storm calmed as quickly as it came up. We all loaded up and hiked on perhaps two hundred meters. Our friends were set up in business beside a UN Supply Issue warehouse tent. We piled all our stuff next to our friends' rug and lean-to. I was now properly introduced, and we all sat down lotus fashion around their little fire to shish-kabob and tea.

We ate and everyone talked and laughed and reminisced. I expected to just listen as they relived old times together. I was wrong. Each adventure, someone would recount the whole story for my benefit. By the time we were settled, it was late and the fires had all burned out all around. Still the smoke hung low over the dead calm camp. It was painful to my eyes, but I suppose if you're a refugee paying no rent or taxes, smoke-in-your-eyes is a small price.

Bedtime, both families lay down on the market rugs. It was clear they had done this hundreds of times before. The four adults lay in a hollow square facing each other. Nearby, the two girls, Benji and Ruth, were facing each other, laughing and chatting. There were also two young boys in the family, seven and ten. They had me in a small, lie-down circle talking major league baseball. Things just slowly faded away. Nobody around lilt a lantern. No one counseled anyone to quiet down. Normal sounds of people just lowered and softened and finally just went away.

Five

Business at the camp the next couple of days proved to be less than hoped for, so about mid-afternoon of the third day, Abu began getting restless. My strategic plan called for leaving my crafty family here. We were just south of the confluence of the Little Zab, up whose course was my planned route to Iran. I should explain.

Along the Little Zab River runs a century-old flock migration route. In the early fall, as now, the Kurdish shepherds drift their sheep, cattle and goat flocks down out of the Zagros heights. The mountain grasses have been lush all summer, but are now much spent. The shepherds and flocks migrate down to the Tigris then cross the river to winter on the desert valley grass just coming green. The desert-plain greens up and flowers with some rainfall during late November, December and January. This rainfall comes as a kind of monsoon off the Mediterranean, across Palestine, across the flat Syrian desert. This *monsoon* drops moisture as it is pushed up the western slope and against the Zagros mountain wall.

I estimated I had brought enough trail lore out of my youth in the Montana mountains plus what I had gathered on weeklong hikes here and there to find my way up the wide migration trail. The major obstacle was crossing the notorious Prince Ali Bridge at the top. The Prince Ali is a notoriously rickety suspension across a hundred-yard-wide gorge, two thousand feet deep. But the good news, just beyond the bridge, I was told, is the border checkpoint. As

91

I've mentioned before, the Shah had a major U.S. military assistance program going in Iran. I envisioned reaching the border and phoning a U.S. Army unit for wheels. My vision: A U.S. Air Force Major, once in contact with a U.S. Army detachment at the border, should be supplied a clean uniform, a good night's sleep and transport to Teheran. With luck, the attaché will be free to fly me to Beirut. I could be back in college by Saturday.

Journal, 27 September 1952, Shar-gat Refugee Camp, Iraq

Suspecting this might be our last day in the camp, I took Benji and Ruth as Kurdish/Arab interpreters and guides on a local culture, photo-op sortie. We had invited the boys (timid refugees will pose with kids). But their Mom had whispered to me that the three were needed to help pack and carry stuff to the boat.

I got the idea (unintentional eavesdropping) that there was just no money and little barter in the camp. It was time to move on. The old man had seriously discussed his experience with Abu during breakfast. They had tossed around the options. Both women liked the ancient camel caravan river crossing at Samarra. Samarra, a hundred miles south, is a river port and crossing with a lot of spiritual connection—huge Sunni mosque, school and center. With the two families on the boat, there was enough manpower to handle the work and enough women and kids to accelerate the crafting plus abundant caring fellowship. I could drop out without guilt. So Ruth, Benji and I set out to shoot a variety of camp pictures. I needed some live-action photos to supplement my words in a paper on refugees I planned back at college.

I got some great shots of one, very old Arab asleep with a hashish pipe in his mouth. I shot a gathering of women doing their laundry at the edge of the river. I caught some black-veiled women in chadors that completely covered their bodies. But I also snapped some colorfully scarved girls drawing water and carrying the jars on their heads just like in Bible times. I got the UN supply point distributing rations of flour and sugar. I shot kids at joyful play under unbelievably, unjoyful conditions. This helped support one of my favorite worldwide notions: Kids' happiness is "nehil ad rem" to conditions.

When Benji and I were shooting, we decided to include a series on the pier. We shot a set of the check-in office, and I was looking out over the river thinking of a shot of the colorfully assorted traffic. I was thinking, *Shots of rivers and oceans always look great on site, but the prints usually come back unexpectedly far off and objects tiny.*

As I surveyed the panorama from the dock, I could see far upstream and about ten miles down as the shoreline fell away to a flat, grassy swale to the south. I got the feeling that the light was not right for photography. There was a sort of greenish yellow look about the river scene. I noticed it was deathly calm, and I concurrently felt an inner tension. I passed it off as part of my lurking guilty conscience.

I noticed also as I looked south downstream what appeared to be a lower or subsidiary dock. I guessed it was 150 yards away and right on the water. In fact about a third of the lower pier seemed to extend out into the water. There was no traffic tied up there, nor was there any traffic coming or going, and no huts, shacks or other infrastructure had been built either on it or adjacent to it. I wondered why. Also, I wondered why I had not noticed the dock earlier. I charged it off to the drawing darkness when we had arrived yesterday. Then also we were very busy with unloading and moving goods last night.

At this moment something strange happened. The pilot of the dhow we had dinged upon arrival walked onto the pier and headed toward his boat. Benji apparently knew him and exchanged a greeting and surfaced a polite apology. I felt uncomfortable, so I jumped right in. "Sir, I am very, very sorry. I'm an American sort of student-tourist. I'm new at this river work, and I just couldn't handle the ropes."

The man was very pleasant. He introduced himself, extending out his hand to me. "I understand. My name is Ibn." He followed it with a long traditional Arabic name which I missed completely. We walked toward his muhelah. He pointed to the almost indiscernible crash point. "It is nothing. My daughter has sloshed away even the mark. No, this boat is too strong to be hurt by a gnat-bite like that. I built this dhow." His index finger popped his hairy, bare chest. "My brother and I build dhows in Kuwait, down south. Look!" Ibn's arm swung out across the mile of heavily trafficked river. "All the sturdy boats are ours. I'm up here taking orders. You want muhelah? Of course, every rich American must have Kuwait muhelah. Yes?" We stood now where his bowline tied off looking out over the river.

There was a moment of quiet. I filled it with my lurking question. "Tell me, Ibn, why is there no traffic at the lower dock?" I pointed.

"Oh, no sir. That is not a dock. Ha, ha, ha, that is not a pier or a dock at all. That is ferryboat." He laughed at my ignorance of river things. Then he explained that the lower float was a river ferry. It had been totally fabricated from logs—fir logs from the Taurus Mountains in Turkey. Apparently Ibn's father had been in on the project. He now narrated with gestures how five Kuwaiti river men, along with the Kurdish seasonal herdsmen, had harvested the logs up north, just below the notorious rapids at As Qosh. They teamed up and had floated them down the river lashed together by braided reeds.

Ibn, like many boatmen, was a veritable Tigris encyclopedia. Moreover, he was thrilled that someone appreciated his knowledge and would listen. I noticed Benji and Ruth soon lost interest and drifted away toward the camp. Ibn took me by the arm and walked me over to where we could look out and down upon the raft. He explained that the raft was 100 meters long. I thought, *Holy Mackerel! A raft as long and half as wide as a football field!*

Ibn continued, "The raft came after the flood of 1910. Look." He pulled me down onto a gray, weathered bench. "Look! Since Bible times, the herds have come down to the river from Zagros highlands at the change of seasons."

He pointed to the northeast. "In the fall, the rains bring grass to the river valley and the plains to the west. The herds traditionally swam the Tigris and followed the grass. Then when the season changed again, the shepherds swam their flocks back across to climb back up to the mountains. In the spring, the snow-melt make grass and willows."

As I say, Ibn told the story with great enthusiasm and elaborate gestures. I thought, *Here is a true, any-age, Arab storyteller.*

He continued explaining that the crossover-point was normally just above the confluence of the Great Zog with the Tigris where the river narrowed. Ibn remembered his father telling him the migrating herds seemed to enjoy the swim that carried them about five miles downstream to a flat swale which led to the rich meadows of the al Qaiyara depression. This clear topographical featured started right where the refugee camp now stood.

Ibn jumped to his feet for emphasis. "Nineteen ten, all change. Tigris broke banks like flood of Noah. Most of flocks—sheep, cows, goats—most try swim, but rains keep rain. River get twenty-mile-wide—fill great depression. Many herds lost. So shepherds talk to river boatmen. Boatmen mainly from Basra, Abadan, Kuwait decide built raft." Ibn pointed down to the thousand-log field below. The loquacious pilot concluded his historic presentation with the note that after they built the raft, the boatmen and the shepherds together floated it down to this area where now they normally operate and store it on off-season. Each fall the migrating herds gathered on the east bank just above the Little Zog—about a thousand cows, two thousand sheep and an equal number of goats. Then all together, they poled the massive raft across. The raft was now going back for its second load of the fall. The flocks were already assembling at the base of the migratory path across the river. He pointed upstream, northeast. When my boatman-storyteller mentioned this imminent passage east, I became totally alert. I had been worrying since arrival here at Ash Shar-qat how I was going to get back across the river? Now I knew. As this friendly fellow finally turned to board his dhow, I asked him my last question, "Where do I get my pole if I want to hire on?"

Thinking I was kidding, he laughed, but he pointed down toward the raft and from his deck, he shouted, "Sir, it takes no skill. You learn on the job, or the man throw you in river. Ha, ha, ha. Even an American can do it!"

He sounded like Abu. His shouted laughter filled the air. "Ho, ho, ho—good luck!"

With that encouraging news, I turned directly toward the path down to the massive log raft. I would go down and investigate the monstrous thing and make a judgment. Then, if it appeared sensible, I would inquire into joining the crew.

Suddenly behind me, on the roadway that led to the pier from the camp, a loud ruckus broke out. I turned and immediately froze. A squad of military police stood in a circle around the port officer. Everyone was talking at once. One of the police soldiers who seemed to be in charge was shouting and gesturing. The port officer was shouting back and gesturing down toward the camp.

I quickly ducked behind an upturned riverboat that was drying on the dock. I could not hear any words, but it was obvious that the uniformed squad were hunting for someone. From the way the port authority and the police squad were responding. I immediately drew the conclusion that they had a lead and were after him. More, I surmised that "him" was "me"! I precipitously slid on down the trail to get totally away from the dock and out of sight. I scuffed and slid down the sandy incline. At the river's edge I came upon the pile of poles. Each pole was smooth and black and as long as, and twice the diameter of an Olympic pole-vaulting pole. I edged around the pile glancing at the western sky. I think I was trying to get a quick fix on the time. The sun was a hollow ghost in a swirling yellow sky. It was uncomfortably hot and humid and very still. Though I was totally preoccupied with the new platoon threatening my survival, I, nonetheless, noticed a sort of eerie feeling in the atmosphere. I thought, *Storm coming.*

I found the side of the raft about four feet out from the riverbank. I wanted to inspect the massive structure. I wanted to see if it looked like a sensible and safe way across the river. I stood for a moment surveying the mass of logs from close up. I decided I needed to walk out on the deck rather than just look from the shore. I had expected someone to be in charge or guarding. I was wrong. There was no one in sight. There was no fire where men might hang out, no tent, just the long, wide, flat acre or two of logs, logs, logs.

I did notice far out near the center of the raft a rumpled pile of gray tarp, nothing more. I could not see where or how the raft was secured in place. It appeared to be pulled just far enough out of the water to keep it from floating away. I wondered idly what kind of machine had been used to drag it up there. Or had it merely been guided ashore as it drifted down. No, it was far too high aground for that.

I decided to risk it, so I took a short burst and WHOOM! I leapt the gap onto the raft. Hardly a log moved at my rather clumsy landing. First, I walked along the northern edge. I noticed that being the upstream side, water washed onto the deck for about ten yards. I jogged to the corner and turned south. I continued my jog down the south side trying to imagine myself as a poler. I could not see the river bottom, but it seemed to me I would be able to hold my own if, as the man had claimed, the crew was only modestly experienced. The logs were indeed firmly lashed with a heavily braided webbing of either reed or sisal or both.

The entire expanse moved up and down in sort of waves as the river surged under the huge segment afloat. About halfway to the downstream corner, I decided to cut back to my jump-on point. I glanced again at the western sky and once again was gripped by a strange feeling that often seizes one when a storm is gathering. I had not experienced any sort of weather on the river other than hot and fairly dry and always fraught with small, aggressive river flies when close to civilization.

I jogged across the ferry toward my entry point. Now and then I glanced up toward the main pier. The dust-up had apparently quieted, and the little clutch of uniforms had moved off into the camp to make an arrest. As I trotted toward the middle of the log-field, I came suddenly upon the mound of abandoned tarp. I saw at once the huge UN letters on the gray canvas. I quickly concluded that the canvas had been blown down here from the camp above. As I came up to the mound I decided to jump it. But I was out of synch with my footing, so I gave the mound a huge kick and immediately found myself momentarily airborne then sprawling on the logs.

Instantly, the ambient air exploded in an angry, articulate mass of loud Arabic profanity. A bearded face appeared from under the tarp. "You goddamn, clumsy, camel-shit, Mother-of-Satan. Can't you let a tired captain nap? Up all night hunting crew! Damn!" Then, when the irate raft-master saw I was not some tormenting teen from the camp, but a grown man, sprawled on his butt on the wet deck, he pulled the tarp back over him. His last shout: "If you're a poler, report on deck at first light. Bring your friends!"

I pulled myself up and jogged back to my entry point, praying, "Thank you, Lord. You got me a job from the Captain himself when I didn't even know where to look. Now if I can just lay low until dawn tomorrow! I'm safely outa' here!"

I had expected a quiet sadness when it was surfaced at breakfast that we were packing to move on. Sophia confirmed to me that both families had decided to leave together. She apologized for not including me in the discussions.

A yellowish mist lay over camp and river. It was still not light, but the camp was slow-moving and low-growling, so I kept a sharp eye on the streets and between the tents near us. As we finished our fish and thick coffee, everyone began pulling things down and rolling them up in the rugs. Abu slipped away to say good-bye to a relative in the camp. I took a few character snaps of people and places coming awake—stuff I needed to illustrate my journal stories back at school. Then we began the safari to the muhelah. I carried a load, but when we all had arrived beside our boat, I took

Abu's hand and gripped it tightly. "Abu, I love you all, and thank you for taking me in, but I must leave now." Abu dropped my hand and took me in a huge bear hug.

Both families gathered around saying nice things that didn't make much sense. Everyone seemed to know that I would be leaving. I was not surprised, as there is a sort of mystic foreknowledge among river pilgrims—when someone will appear, when someone will disappear. I was caught by surprise and deeply moved to see Benji and Sophia behind me hugging one another and quietly weeping over my departure.

Abu held me tightly for a long time. He too was crying like a child. He asked Allah to guard and protect me. We held each other at arms length for perhaps a minute, just smiling into each other's eyes. Then I turned away. We all scattered toward the next event. No one looked back.

My daypack was already on my shoulders. I jogged across the flat pier, around the upturned fishing boat and down the sandy path. Beside the pile of poles scowled the bearded Captain.

"Are you zee one?"

I knew what he meant. "Yes, Sir. I am zee one."

He pointed to the pile of teak poles. "Take any pole and let's go! We need to cross now. A Sacre-barrak is there!"

He pointed west. I did not know this word of horror on the desert. Sacre-barrak was satanic, Arabic for total sandstorm! I looked out and up. I could see a boiling wall of gray bleed to yellow then orange, twelve miles high—up where the sun was painting the coming holocaust with fire.

I selected a thinnish pole. I grasped it firmly with both hands near the middle. I stumbled under the surprising weight and lurched toward the gap dimly visible in the gray. I timed a mighty leap. I was short. With a yelp and loud splash, pole, knapsack and I went unceremoniously into the drink.

"Ha! Ha! Ha! Allah has repaid you, Clumsy One! But you are baptized, so go!"

The Captain leapt aboard ahead of me, grabbed my arm and helped me onto the wet logs. I was truly thankful that a new dawn was breaking a new chance to escape into a new direction. Of course it was hot and still, but I felt only a flood of expectation and hope. I would be back in school by Saturday.

"Go there!" The master pointed. "And when you hear my shout, pole for Allah!" The bearded one pulled on a Greek seaman's cap and jogged at the center of the vast log raft. Cupping his hands, he let out a bear-like bellow, and fifty poles splashed toward the river bottom together. Fifty more dug into the dry sand and shrubbery along the western side. I lost balance and fell to my knees as the giant raft tipped up. Many, I noticed, were down. Then came a violent, scraping roar, and we were away.

Slowly at first, then more quickly, still more quickly, we swung totally free into the massive hydraulic of the Tigris. WWHHOOOSSHH! On this first wide swing of the log football field, about half the polers, as new at this as I, fell flat again. Chaos reigned! The massive log float was momentarily a frantic scramble of bodies and poles. The captain was not dismayed. He shouted encouragement. The second effort was noticeably more effective.

When I felt like the shame-of-the-novice had passed, and it was light enough to see the water clearly, I looked around. There must have been a hundred Arabs dressed mainly in just black pajama bottoms. Bare, hairy chests were everywhere. We were almost evenly spaced along the three sides leaving the east free. The east side was in the main current and, for now, rode too high to pole from.

101

We were moving downstream and slightly crosscurrent at an amazing rate. From time to time the Captain bellowed out a command. He spoke a mix language of Kurdish-Persian and Arabic common on the river. No one seemed to have any trouble with his orders. I caught onto it after watching the nearby crew's response to a few commands.

Plus, I found the captain's shouts were mainly for encouragement. What needed doing was pretty obvious. I had taught "teamwork" at the Air Force Tactical School, and I was in absolute awe watching this single man, totally without staff of any kind, standing near the center of a football field of lashed logs, constantly and violently undulating, with no sound system whatever, keep a hundred itinerant strangers not only working together at a harsh and difficult job, but in peak morale, happily laughing and shouting.

Although the man had an unusually pleasant, robust and humorously obscene personality, which appealed to this cadre of male ruffians, his main leadership qualities were: He was loud. He was decisive. And he was effective. He kept this log rug moving in an orderly manner across a mighty river. He knew the secret: Let the Tigris do the work. He knew the river, and he understood its enormous hydraulic power. His main task was timing our efforts. He managed this superbly. In fact the pitiful little poling we did all together was just slight enough to allow the river to float the ferry into the main stream and at the first big bend, head across.

With the crossing progressing extremely well, about noon, the storm hit us. For half an hour we could hear it coming—the rumble and thunder of the most violent force on land on this planet. A stage seven tornado came out of the west tearing the desert carpet up, sucking it twelve miles into the stratosphere. Here and there the whole onslaught was randomly and momentarily ripped apart by half-million-volt, jagged shafts of lightning probably fifty yards thick and each putting a hundred thousand degrees of temperature change into the brown, boiling brew.

The Captain kept glancing west watching its approach, but he showed no anxiety either in voice or demeanor. He just kept shouting encouragement and mid-course corrections. I found later that he had never before crossed in a storm of any sort.

As a career military pilot, I have flown through thunderstorms of unbelievable violence. I have had a tiny fighter flipped and rolled and turned end-over-end in a south Asia tsunami. The gyros tumbled and the instruments rolled and spun. I was 60,000 feet up and totally out of control. Worse, I had no way of regaining control. I was thrown wildly around the cockpit. My boots were up, my head was down with the rudder pedals. I was violently sick to my stomach. My jet helmet banged off the armorplate. My neck snapped. I screamed in utter terror, I prayed.

One day in the summer of 1943, I was on the ground refueling a PT-19A trainer when a tornado swept through Enid, Oklahoma and piled up a dozen airplanes lashed to steel loops in the concrete ramp. They haven't found my little bird yet.

I have been typhooned at sea off Okinawa at night on, of all things, an LST landing craft. The craft was tossed, even somersaulted. On deck, a dozen tanks were breaking their chains and sliding into the East China Sea. Below, a hundred absolutely terrified, soldiers, sailors and marines facing certain death drank Aussie beer and sang "Roll Me Over, Lay Me Down and Do It Again." That's American GIs at war.

But forget all that! This Iraqi desert sand-blow was to take the all-time prize. If you can imagine a dozen ants caught in a washing machine full of really dirty baby diapers and Lincoln Logs, throw in a kid's jeans with pockets full of sand in the full-wash cycle. You have it right. The Sacre-barrak swept in off the desert like a savage, hungry dragon. No, no, no—no comparison with something savage, and ruthless, uncontrolled and consuming everything in its path. In fact, no comparison is in the ballpark, including cyclones, hurricanes, tsunamis, typhoons, you name it. We're talking about a twelve-mile-high wall of sand moving east at roughly sixty miles an hour, spinning and boiling, swirling and sucking. The wind was not the weapon. And there was no hail, not even torrential rain. And the thing didn't twist. The sand was the weapon. Literally hundreds of millions of tiny sharp diamonds with razor-sharp edges—spinning, swirling, cutting and tearing everything in its path. It was virtually a million tons of high-speed, shattered glass. Everything—and I mean *Everything*—was cut down and ground up. Virtually nothing in the swath of this storm remained unshredded.

This wall-of-death hit us in mid-river. We could see it coming, of course, but there was no getting ready. Besides, everyone was fully employed with a pole and the river. The front edge of the Sacre-barrak was a mammoth, sucking vacuum cleaner. It lifted the Tigris twenty feet into the air as solid water. It picked up our ferry like it was a toy. Can you imagine a hundred men watching our football field-size raft, with us on board, lifted right up into the air?

First, the whole thing tipped violently. Then it broke in two or three pieces. At about twenty or so feet of altitude, one end continued on up at a forty-five degree angle. Screaming men slid and tumbled. Others, like me, were simply shocked speechless—scratching, grabbing, clutching anything, trying to survive.

The dry sand, lashed by the whipping wind, cut and burned. It struck with satanic furry blinding us all. I couldn't hear any meaningful human sounds even close to me because of the terrifying hollow, RROOOAAARR! of the storm, and simultaneously, the WHOOOOOSH! of the shouting wind, overtoned by a high-pitched singing, SWIIIISH! of sand, wind and water shouting back.

Soon, the lower end of the giant raft broke off, and then the lashings began giving way. Perhaps ten minutes of this airborne drama, and the whole thing disintegrated into a million, random flying logs. For a minute or so, the air over our stretch of the Tigris was filled with tumbling sand, tumbling water, tumbling logs and tumbling bodies.

Very quickly, the main storm-wall passed on east—on ashore—ravaging the foothills all the way to Kirkuk. It splintered oil derricks, broke windows, large and small, kited roofs and filled the city streets with muddy sand, hunks of destruction and general debris.

I just cannot fully describe how the driven glass grains cut into our eyes and nose and ears. We were all blinded and many were in screaming pain from the glass-sharp sand, to say nothing of the flying logs and suffocating water.

The shouting roar of sand, crashing water and flying logs ceased as suddenly as it came. Storm passed, the shouts of the poling crew and the frantic commands of the captain who, would you believe it, was still—even without a ferry to command—doing his best to get his charges ashore safely on the downwind, eastern side of the river. Many of the crew could not swim, but were hurled from the raft into the water with only their heavy, black teak poles too dense to float. My eyes, and I suppose everyone's eyes, were jammed tightly shut from the obsequious, cutting grit.

Once down at river level again, I found myself on a small, irregular-shaped, five-log raft cocked up at a thirty-degree angle and plunging downstream. I was forced to lie down flat. I lost my pole and just clung on, eyes jammed shut and burning violently. Even though I could swim and was Red Cross rescue qualified, and while I could hear grown men screaming for help all around me, the grit and pain would not allow even a tiny peek to see where I was, where the others were or where we were headed. I had never felt so totally terrified and frantically helpless before in my life.

Then my five logs gave way, and I was swimming free in the chopping, rushing river. I sloshed my eyes for about a minute before the grit and pain allowed me to look out. Then I floated, holding my breath as long as possible, then refilling my lungs anew to repeat. I bobbed about in the yellow, muddy river for perhaps a minute of blinking sight. Then the swishing sand and grit again forced my eyes shut in reflexive pain. My glimpses, however, had shown me that I was drifting rapidly south in a tumbling, chaotic, chopping yellow sea of logs and men.

The men were mainly gripping single logs with arms and legs, yelling at the top of their lungs. A log whammed into my back and knocked the wind out of me. As I choked for air, I thanked God it had not hit my head. Another log, with a man attached, rolled over me and swept on. I saw the man's bare back, then his face. His eyes were wide with fear. He saw me and screamed, "Help!" and was gone. His log pitched up with the loss of weight, rolled, then it too was gone.

The air following the storm-front was so heavy with sand-dust that the visibility even now, was only perhaps fifteen yards. Although I had learned the secret of sloshing out my eyes with river water, the chance to see lasted only a couple of minutes.

I don't know if your experience has taught you the importance of *seeing* in controlling *fear*. It is crucial. When you can't see in a condition of chaos and danger, you imagine the worst, and panic is right there to pounce. The victory over panic is absolutely essential in controlling fear, yet it is almost impossible if you can't see what's out there. That, of course, is why a blind man in serious danger is the nadir of terror.

I mentally visualized myself being about midstream. I could see no shoreline, no skyline, nothing but a sea of thousands of singles or pairs of logs pitching up then sliding under, racing with the current. Once in a while a clinging, half-naked body would pop up, scream pitifully, then disappear. I felt wrenched with guilt knowing I could and should be doing something to help. I was an Eagle Scout. I could swim. I was a Red Cross Life Saver. So far I was zero for a thousand in helping save anyone's life.

Oddly, I had been near to death myself recently and returned. I was thus armed with a very special mystical assurance. And, with this, I was also somehow armed with a compulsion to reassure the others. This surfaced as a shouting-out. I kept shouting-out against the storm, "Mishaw-ab-sonica! Mishaw-ab-sonica! Mishaw-ab-sonica!" which is a Kurdish baby soothing expression meaning "There, there," or "Don't worry, my child," or "Everything will be all right." Frankly, this profound sense of faith that I had unconsciously drawn from my earlier, near-death, experience, namely that "All things work together for good and will come out all right in the end if you just don't quit," helped me immensely in controlling my own brushes of terror.

Suddenly in the midst of all this chaos, I heard the howl and felt the powerful swirling blast of a final wind. The sand laced my face and shoulders painfully. I squeezed my eyes shut. Now, in this defensive, eyes-jammed-shut mode, I felt myself squeezed between logs. I couldn't breathe. I thought, *I've survived this storm's main punch; now am I going to be done in by some minor aftershock?* I determined that I would not be squashed between a ton of logs inadvertently pressed by the

107

wind and current. I quickly sloshed out my eyes. The log press was a pulsing squeeze, now tight, now loose. I waited for one cycle to pass. Then, as the squeeze relaxed, I made a huge surging leap upward. I opened my eyes on a sea of wet logs pressed together along with palm trees, willows, some cat-tail-like reeds, an ordinary sand dune, and a voice behind me which I immediately recognized as that of our Captain.

"Well, hello! One survivor!—Wait a minute!—Aren't you the one?"

"Yes, Sir, I'm the one."

"Well, my friend, we're there. You're discharged." The captain saluted me in dismissal. I climbed out of my log nest and waded ashore. A small log pile gave me a place to sit down, collect myself, check my daypack and plan. Objective Number One achieved. I was safely and permanently on the east bank of the Great River.

Six

I had often drawn mental pictures of a hike across the Zagros to the Iranian border. I had always thought of the trip as a minor hike for a professional athlete like me. I often foresaw arriving back at the college by Thursday, or Friday, or Saturday at the latest. This was a major judgment error. Hiking along the road in places, the desert in other places, my court shoes quickly became moccasins and my clothing soon became very worn and torn.

I hiked north along the river to the confluence of the Little Zog. This was a cross-country hike, no road. Now I turned my eyes to the hills. I joined the migration trail recently worn dusty by the hundreds of sheep, the shepherds of which, had not yet discovered that they must now, once again, look to the shallows at al Paola and swim the mighty Tigris this year. No free ride across on the ferry.

In exactly four days I found myself on the outskirts of Kirkuk. I was hungry, tired and conscious that I was wanted and thus unable to knock on doors and beg for food or look for work. However, I found that as hunger increased, my survival edge sharpened. The alleys behind the wealthier homes and businesses all had garbage cans. I found gobs of leftover, cooked rice. I found whole river fish and whole, withered garden vegetables. It's amazing what hunger and fear will do to a man's pride. Of course. Evasion and Escape training in the service makes it easy to gear pride to circumstances in combat or *virtual combat* such as this. Fortunately

I also found an abandoned, ragged kaffiyeh and later, a piece of rope. Also under a bus stop bench, a worn pair of Kurdish baggy pants that looked and felt much like American sweats.

The storm had, of course, dissipated, and the sun reestablished itself as king bringing with it the heat and the flies. I could not believe it was early October. It certainly didn't feel like autumn. After taking two days to figure out how a prey animal can survive almost anywhere these days, I filled my daypack, left the city and headed for the high country.

The Little Zab is a picturesque and very noisy mountain stream. It snakes down out of Lake Diza, in turn snow and spring-fed by a cluster of 12,000 foot Azerbaijan mountain peaks. The migration trail is wide and dusty and snakes pretty much beside the Zab water as it plunges toward the desert. I climbed alone. There were a few straggler shepherds with small goat flocks headed west and down, but no one climbing east and up. I found the sand in dune-like drifts where the storm had petered out in the foothills. Once in the forest, I set a strong pace. The trail switch-backed across the creek. I had a map sketched by Abu as we discussed the route. The rough distances told me that if I kept moving, I could reach the famous Prince Ali Gorge at the summit in about a week.

This gorge or chasm is a notorious, natural barrier—a two thousand foot sheer cut lying north and south along the ancient border between Persia and Assyria. Historically, from Biblical times up through the Middle Ages, the chasm was considered impassable. Traditionally, the Tigris Valley herdsmen who chose to take their flocks into the thick complex of mountains for the summer had to detour a two-week's journey north to Rawanduz Pass. During the Kurdish uprising in 1923, a Kurdish engineer, educated in England, built a bridge across the gorge to allow swift guerrilla movements.

110

This bridge is a remarkable 100-meter long suspension bridge set in the stone faces on both east and west. Four twenty-foot-tall poles anchor the braided hemp cables. Long, lashed poles form the sides of the deck. The deck itself is woven matting repaired and replaced as needed by shepherds that use the crossing. Abu told me that he had crossed over once, and would never do it again. He claimed the bridge swung in a terrifying jerky way because of the gusty winds that constantly move the air up out of the sheer rock chasm to spill down the foothills out onto the desert.

The third day on the upward trail I had already been alone for a week and was beginning to feel the loneness. I camped each night beside the stream under some kind of berry bush. I was rationing my grub and was without a coat or blanket, so the term camping is a stretch. Everything in my body, mind and heart was concentrated on reaching the pass, crossing the bridge and reporting to the Iraq-Iran border station.

Abu and several other travelers had told me that the border station was manned by Iranian military, which I knew were being assisted by U.S. Army soldiers. I counted on the border guards having a jeep and thus getting me to an airport shortly and thus back to the college. This time-gap was my major concern now because I knew if I were absent too long, questions would surface and the security of my mission would certainly be compromised.

Middle East Journal 4, October 1952, Little Zog Immigration Trail, Iraq

It was just before noon. I could see and hear a waterfall on up. I rounded a high granite corner hiding the path ahead. There lay a flat slab of stone the size of a large city parking lot below a 100-foot, picture-perfect falls. For perhaps fifteen minutes I just stood there in awe of the scene. Then as I walked slowly toward the falls, I saw them. Six black figures in a small cluster lay prostrate on the flat stone lanai. I crept forward and became aware as I approached that these were probably Islamic religious men. Their dress said, "Dervish Order." They had paused for their second of five-daily prayer rituals. As I cautiously tiptoed onto the huge stone ledge, one of the worshipers jumped up and ran to me. He hugged me fondly and led me forward to where the others were now finishing up and standing up. These men now greeted me as though they had been expecting me.

Although uneasy at this familiarity, the chatter quickly disclosed my role. Apparently seven of them had signed up at their city below for a mountain prayer retreat. Only six had appeared so far. I must be the seventh. There was so much loving chatter that I could not, and in a moment decided that I should not, demur. I was fitted with a black shroud and the man who had initially come to me, stayed with me. He had apparently earlier been assigned as my prayer partner for the five-day session. His name was Ali. He took me to our leader or mufti whose name was Sufi. Sufi hugged me warmly and welcomed me, noting his relief at my final arrival.

I was not disappointed when after a half-hour of chatting, most of which was a description of the what we could expect on this climbing retreat—activities and observances—rations were issued in a sort of military fashion and we ate. It was a page out of the sixth century for me to be sitting lotus fashion in a circle of black monks eating something I could not identify. It felt and tasted standard Middle Eastern, so I gobbled it down for survival.

I gathered that we were to hike up this mountain trail for about two more days. The physical objective was a hut further up where a hunchback dervish holy man would pray with us. This mountain holy man was apparently a noted healer who would heal one or two who had infirmities as well as perform other miracles during our stay. The plan was to return on the fifth day to the pickup point in a village below and thence by bus to our city of origin, historic Irbil.

Following the meal, we climbed on up away from the noise of the falls to a little cove in the rocks. There the mufti led a discussion on meditation. His brief message conducted in Persian was extremely thoughtful. He explained that at one of his very first discussions with Allah, the Prophet Muhammad had asked Allah's desires concerning prayer and meditation. In his discussion of meditation, Muhammad wrote in the Koran that Allah had promised that any time under any circumstances Muhammad or any of his faithful would desire to meet with Allah, they should go *halfway out* to a still and peaceful place and wait. Allah promised to come *halfway in* and meet with any believer there at the *halfway secret place.* Moreover, Allah promised that he would always make His presence known. This could be by a clear vision, by an inner or audible voice, or by a holy sound such as wind or rain or thunder, or by a mystical sensation such as an affirmation of bright light, warm feeling, inner peace, whirlwind passage or other clear indication of his supernatural presence.

We faithful then each found a quiet place. Each in his own way meditated for perhaps an hour. Ali hovered a little apart from me—meditating and guarding. As this fulfillment was winding down, Mufti Sufi came around and touched each of us, and we gathered in a lotus circle again. Here many of us shared what had happened during our time of reflection. It was a most fascinating, sensible and edifying retreat session. I was spiritually encouraged and felt a genuine inner lift. I set my attitude to participate fully and with good heart. When night fell, the faithful built a small Indian campfire, and we cooked lamb and camas bulbs and ate. Evening prayers followed. Ali laid beside me and helped me to learn to prostrate myself on the stone and stay there. Ali seemed to sense that I was new at all this. He took time to demonstrate each new move slowly and carefully, then watch and encourage. I was issued a warm woolen blanket. Ali showed me how to fold it just right for prayer. Following vespers, the group blanket-rolled in a row on a grassy patch under an ancient acacia tree and slept.

Perhaps the greatest service any nomad can offer another is to find him with sore feet, needing to continue the march and provide him shoes. This is exactly how Ali won my heart. The climb was getting steeper and the view more breathtaking as our little file of pilgrims crawled on up the Zab. But much as I enjoyed the spectacular environment and the company of the holy band and felt lifted by being considered a part of the troop, my court-shoe sandals were dying fast. I could not keep small, sharp pebbles or spoons-full of sand from creeping in under my arch.

Moreover, the makeshift lashings laced through holes cut in the sole had begun to tear out. My feet were breaking down with tiny cuts and bruises underneath. I was hobbling along obviously in trouble and falling behind. Loyal partner, Ali, stayed with me. I was actually pondering casting away my Keds and going barefoot. I was sure that if I watched carefully where I stepped and stayed on the path or at most padded only through the fine sand on the sides of the trail, I could toughen up my feet, and in a day or so put the pain behind me.

But God works in mysterious ways. When we paused for noon prayer and a snack, Ali went forward and returned with a fine, almost new pair of mountain boots that one of the men had brought along as spares. God's grace, they fit.

It may not be surprising to everyone, but it was to me, how quickly my sore feet healed. Equally surprising, I discovered how much more buoyant my spirit became once my feet were comfortable. Now I could climb with the strongest and clamber over the huge creek-edge cubes of granite like a squirrel.

Of this long hike up the western slope of the northern Zagros, the memory most stirring to me is that of the awesome views that came with each rest stop or prayer stop as we ascended. Honestly, we could look west out over the foothills below and see the tiny people working at or driving to their tiny tasks. We could see the millennial history of the mighty Tigris. The several paths where the river had once and anciently flowed contrasted with the clear blue path fringed by palm, willow and reed. From our pause on high, the rafts of logs, the dhows and the sailboats looked like tiny toys on a backyard rain pond.

About dusk of the third day, our band mounted the crest of the series of ridges we had been battling since leaving the waterfall where I had joined. I had in my mind that here at the crest we would find the Prince Ali gorge and the notorious bridge across to the border. I happened to be with my partner Ali up near the front of the column as we came to the top and looked out beyond. The view ahead was not the shocking two-thousand-feet-deep gorge I had expected. One glance and I dropped to one knee. Holding my stout hiking staff in both hands, I just gasped. There was indeed no shocking gorge with a bridge directly across to a border station. There was instead a depressing view of miles and miles more of complex mountain ridges cut by sheer canyons, as far as my eye could reach. The furthest peaks were snow-capped even in early October. I breathed heavily in disappointment and disbelief. I had this whole escape planned out to a timetable of days. Reality suddenly, in one glance, exposed a timetable of weeks, perhaps months. I was so totally shattered and confused that I just hung there on my staff, kneeling and staring and gasping.

Sufi came up from the rear. He had been there before, so he took charge and led the file north into a narrow pathway through some berry bushes and sage. I was unable to move. I just knelt on my stick, totally depressed. Ali came over and stood beside me. I could feel his black chador brushing my shoulder. He sensed my mood and was just being there for me. I was thinking I had been here before and should not have been surprised. It was sort of, as Yogi Berra says, "Deja vu all over again." Then I realized it was not a repeat for me personally. It was an historic repeat that most Montana outfitters and wilderness guides grew up on. It was right out of Lewis & Clark's Corps of Discovery Journals, August 1805.

"Meriwether Lewis, with three men, had gone on ahead of the main Corps of Discovery to find the Continental Divide and the Shoshone Indians. The Corps badly needs the Shoshone horses as well as information concerning the best pass across the Rockies and the shortest portage to the headwaters of the Columbia River." Lewis's journal describes further how thrilled he and his men were to come to the spring where the Missouri River's west-most tributary arose. They stopped for lunch at the pool of clear, fresh, ice-cold water which gushed from the rock and then wandered, some west, some east. His journal records his feelings: "I realized that right here, right now at the very top of the Missouri River, I have accomplished one of those great objectives on which my mind has been unalterably fixed for many years. Judge then the pleasure I felt in allaying my thirst with this fresh, pure and ice cold water."

Now was his moment to go to the top of the pass to become the first American to look west of the Louisiana

Purchase into the great northwest empire. He had been conditioned by President Jefferson, encouraged by vague discussions with the Mandan Indians in the Dakotas, unhelped by contact with any Montana Indians. He expected a short, green sweep of foothills down to the mighty Columbia with the Pacific Ocean visible in the distance.

He actually saw: "From the spring, we proceeded on to the very top of the divide. There, instead of the Great Western Sea, I discovered immense ranges of high mountains cut by severe canyons on to the west as far as my glass could reach. Their tops were all covered with snow." Historian John Logan Allen writes, "Imagine the shock and surprise that struck this travel-exhausted man. From the top of that ridge were to be seen neither the great river that had been promised nor the sweeping, open plains down to the shores of the Pacific." Allen goes on to say, "The geography-of-hope suddenly gave way to the geography-of-reality. With Lewis's final step to the top of the Divide went decades of theory about the nature of the Rocky Mountains and the dimensions of this Continent—theory shattered by the single glance of a single man."

After a few moments to accommodate, Ali helped me to my feet. We jogged after the disappearing file of black clothespins. Almost immediately we came upon a natural gate in the bushes. The mufti led us through. There we came upon what appeared to be a huge hat left on a pile of brush. Suddenly the hat-on-the-pile moved, raised one arm and shouted. It was the fat, round hunchback. Believe me, he could not have been more than three feet tall. He welcomed us with a sort of Praise-God chant in Kurdish. Then he directed us to follow him.

We wound down a series of switch-backs and along a traverse north and came out in a flattish clearing about twenty yards across. The clearing was completely surrounded

117

by Juniper bushes. The hunchback's two wives were there laying out lunch on a Persian carpet in the center of the clearing. Our group made its way to the carpet and formed a loose circle around the carpet, the tiny fellow and his ladies. Sufti introduced the holy hunchback. His name was Gerhedi. I immediately recognized the name as that of a very important Independent Kurdistan activist. In a moment we were all in our traditional, lotus-legged circle. The girls served us what looked and tasted like taco salad that came on a flour tortilla. I wondered how I had so quickly gotten to Mexico. Then Ali, noticing my querity, whispered a name and explained that this was regular Kurdish mountain picnic stuff.

Gerhedi stood beside our circle and told us that this clearing was a secret hideout and resting place for the Free Kurdish insurgents who were out continually on raids. He pointed up the ridge a couple of hundreds yards where we could see the hunchback's cabin and a shed barn behind. He also told us that the creek that ran through the clearing was an overflow from the Little Zab whose main plunge was through the granite boulders behind his cabin.

Following lunch we of the holy-band took a siesta. Without direction after perhaps an hour of rest, the dervishes moved again into meditation. This session was not in our usual circle, but each holy man, as he awoke, wandered off to a secret place of his own. Ali, as expected, waited for me. I explained to him that it was okay, I could handle this alone.

I was working on a plan to secede gracefully from this retreat group during the coming night or early the next morning. I needed to fill my pack with food and if possible find a donkey, camel or horse to move more rapidly and with less effort than so far. I was already having leg cramps at night from the steep hiking. Now that I knew the migration trail continued on some distance east and the mighty gorge was apparently far ahead, I needed to decide whether to go back and try to get into the embassy in Baghdad without being caught by the Revolutionaries, or I needed to set my mind on a long, arduous trip through this north Zagros wilderness to freedom. Either way, I was becoming aware that it was not going to be either as quick, as easy or as safe a venture as I had originally surmised.

As in high mountains worldwide, darkness came down rather suddenly. I had been in deep sleep for several hours when I heard my wristwatch click. I cautiously peeked out of my blanket. It was pitch dark except for a half moon rising through the juniper. My blanket-rolled friends were scattered in disorder around the rock circle of the Indian campfire we had used to cook and around which we had earlier held our vespers.

I slid out of the blanket and silently folded it and slid it into my daypack. I stepped carefully to the supply pack and lifted out a sack of coarse-ground meal. It almost filled my pack. That would have to do. I gave one final glance at the group. No one was moving. I stepped over Sufi and slid up the slope and out through the hidden clearing entrance.

The moonlight was critical. It allowed me to slip along the corral rail below the cabin. The brush was dense except close to the fence where a path seemed to lead from hut to barn. As I leaned down to enter the barn-shed, something inside snuffled a greeting. My heart leapt, "A horse!" Immediately, in the pitch dark, I felt with my reaching hand, the soft, wet, aquiline nose of the snuffler. "Good Boy," I whispered. My Montana lots-of-horses youth was now going to be tested. I scratched a forehead and with my fingers combed a long forelock. This gesture brought another quiet, fearless snuffle. My eyes were getting accustomed to the light, plus the half-moon was coming over the junipers and leaking in through a square shed window.

119

On the pole beside the head, I found a snaffle. "Aha! This must be attached to a bridle. And here it is! And that takes some of the risk out of this move." I had worried since in the afternoon when I reasoned that the presence of a shed should mean the presence of an animal, that whether it was an ass, a camel or a horse, it might not be a riding animal. Here was a major breakthrough in the risk department. "A bridle meant a riding horse."

Some things you never forget, like how to ride a bicycle. The same goes for a horse. I also found I was drawing from my youth on the western range a series of know-hows that just came along naturally as I moved. I scratched his withers gently and called him by name. This came to me also. From my little Nez Perce third-grade schoolmate, Li'l Bear, any strange horse will respond to the Serhaptin word *"Shopuni."* Actually, I was told by Li'l Bear's grandfather that when a Nez Perce warrior was gentling a wild horse he found on the loose, if he would call him Shopuni, the horse would not only be quiet and obedient, but often would follow him home. One night the three of us were sitting around a campfire talking horses. Grandpa Blackfeather told me *"Shopuni"* is the mystic name all horses are called in heaven. It worked for me as advertised, and in short order, I was leading my new horse Shopuni along the path beside the corral, across the small clearing in front of the hunchback's cabin.

The moon was high now, and I expected at any moment to be forced to mount and make a run for it. I was wrong. No one, either in the cabin nor down in the hideout, awakened. I walked quietly beside Shopuni west along the approach trail we had followed yesterday. In maybe half-an-hour I came out through the natural gateway and onto the moonlit, wide, dusty migration trail. I turned east. Riding a horse is normally fairly easy—with a gentle horse. This horse fortunately was very gentle, but riding bareback (there was no saddle in the shed) if you haven't ridden at all for twenty years, is a challenge.

I did remember how to move with the rhythm of the horse, and in only a few minutes, I found that this steed and I were going to be a fit. I walked him for about an hour, riding under tight rein. He wanted to go. The main trail followed a gradually descending open plateau for about five miles. I talked in a quiet, soothing voice almost constantly calling him by his new name, Shopuni. He seemed to be enjoying the freedom, but, as I say, he wanted to run.

As dawn began to pink the stratus along the farthest eastern horizon, I found that my horse was an iron gray Arabian. I loosed his rein some and spoke the word, "Trot." He trotted with long, even strides and maintained gate reasonably well. I had some trouble moving my hips with his trot, so I was very tensely trying to keep my balance and not bounce perceptibly. I was pulling a lot of main to stay on, but I knew my escape depended upon my mastering this exercise quickly. We kept trotting.

In an hour I was beginning to relax so I moved us into a soft canter. This was easy and a welcome relief for both horse and rider. Now we were moving out, covering a lot of ground with an easy rhythm. By noon we were up out of the first canyon and traversing the second major ridge. The trail came back to the river here, so we paused for a snack and a drink. I searched the back-trail but could find no evidence that we were being followed. I thought it was possible the missing mount had not been discovered. In any event, on foot, it would be impossible to catch us.

By evening we had covered astonishing miles. We camped five ridgelines east of the retreat site. At dusk we came out onto the high lake that fed the Little Zab. As I had done before, I hobbled Shopuni and turned him out. Our campsite lay on a rich, green, grassy meadow. While twilight passed, I collected an armful of reeds along the lake edge and twisted and braided a decent rope. From my rope, I fashioned a figure eight hobble. Now I would not have to break down my bridle for hobbles at each stop. Also I had enough for a lead-rope to allow me to temporarily secure Shopuni to a tree during brief stops.

One of the strange aspects of this relationship, Shopuni didn't seem to desire to run away. My feeling was that he was being well treated (perhaps unusual), well fed (also perhaps unusual) and he had lots more freedom than the little shed by the hideout provided (very unusual). Here on the evasion and escape trail, he seemed to be happy as my partner in crime. When he wasn't grazing, he lay beside me at night, which was an added bonus of heat. The days across the high country as we followed October were still warm, but the nights with only a light prayer blanket were chilly.

I should pull a paragraph from my journal about my general morale during this stretch. I had been very buoyant and positively "can-do" from the dhow on the Tigris to the sandstorm. True, I was periodically struck with brief spasms of terror at the appearance of nearby authority and I was often plunged into short but deep "missing Najua" depressions, but my morale was generally high because I was ever certain that this whole bad dream would all be over in a week at most.

The Sacre-barrak had put me down, but only briefly. Then again, once I was out of the city and on the trail to the Iranian border I was full of hope and confidence. The view from the ridgeline at the hideout severely tested my grip. I was so sure this was to be a couple of days hike. But now with my new friend, Shopuni, an Arabian colt with unusual personality, I was again having fun. A fighter pilot in the midst of adventure in an unknown venue creates fun even without any of the normal amenities of the good life.

I had long ago made a solemn commitment to play the hand I was dealt, giving it my very best, to learn from, rather than complain about, each adversity, and to resolutely believe that God would somehow deliver me in His time and under His conditions. The unusual warmth of our friendship and the surprisingly humanesque interplay between Shopuni and me was of singular value in keeping both our interests and enjoyment high.

My Journal tells me we had been traveling together for four plus days and found ourselves halfway across a deciduously wooden plateau. The trail followed along a pretty trout stream. By late afternoon we were both physically tired out. I decided to stop for a break and see if I could catch some trout by tickling. I turned Shopuni loose to graze. I no longer hobbled him even at night. I found a shady place where the brook came off a pretty, foot-deep eddy. I lay down flat on my belly on the bank where a nice riffle chuckled into another eddy. I was trying to remember Grandpa Blackfeather's technique. He first taught Li'l Bear and me to tickle trout on Clear Creek in the Bearpaw Mountains in Montana. I reached out and trailed my left arm in the brook. I was surprised at how warm the water felt. I moved my fingers lazily and, sure enough, from out of the riffles near the creek center came a nice size speckled trout. He curiously approached my moving fingers and then made the mistake of passing over the top to get a closer look.

FLIP! Up and out into the air flew the surprised fish. I snatched it up as soon as it dropped into the grass along the bank. Eureka! I had my dinner. And, as it was nearing sunset, I decided to RON there and try the same trick for breakfast. There was plenty of grass for my partner, and the rustle of the high country breeze through the cottonwood leaves made a comfortable camp sound. I collected some squaw wood and made a tiny fire. Trout is just as good at sundown as it is at sunup. And if I thought that good tasting fish had to come out of ice-cold water, I was wrong.

Dawn came clear and crisp. I rolled over onto my belly and raised my head. There was Shopuni rolling on his back some twenty feet away. It had been his joyful grunting that had surfaced me from a pleasant dream. I don't know what made me look back to the west—just a general instinctive prey reaction, I guess. It was fortuitous. Far up along the slope facing me—the slope we had just descended yesterday—a cloud of dust arose. I watched the cloud lift straight up whimsically wondering—then it hit me! "Someone is hard on our heels, pal." I spoke it out loud to my friend who had righted himself and was shaking violently. I moved quickly to the fire and covered the ashes with sand, then creek rocks. I hurriedly donned my pack, rolled my prayer blanket, and laying it over Shopuni's withers, jumped on. In a trice we were in a soft canter east along the well-worn, old trail. The terrain was flat, and as I rolled with the horse's rhythm, I worked on our *"follower" problem.* Coming at this time of morning and fast enough to raise dust, told me it must be a pursuit. Now the brainer is: Should I try to outrun them to the border, or hide and let them pass. I tried to search up ahead to see if I could make out the texture of the vegetation and the rock shadows at the spot where the chasm narrowed, a bridge site. The rhythm of the horse, while smooth and easy, was not such that I could clearly define anything more than 100 yards ahead.

I decided to move on out at a full gallop and see whether we could maintain an opening speed without dust. Also, I tried to see whether the posse was closing. I couldn't believe that a gang of horsemen could long maintain any great pace without slowing periodically to a walk. I thought the troop might have put up that dust cloud descending a steep drop. I remembered at least one steep descent on the trail. Still I couldn't dawdle and find out too late I was wrong.

I was immediately startled at the vigor of my steed. He jumped from a gentle canter to a full run in one squeeze of my legs. I grabbed a healthy hunk of mane and hung on. I was feeling very uncomfortable as the trail was neither level nor straight. So I put the reins, which I had knotted, over my head and grabbed mane with both hands. Shopuni was in his element. He laid his ears back as if to say, "Don't worry, Boss. They'll never catch us. Watch my smoke!"

We were making smoke, but as I say, I was not riding easily. I was, in fact, tensely hanging on for dear life. In a quarter of a mile, with Shopuni showing no signs of tiring, the trail turned around an ancient oak tree and started a curving descent. At the turn, I went off the right side and into a large growth of what in Montana we would call buffalo berries. The bushes were grayish in color, with small pointed leaves, red berries and lots of thorns. I rolled nicely as though I had practiced. Recovering safely from a spill all sort of came back instinctively. I had bit the dust a lot as a kid. We played a kind of Texas rules polo with baseball bats and a softball. It was vicious, but we learned how to balance and how to fall and roll. I came to a stop with no signs of major injury, some scratches from the thorns and a scrape on my hip from sliding on the gravel. I called in my best shout, "Shopuni!" The Arab skidded to a stop below and circled directly back to me. I limped a few steps and realized that my right hip was too tender to ride. I would have to lead.

When Shopuni came up to me, I scratched his withers and poll and talked reassuringly. "Good Feller. That was not your fault. Nice Boy." I led him out on the trail and noticed that because of the trail's descent, I could not see far behind. Any pursuers were hidden in both sight and sound by a long stone ledge. The trail ahead continued to drop away to a bushy wash below, after which it turned north and traversed up to the same level we had just departed. We were in a natural erosion-cut in the broad plateau. I continued leading on down the trail, sort of soft-jogging along beside Shopuni. I soon realized that I could not continue far with this acute pain. We would have to hide out at least temporarily until my hip eased.

The heavier brush near the creek at the bottom of the cut looked promising. Down, down, down, I decided not to cross the water as it would leave a telltale sign of passing to a sharp-eyed tracker. I turned Shopuni's head between bushes and limped along zigzagging between the thorny sage-colored chaparral. The bushes were eight to ten feet tall and very thick, so I felt confident we would not be seen. Thirty yards off the trail, I turned down to the creek. We both drank, and to relieve the pain, I stretched out on the sandy bank.

Almost immediately I picked up the echo of clattering hoofs behind us. The posse was descending the same difficult stretch where I had just been policed. Down, down, down, the troop made no effort at quiet, so I decided it was apparently a palace guard detachment of some sort—not a regular military cavalry unit. I remembered the universal equine instinct to communicate, so I squeezed Shopuni's nostrils gently with my right hand as the pursuers splashed across the creek below us. I counted seven horsemen. They did not stop to drink but cantered on up and out of the ravine. I caught scattered glimpses of gray uniforms. Then they were gone from sight and sound.

I let half-an-hour pass. Then I tried my hip. The acute pain had eased. The hip was sore to the touch, but I could ride. I led Shopuni out of the bush by descending the creek. Once on the trail, we climbed up out of the ravine. My thought was that we could move along behind the pursuers and, at their swift rate, we would not catch them before they arrived at the bridge or changed course to search in a different direction.

At the top of the traverse the trail headed once again east toward the border. We walked now as trotting was painful. We passed through a grove of oak and came out onto a straight stretch when, looking up, I saw we were walking right up on the posse. It was too late to cut and run. The soldiers had dismounted and were standing beside their horses on either side of the trail. There were more than I had earlier counted. On each side of the trail, lined up as for parade, but facing toward each other, were two rows of silent, uniformed warriors, at attention. Standing at the far end of the rows in the middle of the trail, his booted legs apart, his hands on his hips, his gold braid shining elegantly in the morning sun, a commandant of some sort faced me.

While I was deciding to just casually walk straight on through as though I were just a journeyman passing along the trail. Shopuni picked up a very casual jog that perfectly fit our act. He jogged without noticing between the two rows of soldiers and horses. Nearing the end, he slightly side-stepped to avoid the commandant's person. The outraged commandant shouted "Halt!" in Arabic. Shopuni apparently did not read Arabic. He jogged steadily on. The air was filled with a wild burst of orders mixed with inelegant profanity. There was an equally wild scramble as all the soldiers simultaneously broke ranks to mount their steeds.

Then I noticed the commandant's elegant, gray Arab mare was not beside him, but rather her reins were tied to an oak branch perhaps ten yards beyond. Shopuni headed directly toward her. Once alongside the mare, Shopuni bowed his neck, began his mating dance and let out a very horny stallion roar. The mare responded. Rearing, she broke her tie. She nuzzled Shopuni once, whinnied something about "Come with me, Big Boy!" and broke into a romping gallop west, right past her master, right between the mounting ranks and straight back through the oak grove toward the ravine in a gathering wild dash for home.

There was a violent chaos of men and horses! The commandant shouted a series of commands. I tightened Shopuni's reins, and we watched the entire platoon in pursuit through the woods after the fleeing commandant's horse. Turning east now, we eased into a soft canter and headed down the trail toward the bridge and the border. The braided commandant was still standing in the middle of the trail shouting obscenities after his men—once again raising a cloud of dust—this time in pursuit of a horse headed west. His cute little trap had been deftly set. We had taken the bait. The trap had sprung. It had simply snapped empty. And we were on our way out the other side.

After an hour we slowed to a walk and I saw up ahead perhaps a mile or two, the tall red stone pillars that mark the approach to the notorious suspension bridge at Prince Albert Gorge. We would be across the border to freedom by nightfall. I began singing out loud one of the few cowboy songs I knew, "I'm a lonely cowboy, far away from home." At the approach to the famous bridge, a huge open area lies off to the north. This is apparently a holding space for herds or flocks who arrive to cross east and must wait their turn. The narrow, swinging suspension bridge is definitely a defile in the classic sense. Although the trail proper makes a slight turn and drops a few feet onto the bridge itself, I had decided that because of the fear psychology connected with the crossing, I would just simply ride Shopuni directly onto the bridge and across. I knew horses well enough to know that if the rider starts vacillating, the horse will read the indecision and lengthy negotiation will ensue.

Shopuni walked without falter directly to the bridge. I was very proud of him. I watched with some trepidation the 100 yards of braided hemp swinging from its high stone posts. I noticed the deck of poles covered by woven reed matting, grass growing through in spots. As we came up onto the approach, I made the further mistake of glancing 2000 feet down the sheer rock wall into the awesome chasm below.

My gut cringed, and I clutched not only main, but also a hunk of Shopuni's neck. Shopuni planted his two forefeet directly short of the bridge matting. The sudden stop slid me to the ground beside my horse. There was no other living person or thing in the vicinity. I decided to keep up the momentum. I held the reins in my hand and walked ahead of Shopuni onto the bridge. My feeling was very uneasy, but I played brave. I looked down and could barely see the tiny river as an ink mark winding through the rocks far below. Shopuni would not follow me onto the bridge. He pawed the approach. When I pulled, he reared. He snorted and bowed his neck and threatened to break away and go home. I did not edge or raise my voice. I simply tried all the tricks I knew to induce a horse to follow me. We had developed such a mutual trust and respect I was not going to try to force Shopuni to cross. Rather, we would part there.

After some time, it became clear to me that Shopuni had never been across this bridge and was not going across now. With a giant lump in my throat and tears coming, I walked him back into the clearing, lifted his bridle off his ears and tossed in on the grass. I patted his neck and withers, said goodbye and turning, walked out onto the four-foot-wide bridge alone. I thought maybe if he saw it was safe for me, he might change his attitude. I got about halfway across periodically clutching the handrails and feeling far from secure. Suddenly without warning, I heard a WHOOOSH, and a small gust of wind struck the bridge's rigging. This started the bridge swinging and rippling. I grabbed the side railings! The twisted cattail canes provided less than abundant assurance. Because of the irregular motion, I lost my balance and was thrown down on my knees on the grassy deck. This tore loose my death-like grip on the rails. I screamed out loud as I caught one glimpse of the tiny blue snake thousands of feet below. I clutched the edges of the deck now slanting at a severe angle. I felt myself sliding off the north side. I cannot express the icy surge of sheer terror that swept over me. Suddenly I was very sick to my stomach.

It was as though without any warning sound, they were right there, close up. I was too busy with my awkward terror to notice approaching dust. The clatter of steel-shod hoofs rang on the rocky approach to the bridge. The well-known voice of the commandant shouted orders.

Simultaneously came Shopuni's sharp whinny. He was trying to warn me, I know. Then with the sound of boots and spurs and leather, riders dismounted. I could hear voices approaching. Still I was frozen with the instinctive fear of sliding—falling. Plus the ultimate terror, my grip was failing. In fact my deep soul was begging my pursuers to hasten their rescue before I was swept two thousand feet to my death on the rocks far below.

In seconds I felt leather boots stomping my wrists and fingers forcing me to let go of the bridge edges. I could not believe how sure-footed were these guards. Booted and spurred and in fancy uniforms, they spent no effort at all looking to their own safety. They dragged me the thirty or so yards back off the swinging bridge and stood me before the commandant.

His Excellency sat astride the same gorgeous, gray Arab that I had insulted two hours before. The commandant wore the surly sneer of a movie bad-man with the drop on the hero. He spit out a ripple of instructions. Six feet of rope appeared, and I was rope-cuffed behind my back and tossed bodily back onto Shopuni.

The column jogged at a very uncomfortable gait back down the trail we had come—back through the grove of oak, back down the ravine, back across the creek, back over the wide plateau. I was totally sore, sharply pained, deeply depressed, thinking, *Spies get hanged.*

Darkness slid down the slopes of the blue Zagros as we turned southwest off the wide, main migration trail. A wooden sign pointed west to Kirkuk. My mind flashed to an aerial view, Sulaymaniyah and the Diyala River, down the foothills to the Tigris and the eight-mile-high column of dust, Baghdad.

The commandant pulled off the road and reined his horse. He watched the column clip-clop by, and I heard him fall in with his rear guard. "We'll camp at the lake and go on in tomorrow, Captain. You arrange a watch schedule for the night. Abu is pitching my quarters and his assistant will make supper." He spurred his Arab and rejoined the point.

You have probably never been propped against a pine tree with your hands tied under your half-full daypack. It is okay for about thirty minutes. Then it becomes a series of complaining muscles. My arms, no matter how I shifted my position, insisted on cramping. My back was already painfully torqued from riding off balance and trying to stay on my faithful Shopuni who did his best to make the trip smooth. Someone threw what felt like a GI blanket over me. It slid down so I could breathe—breathe and see. The sight of the night-camp reminded me of Troop 39 in scout camp by a lake in Glacier Park a thousand years ago. I could hear the soldiers bathing or swimming. I could see between the trees, the light from the long-set sun reflected off the water. Abu's assistant had a small campfire crackling and the smell was meat-on-a-spit. A light shone through the commandant's tent wall. There is a point in time when a man gets to totally depleted, exhausted, depressed that though painfully hungry, in sharp dread and aching all over, he falls asleep. Have you been there?

It must have been an hour or so after midnight when the dust-up started. I jumped awake. There was a prolonged earth tremor underway. I instinctively tried my wrists again. They were tighter than before. I could see in the half-moon rising, several wrestling matches between black forms in the open area near where the fire had been. For a moment I thought I was dreaming as there was no sound of voices, just grunts and ughs and whispered profanity. Then I saw to quick flashes and heard the reports, "Bang! Bang!" I now recognized the voice of the second-officer of our guard unit over there, yelling for help.

At that instant someone cut my rope-cuffs with one slash, grabbed my arm, and I was suddenly on a saddled horse running hard through a brief clutch of brush and trees then out onto the main road. It all happened with such commando precision and speed, I was disoriented. I was not sure which way we were headed. Two men in dark coats on dark horses raced ahead. One in a black chador and mask or hood rode full-gallop beside me. The sound of two following some distance back told me they had remained a few seconds to secure our departure. Then we broke into a clearing, and a half moon rising lit the night. A flurry of rifle shots! I lay low on my horse. In the dim light, I recognized that we were retracing our steps east along the main migration trail. I found I had reins, but was still confused, off-balance and running hard. I was mainly holding onto the cantle of the saddle and some main. It was what we would call in Montana an Eastern saddle, no horn. I felt my feet steady in both stirrups as I rose and fell with the horse's rhythm. I wondered how I had managed that. Now a burst of AK-47 fire behind signaled the rear guard was discouraging pursuit.

For over an hour, we thundered east through the moon-lit woods, then out across the high plateau. I had no clue who these guys were. I knew they must be very familiar with the terrain. We had left the commandant's lake camp at a full run, and we had not slowed a hoofbeat since. I could not believe horses could run, not canter or gallop, I mean run hard as though scared, and through this weird, shadowy darkness. There was nothing I could do but hang on and try to accommodate to the shocking pace. I recognized most of the terrain features as we passed, even in the ghostly, bluish moonlight.

The leaders slowed a bit when we came to the cut down the ravine. Then suddenly we slacked to a trot and turned sharply left—north. This turn took our mounted squad down the main course of the rushing stream where Shopuni and I had earlier hid out to let the commandant's guard squad pass. I knew this meant we were about two miles west of the bridge across the gorge. The turn told me that the leader did not intend to cross the bridge. I heaved a major sigh of relief. The squad of eight bled into single-file as we splashed down the stream. Half a mile and the terrain broke away sharply down a cascade. Here, the leader took a deer path that followed beside the creek down, down, down. Here the pine changed to the same type heavy brush in which Sho-puni and I had hidden way up on the main migration trail. The file cut back to the east, and the moon, now high, dis-closed we were passing through a badland of building-size boulders.

Half an hour at a quiet walk. Suddenly, up ahead, the night was cut by the sharp voice of a sentry challenge. We paused for identification. Then we moved on through what appeared to be willows to the edge of a pond. It was black dark here. The moon was now hidden behind a sharp bluff, high to the south. We paused again and were immediately surrounded by a squad of men. Everyone in my party dismounted. When my feet touched ground, one of the men took my upper arm in a tight grip. "Fear not. You are among friends." He guided me in behind the others who were following some sort of trail in the pitch dark. We wound through the willows a hundred yards. Up ahead I saw a campfire, around it a group of men stood in a circle. Their faces reflected orange from the firelight.

When we broke out of the willows into the open, one of the men by the fire sprang toward us shouting a challenge. Our leader, up front, called out a password. Our squad moved in, circled the fire and joined the others. Everyone was greeting and laughing and talking, narrating the encounter earlier in the night and pointing at me. Someone brought some hot food. A huge Kurd in a long, rough-out, leather coat, a scarlet turban on his head, came through and grabbed my right hand to shake.

"Shalom! Welcome to Shanidar Cave, Major." He spoke in heavily accented English, pointing up and back. Only then did the firelight and shadows disclose that the nightriders' camp was under a vast, flat-stone overhang. The Scarlet Turban continued, "I am your host, Mullah Mustapha Barzani. You have had a brisk ride. Ha, ha, ha. I apologize, Major. We have to strike like zee hawk and ride like zee wind, or we die like zee dog. Ha, ha, ha, you understand?" My memory flashed back to the desert refugee camp, *Shar-Gat*. He turned to a heavily black bearded man at his side, also in a long coat but of course wool or goat hair. "Sergeant Kabir, you have zee honor of escorting American hero. Right now, get the Major some hot food and a place."

At that moment, a furry fellow slid out from behind, grabbing his arm. Barzani turned. The fellow held his fist up to his ear like a telephone. Barzani turned back to me.

"Pardon Sir, that's the zit-net, our radio. We have two hours 'til daylight. Get some rest. We'll get you across by noon, I promise." He slapped my shoulder. "Excuse me." The Mullah Barzani walked with the furry fellow back toward the horses, and I never saw him again.

Kabir stuffed a torch into the flames. It lit. He took me by the wrist, and we headed back into the velvet black part of the cave. "That giant is Mustapha Barzani. You know about?"

The torch was not a flashlight, but its flickering light disclosed rows of men asleep in blankets along the walls. I knew the name, Barzani. The desert refugee camp-city. "Sorry, my friend. I do not know of your leader."

"He is the immortal Kurdish nationalist activist. He leads our fight for a nation, Kurdistan. He most wanted outlaw in Turkey, in Iraq, in Persia, in Azerbaijan. Zee cave, only one of seven secret hideouts. He will get you across, fear not."

"How did Barzani know I was trying to get back? Why are these insurgents interested in me?"

Kabir indicated a straw mattress between two snoring bears. "Zee Mullah know everything. You hot item on zit-net." He laughed. "I bring beans and coffee, Shalom."

The torch flickered back toward the campfire. I dropped onto the straw and found there a coarse wool blanket to pull up. I never saw Kabir again.

Dawn came up like thunder, literally. A violent earthquake awoke me. I dashed to the mouth of the mammoth cave and looked out across the clearing to the chasm beyond. Because of the sheer, vertical stonewall to the east, the sun would not appear for another half-hour at least. The mountain shook again. Building-size blocks of granite crumbled and crashed down from the cliff opposite and large gravel fell from my cave roof, a hundred feet above. My vast bed-room was in partial light now. It was a gymnasium-size bar-racks. But, surprising to me, not a soul slept where I had seen the lines of bodies earlier. The commandos had been awakened, had eaten, saddled up and slipped silently out.

I stood for a long time at the edge. The view from the opening was absolutely breathtaking. I was looking east along the trench of the mighty Prince Ali chasm. This camp hideout was about halfway down—between the bridge at the top and the white water river snaking below. The paleozoic rock showed intense folding here. The central gorge was fed into by numerous deep, narrow cuts. I thought of a very narrow Grand Canyon. Small lakes were visible in notches out and below. Constant volcanic and fault activity brought hourly tremors as well as the daily shake-of-consequence that had just rattled our bunkhouse. Someone appeared to be the sole remaining life at the camp. Someone was stirring the fire in the clearing outside. I thought it was Kabir—same size, same dress. I was wrong. When I called his name, a young Kurd with his left arm in a sling turned as I ap-proached. He saluted with his good arm.

"Ah, no, sir—a raid. They all slipped out before light. The mullah got a call on the zit-net. A raid. He gave his son, Masoud, order to make you happy." He tapped his chest. "He return soon. You hungry, Major?—Food here." He stirred some chili in a hanging cauldron. I was very hungry. I ate the meat and beans with relish.

"Where are we?" I asked the question without thinking that the location of this hideout was undoubtedly top secret. Masoud merely pointed almost straight up, slightly south. I looked through the leafless branches of a tall cottonwood, and there, probably a thousand feet up and half a mile south along the wall, like a tiny shadow across the sky, connecting one sheer stone cliff, painted orange in the morning sun, and the opposing stone cliff, brushed velvet purple in deep shadow—*The Bridge.*

At that moment I heard a loud, plaintive whinny!—a horse whinny I recognized. I dropped my empty bean plate and jogged across the clearing to the path leading down to the horses.

"Where is that horse?"

Masoud following at my elbow, replied, "He came in during night. Strange horse. Runaway—broke loose somewhere. Mullah afraid he trained RCC spy-horse. Sent to find hideout." He pointed up ahead to a break between two trees. "Broke fence—join herd. Only few mares now—the raid."

Masoud Barzani kept up a line of chatter as we trotted together down the trail to the meadow. We did not reach the meadow. Still perhaps thirty yards from the woven-vine fence that, tree-to-tree, circled the meadow, crashing through the heavy chaparral and upon us with another loud whinny, Shopuni!

"Shopuni!" I shouted his name. He reared up, whinnied his enthusiasm, recovered and snuffled my shoulder. I cried like a child cries when a lost friend returns. I was deeply touched by this unusually sensitive horse's display of loyalty to a master he had only known a matter of days. It fed my self-esteem. I was reminded I had something going at least with animals. Young Barzani had pushed back against a tree to stay out of the way. "He your horse?" I turned to him nodding my head.

"Masoud, is there a way across the river?" I pointed to the east. "Direct to Persia from this camp?" I stroked Shopuni's forehead and patted his neck and scratched his withers. He was ecstatic. He pawed and circled around and came back and rubbed his face against my chest. I hugged his neck, kissed his nose and kept repeating, "Good boy, good

137

boy, good boy." There was simply no understanding the strange electric charge between us. The young guerilla watched this drama with disbelief. "Masoud?" He was not answering me.

Then, "Sir, the Mullah Barzani told me to watch out for you."

"Of course, Sergeant. Isn't part of that watching out also helping out?"

"Yes sir, of course. You are American flier, I must help out."

"Masoud, I need to cross over the border as soon as possible. This horse can take me if you can tell me how. Is there a trail down to the river?"

Masoud pointed down to the north. "Sir, some of the shepherds bring shaggy goats across river." He pointed up to the south. "Goats hate bridge. No one uses low trail except goats and guerillas. I can show you. Kurds cut a zigzag trail down to water, but too steep for horse. And, Papa!" The boy shook his head.

"Lieutenant Barzani, your father will knight you. You are helping an American jet pilot. I need a pad, a saddle and a bridle."

Masoud squared his shoulders with pride and started back up the trail. "Horse stuff in cave. I don't know, Colonel Barzani mean."

I cut him off, "I guarantee he will promote you to Captain for your help to an American officer."

We crossed the clearing where the campfire now smoked under the bean pot. Just inside the cave, we found an ancient and badly worn McClellan-type cavalry saddle and a rawhide, hand-tied hackamore to slip over Shopuni's ears. I took a rough woolen blanket from a nearby straw mattress. Back at the woven vine fence, Shopuni would hardly stand still to tack. He wanted to go, go, go. I gave my still-doubtful lieutenant a hug and we were off.

Seven

Midmorning found Shopuni and me following the zigzag trail that was more a stairway than a trail. It was, as Masoud had warned, too steep to ride. But Shopuni understood. I led him down, down, down. A dozen switchbacks and we were on the clear, rushing Zab-e Kuchek. Shopuni drank as though he had just crossed the Sahara. Then, as he was tired of being led, and I was tired of hiking the downhill trail, I climbed on. The saddle was a cavalry, one-size-fits-all, and Shopuni accepted the bridle without a bit, so we trotted off east along the goat and guerilla trail through the tall willows beside the river.

I was not familiar at all with this Zab tributary, and I was a bit apprehensive that it seemed to be winding generally northwest. I wanted to go east to cross the border and find some authority in Iran (still Persia to the locals). I kept wondering if I might be on the right trail but going in the wrong direction. The trail appeared to be, as Masoud had ventured, a migration route for mountain game; small, tough military units, and goats.

This observation became reality about sundown when we came upon a scruffy-looking highland Assyrian driving, or I should say walking behind, a covey of about twenty shaggy-haired, black, mean-looking goats. The man was chewing hashish and singing some kind of off-key, tribal chant as he scuffed along. Shopuni seemed to have picked up their smell sometime before they came into view. He was acting nervous

140

and didn't want to advance. I had to keep encouraging him although he and I had such a relationship that I didn't do any more than squeeze him with my legs to let him know I meant to move out. When we and the goats finally arrived together at a small clearing, the goats were immediately into the water and Shopuni turned his head into the willows along the cliff. The smell was atrocious. The horse would not show them any respect. I exchanged cursory greetings with the hombre, and we passed in peace.

The sun set early because the chasm wall blocked the sun shortly after noon. My journal says it was four o'clock local when the trail left the river and followed a narrow canyon heading east. There was a nice little trout stream cascading down the tributary canyon into the Zab-e Kuchek. We followed the creek up, up, up. The trail did not zigzag. The canyon simply climbed fairly steeply up a wash toward the high plateau.

I found we were more comfortable if I got off and walked beside Shopuni for fifteen minutes of each hour. Soon the tall willows and juniper gave out. Sage and a kind of Hawthorn-looking and flowering low cover remained. And the ubiquitous rocks—huge, dark brown, cubish-shaped and covered with splashes of lichens. Just before dark the trail widened onto an overlook guarding an erosion cave, similar to but much smaller than Mustapha Barzani's hideout. I found a cupped-out place where a fire had traditionally been laid just inside the entrance. This had been a migratory campsite since Bible times. I turned Shopuni loose to forage. I made an Indian fire to heat up the beans and meat that Masoud had insisted I put in my daypack. He also provisioned me with a pouch of dry tea that proved helpful.

I cannot narrate the feeling of contentment that I now found in sitting cross-legged on a flat stone plate beside my tiny fire in the mouth of this prehistoric cave eating my meat and beans looking out over the dying shadows of a scene very similar to twilight on the Grand Canyon. It was the same feeling of "God's in His Heaven, all's right with the world" that I had felt riding Shopuni three days earlier. I reflected warmly on the peace and freedom feeling clip-clopping along the migration trail before we were caught by the RCC palace cavalry. I jotted in my journal that today had been a day of grace because of two improbable happenings: Shopuni's tracking me to Barzani's camp and Masoud's reluctant encouragement, helping us move on alone. Now I had a deep conviction that we were finally on our way to freedom. I pulled the saddle blanket up over me by the fire and good dreams emerged.

Somewhere around midnight, the earth began to come apart. The quake shook me so hard lying on the ground I rolled completely over. I sat up with the kind of wild-eyed terror an earthquake always brings. Rocks the size of basketballs bounded and rolled. Cubish baseballs and sand fell from the cave ceiling, and dust made breathing choky. I don't know if you've ever experienced a serious quake in the dark. It is especially terrifying when it happens in a strange land, worse yet in a cave. The starlight even through the dust gave me direction. Still in my blanket, I rolled outside. I heard Shopuni snorting and pawing nearby. I thought it was a God-sent that he didn't spook and run for it. There were a million stars, and except for the starlight, it was pitch black, no moon. I raised up on my elbows. "Shopuni." I spoke his name in a very low, almost whisper. He whispered a low whinny back and came over to me sort of nervously dancing, pawing. Now the mountain shook again, just a brief aftershock. I jumped up and grabbing my pack, stuffed my blanket it.

As the shaking stopped, I reached out to soothe Shopuni. He kept dancing and snorting and staring across the clearing. I couldn't make out whether it was the quake, or if he wanted to direct my attention to a separate threat of some sort. The half moon of earlier on had not appeared yet, but there was dusty starlight. So when he danced away, I could, though barely, keep the horse in view. The cave entrance and clearing was merely a pool of light-blue wash in the near-black velvet.

My first thought was, *Lion*. But I knew neither of us was safe inside the cave now. Besides, Shopuni was neither hobbled nor tied, so he could cope with a predator. I decided to build up the fire a bit for safety and get some more Zs before daylight pushed us on to the border. I would sleep just outside. I patted Shopuni a moment then told him to go chase the cat away.

I turned back into the mouth of the cave to retrieve my pile of twigs. I stopped dead. There was a series of *something-in-the-bushes* sounds out there near the periphery of the clearing. I froze to listen. Total stillness, except for a lot of night insects buzzing. Then suddenly the insect sounds ceased as if by command of the chief insect. I felt very eerie, and just stood there for a minute listening and feeling.

The earthquake was unsettling enough, but here was something else—something more sinister and not quite real. I involuntarily shuddered. A few feet away Shopuni stood absolutely still, staring directly out across the clearing, listening. Then he pawed the dirt hard, and whirling toward the west, he dashed out across the rocky clearing. Almost immediately, there appeared a tiny light in a huge boulder complex where Shopuni had headed. Someone out there had given a signal.

I grabbed my daypack and flashed up the rock wall between two stone pillars. Once up off the level of the clearing, I ducked down behind a row of sagebrush and ran, as much as you can run ducked down. I ran along and up a traverse.

When I came out a hundred feet higher and sort of above the cave mouth, I carefully looked down and listened. I was not being followed.

Around the mouth of the cave I thought I could hear—but couldn't see—a flurry of activity. Muffled whispers, now clear, now hollow; one was giving orders, several seemed to respond to orders, moving in and out of the cave. Shopuni was nowhere in evidence. I fled on up, up and away.

My daypack was quite light. I had stuffed my saddle blanket in on top of a few rations when I retreated from the cave during the quake. I climbed a very steep course using holds on the rocks and sage bushes to pull me up.

My forming plan was to follow as difficult a route as possible, leaving as little trail as possible, as silent as possible, to the very top of the plateau. I was confident that I would be near the Iranian border, although I knew the boundary had been in dispute all through the Azerbaijan mountains since ancient times. Still, I knew an Iraqi Revolutionary Guard would not worry about a boundary if they were able to make a hit. On the other hand, I was beginning to feel pretty confident that I could fend for myself in a wilderness evasion role. I knew now I could tough it out on foot to some Iranian military or customs outpost.

Every few minutes I thought of Shopuni and paused to look, or rather to listen, out over the vast, Grand Canyon-like chasm that lay mist-shrouded, black and silent behind me. I wasn't really worried. From his recent night escape from the commandant's platoon and free run to catch me at Barzani's hideout, I knew that he too could handle himself at this evasion and escape game.

I found during this climb that my past couple of weeks' adventures may not have been very neat and refined, but they had gotten me into pretty good physical condition. I could rock-climb very steeply in spurts of half-an-hour, by only starlight. Of course, I avoided the hard stuff—the sheer places, faces and chimneys requiring rope and technical work. Every half-hour I had to rest for maybe five minutes. During each rest period I watched and listened below and out over the canyon. I could not discern any activity at all now. I could hear no sound and of course could see nothing except should a light show. I was surprised and pleased at how long it remained dark at this latitude in October. One hour, two hours, three hours—finally a thin line of yellow ribboned the southern horizon. The east was a mighty mass of mountain. I would not see the sunrise.

Suddenly I was on top. There were shelves of sandstone, a few low bushes and one gnarled, lonely pine. I stepped up onto the final or top shelf and immediately from the canyon below three rifle shots rang out. Then another three shots from about 15 degrees further north—and not from down in, as the others, but seemingly from the rim of the canyon opposite me.

I went flat. "Who are these guys? Have they got starlight scopes and can see in the dark?" There was no trail here, and because there was no moon, only starlight, and because I had not heard any sound of impact, I reasoned that who-ever was shooting might not have been shooting at me—rather sending signals. Still, if someone had somehow picked up my appearance as I topped-out on the rim, I would be wise to move some distance. I tried to think through, *Who could be after me at this juncture? Who could know where I might be?* I thought of the Barzanis. *Impossible. They were on my side. The Baghdad Palace Guard? Hmmmm. Could they have sent out Shopuni and then tracked him to me? Hard to believe.* Then I hit on the goat-herd. *Could that hombre have been picked up and questioned?*

I had no way of knowing where my eastbound trail was or whether it was safe to follow a trail. Still it was nearly impossible to just cut out across this rugged mountain terrain. It was all boulders, cactus and sagebrush. Border outposts or military redoubts would be on trails, but then so would any enemy. I had a certain advantage in that I was small, comparatively camouflaged, left no dust and was hard to see. Any mounted force would leave dust and sound and motion which I could see or hear and thus avoid contact.

I made up my mind that I would just hike several miles due east to put some distance between my top-out point and any rest stop. I checked the sky and found the big dipper totally below the horizon. Nevertheless, Leo stood out bright and clear in the north and just below it, Polaris. I checked the southern sky opposite and found nothing I could identify. But there was Orion rising in the east. I would follow Orion and try to stay to the high ground. If the floor fell away, I would move south and then return north when clear. The surface was fairly regular with building-size piles of granite chunks. The sagebrush-size chaparral and cactus was tough to hike through as my black baggies provided little protection.

Miracle! In about an hour, I stumbled out onto a roadway. I found it was not a game trail. It was wide enough to be a stock migration trail and it seemed to be headed easterly. I thanked God for blessings great and small and began to jog. Now, it was beginning to creep dawn—not break-dawn in the usual sense, but the velvet blackness began to slowly give way to a velvet grayness. Then the stars faded, the moon set and the texture of the terrain began to seep into my vision. A high country ambiance of bird, bush, and mini-denizens—rock chucks, weasels, squirrels—all began turning up for a sunrise concert.

I decided I was too easy prey on the main highway by daylight. I eased off, following a game trail up a gentle rise for a quarter mile, and exhausted, I there set up my signature primitive camp. There was nice sage and privet cover, and I was within earshot of the main route. I decided to hang out here for a while—rest and watch and wait and see who was still after me. To stalk me in this stuff, he or they would need dogs. I could pick him or them up by sound before they caught me. I lay on my back with a large smooth hunk of granite for a backrest. My fingers interlocked behind my head, I rested, watched and waited. Of course, I immediately fell asleep.

The distant, screaming whinny was immediately followed by the wild clatter of equally distant hoofbeats running at full speed. I jumped awake! Then realizing where I was, I dropped to my knees. My eyes followed the sound. From out of a huge rock pile to my left, marking the arrival of the main road on top and perhaps a half-mile distant, boiled a rapidly approaching cloud of dust. I stood to get a clear view.

Yes . . . yes! It was he! It was my horse. It was Shopuni at full gallop. In a very few moments he was abreast me but down on the main, east-west road. *But, was this bait?* I checked behind him, off to my left. No one appeared pursuing him. Wildly now, I waved and shouted "Shopuni! Up here! Shopuni!"

Shopuni was focused. His ears were laid back, his eyes glued to the road ahead. He whistled by at I'll bet 50 miles an hour and disappeared where the low scrub masked the road on east toward the border. I spit out an expletive, picked up my pack, stuffed in my blanket, kicked the gravel around to cover any evidence of presence and started down through the brush for the roadway.

At that moment, to the west—around the same huge rock pile marking Shopuni's explosive arrival on top—came a huge burst of dust and the sound of more hoofbeats. Multi-hoofbeats! I dropped down to one knee. With eyes level with the chaparral, I watched the Shopuni pursuit develop. He was indeed bait!

The lead element—five horses at full gallop. But surprise! The riders were no one I had encountered so far. No guard uniforms. Yet all were similarly garbed like a paramilitary cadre of some sort. Leather breeches and high, black riding boots; green or perhaps OD capes flying in the wind, and all wearing purple turbans. The loose, died, cotton turbans common to the Caspian Sea and Hindu Kush mountain area. Russian Cossacks came to mind.

I now had second thoughts about joining Shopuni. I ducked down in the chaparral and watched this platoon pass. Then, a couple of hundred meters behind, the second stick burst into view—eight horses—somewhat less intense, but galloping for ease and distance. Finally, a third string of twelve spent horses and patently tired riders straggled along in an irregular file. This rear echelon barely trotted, trying vainly to keep some dust in sight.

Finally, behind the rear guard and following at about a quarter-mile, a covered wagon pulled by two draft horses trotted steadily. This vehicle we would have called a cook wagon or sheep wagon back in Montana. It appeared to be a sturdy freight wagon with hooped, dirty-white cover. I guessed it contained the food, cook and camp supplies of the pursuit platoon. I decided to wait until this unit got out of sight to the east before I got back on the road to follow. I kneeled there wondering who this guerilla unit might be and why was it chasing Shopuni. This was an official, organized, uniformed, platooned, military unit. They certainly were not holy men representatives of the real owner—the holy hunchback from the foothills out of Irbil.

In this Kurdistan mountain wilderness, they could be a local warlord's militia of bounty hunters. Or could they rather be associates of the Baghdad cavalry unit that lost me to Barzani's Kurdish insurgents three nights ago and let Shopuni escape? Or could they be a troop of Mustapha Barzani's helpful Kurdish allies, alerted by his zit-net and tasked to help me escape?

The supply wagon seemed to have stopped on to the east. When I stood up to see what his problem was, I found the driver had pulled off the road for lunch. He was probably a mile on down to the east, but from my rise, I could see him cooking beside a small fire-holder. Being very hungry, I wondered if it would be worth the risk to just meander on down the road and happen into his little temporary lunch-camp in time for chow. I decided instead in favor of a strip of jerky that young Masoud Barzani had packed for me. As I sat chewing the tough, tasteless goat, I checked my shadow and noticed it was about noon. At that point, while keeping check on the cook wagon, I heard a fusillade of distant rifle shots echo off the peaks.

Glancing beyond the cook-wagon, I found a new cloud of dust on the migration roadway to the east. I thought, *Are those troopers coming back for lunch?* Then I noticed the cloud was small—a single horse—and moving at a rate totally unfitting of any troopers I had seen so far. The billow raced west along the road below and passed the supply wagon without slowing. On he came! My God, it was he! It was Shopuni! It was Shopuni returning. I wondered, *How in the world did he get by the Azerbaijan cavalry that was chasing him east? Ran right through them, I'll bet. That's why the rifle fire.*

Shopuni raced at full gallop until he came to the point below where I had left the roadway to climb up and make camp. At that point he slid on his hind hoofs to a rodeo stop. The colt put his head down to check the gravel or the bush. I jumped up and shouted, "Shopuni! Shopuni! Up here!" and I started down. Echoing up the canyon, on the still mountain air at high noon, exploded the piercing and prolonged whinny of a happy horse! Instantly, horse followed whinny. Directly up the slope, through the chaparral, over the rock piles, head up, tail up. He pushed me down on my butt in his enthusiastic joy. Then he circled around me twice—rearing and pawing out. He tromped down the sage and whinnied like a child. I tried to shush him up—no dice.

Finally, I leaped upon him bareback, grabbed some main, and we took off traversing east down the slope onto the road at a pleasant canter.

Shopuni seemed to recall the earlier disaster that high speed had brought to our partnership. Now, we passed the lunch wagon with a wave and got one in response. The road continued on winding through the brush with here and there a colorful rock formation and, here and there, a patch of high altitude, wind-blown juniper. I kept hoping to come upon a border guard hut or some marking indicating a distance to the Iranian line, but nothing appeared. Suddenly, about mid-afternoon, without any cue from me, Shopuni turned abruptly off into the bush. He slowed to a trot, but kept heading southeast, dodging the larger chaparral and major rock outcroppings. Then I recognized his problem. A long cloud of dust was rising out of the canyon ahead and to the north. It looked like a fork of the main road bent that way. I sat back and pulled Shopuni to a halt. The line of dust was long and moving fast. Now the sound of distant shouting accompanied the clatter of hoofs on stone. I thought, *This is the purple turbans coming back. I wonder why they took so long to turn around.* It was the purple turbaned cavalry. Shopuni again moved out picking up the pace to a gentle canter. Now the cavalry group left the roadway to cut us off. I noticed immediately that, riding cross-country, neither of us was going to keep the other in sight.

We had been following a game trail to the southeast. It wound along the ridgeline then cut down some rocky steps. I had them believing we were on a heading, so I legged Shopuni into a sharp right turn behind a grove of juniper. We headed back toward the main migration road. My thought was that if we got the posse far enough out in the boondocks headed southwest before they discovered our ruse, we could put on some main road miles toward Iran, and they could never catch us.

Shopuni kept increasing his speed while keeping one ear turned back checking me. We were off any trail now, and the dark gray colt was picking his was through the brush and rocks, stumbling and lurching, but never falling. Because of the irregular terrain, I was calling on all my instinctive balance as a crack fighter pilot. I had a death-grip on a huge hunk of Shopuni's ample mane, and I was getting good at this. I was sure with a little luck we would ditch this posse.

In about half an hour we were back on the main, east-west, migration road. I legged Shopuni east, but here I made an unnecessary tactical error. As we came down onto the road, I looked back west and saw the dark silhouette of the cook-wagon trotting along the road behind us. I remembered he had waved when we passed. I thought, *That hillbilly doesn't know what this plot is all about. He just drives along and cooks and washes dishes or whatever.* I was wrong. He apparently had a radio, and tipped off the posse as to our location.

We had not gone another half hour when the thunder of many hoofs called attention to our mistake. I didn't have to spur Shopuni. He heard before I did. He began increasing his pace in gradual increments until we were literally flying. We hit a long, straight, down-sloping traverse where the main trail was sand. Shopuni took off. He raced with the sure-footed genius of a born mountain Arabian. The platoon raced after us. I remembered that clever military cavalry take

151

turns with bursts of speed to out-race a quarry. Once in a while I risked looking back. They were close and closing. We came to a rocky ledge where the terrain dropped away sharply. I thought, *This is what got me last time, I've got to lean in on the twisting turn.* It worked, and Shopuni noticed how I was adjusting. He did not slow but very carefully kept his center under me as I leaned into the turns and lay forward on the jumps. Still the lead element behind was now only a hundred meters. It was too late for tricks.

Bang! Bang! Two shots rang out. I felt the wind of one and Shopuni flinched. He was hit. I rolled off and continued to roll and tumble and slide and roll. I finally came to rest against a rock shelf. Shopuni rolled and slid with me and came to rest nearby. I was dazed and my left hip hurt badly. Shopuni jumped immediately to his feet. Without so much as a glance back, he plunged off through the bush on down toward a grassy gully off to the right a hundred yards ahead.

I crawled to a seat on a flat rock. A gray stonewall rose behind me. The scene around me was now one massive cloud of dust filled with horse snorts and the shouts of my pursuers dismounting. Others were arriving. The language was neither Arabic nor the Persian dialect of the Kurds. I thought, *These mountains are full of marauding bands of highwaymen. I wonder who these guys are and from where. And I wonder how much they think I'm worth?*

I pulled down my pants over my butt to examine my hip wound. I was immediately surrounded on three sides by laughing, bearded horsemen all pointing and hissing at my pants-down condition. Each held the reins of his sweating steed in one hand, a cocked AK-47 in the other. I raised my hands and forced a huge smile. Then, I too began to laugh. A tall, Turk-looking giant in leather breeches came striding through. He wore no shirt but a royal purple satin turban partly undone from the fast ride through whipping brush.

His sweaty black horse followed him without a lead. He put his rifle barrel against my chest and broke a huge laugh. "Ho, ho, ho! It's you!" Then in British English, "My name, Suh, is General Jalal Talaboni. I say, if you can walk, let's walk. We'll make camp down theah where your fine mount and now mine has found some graze." He walked. I limped on down.

Somewhere—I believe on the trail down to Mullah Barzani's Shanidar Cave hideout—I had heard talk of this General Talaboni. It was friendly talk, like concerning an admired ally. As I remembered, he commanded a disciplined, Robin Hood-style army of international soldiers of fortune. His Army roamed from Tashkent in the Hindu Kush mountains of Uzbekistan through the Caspian basin in the Azerbaijan to as far west as the Armenian Knot. His cavalry divisions lived off the land and periodically ran a classic marauder raid on a wealthy seaport.

Talaboni's self-assigned mission was to support nationalistic movements such as Kurdistan, Caucasia, Chechnya, the Uighurs in South China, the Mujahedin or Talaban in Afghanistan. His friendships with Juma Namangani in Uzbekistan and Mustapha Barzani of the Zagros cause them to be locally known as the Three Khans. As I was to learn, Talaboni's Army was made up of assorted tribesmen who loved to ride and shoot. They saw themselves as a carryover from Tamerlane and the Great Khans of the 12th and 14th Centuries. These tribes all spoke four or five area languages and dialects. The army was sometimes hired by and sometimes fought against the local governments in the area—China, Pakistan, Afghanistan, Iran, Iraq, Soviet Union, Azerbaijan, Turkey, and the central Asian soviets Uzbekistan, Tajikistan, Kyrgyzstan and Turkmenistan.

I limped along beside Jalal. We zigzagged down through the sage and privet and finally some willow to an open grass clearing. Talaboni told me as we walked that his friend, Barzani, had radioed him about my rescue two nights before. He asked Jalal to help me if I needed help. He told of a brief firefight with a column of Iraqi cavalry who they met in the canyon the day before. He stated that the Iraqi RCC Commandant had offered him a thousand pounds sterling for my head, dead or alive. Talaboni confided that he chose to take me into "protective custody" because of the several bounty hunting bands currently loose in the border mountains.

When we finally broke out onto the meadow, the general's horsemen were already erecting a typical military camp. Headquarters were designated by a small flag on a pole centered in the eddy of a noisy mountain stream. I counted forty horses turned loose to graze. Shopuni was the only gray. All Talaboni's mounts were pure black Arabians. This was apparently his fast and elite cavalry company. His main force, including artillery, was on duty under a Russian general in Chechnya.

I was not restrained in any way. I was assigned a place by the creek. I tossed my pack and lay out my blanket. There were no tents. The supply wagon arrived about sundown. It went to the center and the cook went to work making a small council and cooking fire. A Hindu medic called Splints-Suh came to attend my scraped hip and deeply scratched scalp. His chemical of choice was iodine.

A black-bearded, scruffy young Kurd with a coarse wool sleeveless sweater and purple turban brought me my issue-kit—a worn saddle; a bridle; and a smelly, rough wool blanket. My rations were a hunk of black bread; about a pound of smelly cheese; some dry meat like jerky only thicker; a bowl of thick, hot soup; and a skin of bitter buffalo berry wine. This was officer treatment. The men gathered in a gang on the ground close by and ate. I squirreled away most of the rations in my daypack.

Talaboni, busy with his tactical officers planning a raid into northern Iraq to take advantage of the coup in Baghdad, came by at dark to see that I was comfortable. He volunteered that my horse was only scratched—Splints-Suh had anointed him. He spoke on his radio to Barzani. While I listened, he told us both he had assigned a detachment to escort me across the border at first light. In less than an hour everyone was down in clumps in the flat, green clearing, wind-shaded by the protruding sandstone slabs. There were no trees. Shopuni grazed casually with the other horses as if nothing untoward had happened in the past year or so. Except for an abundance of snore-like belches, all went quickly quiet. One lone trooper crouched by the dying fire playing softly on a shepherd's pipe. While my heart pitched and yawed in a contradiction of apprehension and excitement, while I tried to relax and hope for the best, while this, that and more, the black-booted, purple-turbaned company and environment around me settled into a most primitive and attractive peace.

I now examined my issued kit—blanket and saddle, snaffle bridle, and saddlebag. Everyone's kit and tack seemed to be identical. A coarse, nearly black wool blanket, neither clean nor filthy but, as I say, smelly from having never touched water but horse sweat. It was nearly square, about five feet a side. A plain McClellan-like, hornless military saddle, snaffle bit and headstall plus braided rawhide reins. The saddlebag was rough-out, tough yak leather, not unlike my own ranch saddlebag back home. Leather loops and horn conches secured the two opposing flaps. Half full, it doubled well for a pillow. As my head went down for the third and final time, I glanced out at my faithful Shopuni. He was befriending a shaggy, black Arab mare munching sleepily on the seed ends of a patch of wild vetch. I noticed as I sank, a very large blue-white planet setting behind the craggy snow of 14,000 foot, Kuh el-Tashin, and I was out of there.

Eight

Talaboni had sort of promised to escort me across the border at daybreak. But here on the Zagros mountain border, just as on each of the other forty-eight rebel fronts around the world, the Saint could not be everywhere at once. Yet, General Talaboni wanted to give the impression to the local authorities that he was indeed ubiquitous. So his MO was to personally lead the colorful, press-covered big city raids and politically significant sweeps while delegating rescues, reconnaissances and small raids to promising young lieutenants.

Long predawn, I could hear the whispers. I could hear the young commandos rustling around—packing, eating, tacking and finally mounting and moving out in column of twos. I was exhausted, I could not bring myself to life. I hung there just under the surface, still in sleep, waiting for a bugle. None came. Dawn, I broke through to consciousness. The now almost full moon was setting. There was not a soul in camp. Nor was there any sign that a camp had ever slept in this high country meadow. These guys were good. A carefully inked note was pinned to my pack:

> Keep heading east. You are north of the high bridge and will come to Persian border station Gamma by sundown. My flank guard will check in with you midmorning. See you in New York.
>
> Gen Jalal

Shopuni was saddled and tied to a lone pole twenty yards

away, casually grazing. I tickled some trout, made a fish sandwich and drank tea.

I checked Shopuni with a fine-tooth comb for a bullet wound. I found only an iodined graze of his left hip. To check him out completely in action, we walked together slowly and steadily east on the main roadway. I felt warm and secure, realizing, as we clippity-clopped along, that this was about the fifth time I had felt warm and secure only to be surprised, chased, dry-gulched or simply beat up by warlords of various sorts. Still, hope springs eternal. And this time I felt added comfort and security because this time I had for allies two decent terrorist outlaws, Mullah Barzani and his powerful ally, General Talaboni. Both were respected far and wide among the common Kurds, the Arab Bedouins and numerous assorted nomadic tribes of north Iraq and the Azerbaijan. *I'll surely be back in college by Saturday.*

And so we picked up the main migration trail and jogged east. Though the migration route wandered about, it followed the crest-line of a rough wilderness plateau. We passed around and under the majestic 14,000-foot Kuh el Tashin, topped with a permanent glacier in its northwest notch. Noon found us in a narrow defile between two rock walls. The cut through of this narrow hallway rose gradually in quarter-mile-wide steps up, up, up. I felt like a tiny ant entering a vast granite temple.

Far up on the horizon about a mile ahead, I could see a stone pillar standing beside the trail. I remembered the report in Barzani's camp that a tall stone pillar called the Talayot had been erected by Alexander the Great to mark the Assyrian-Persian border after his first primitive survey about 330 B.C.

The campfire legend I heard last night told a different story. The soldiers at Talaboni's camp said Alexander had raised the pillar in memory of his boyhood buddy, Clitus, whom he had killed accidentally in a drinking brawl at a camp in the pass during their hot pursuit of Darius following the battle of Gaugamela. In either event, the pillar marked my goal, the Iranian border.

I mused, "Easy Shopuni, my faithful friend, we're approaching a mixed blessing. Iran's border station Gamma means freedom for us both. But, it also means the end of our unusual friendship." And I should have known. In the midst of my complacent, warm mid-afternoon muse the world around us exploded!

From higher up near the Talayot, from out of the Juniper cover at the base of the wall on my right and from out of the purple shadows of the east wall, rode a wild, shouting cavalry charge that momentarily reminded me of reading about the shouting, savage onslaught of Tamerlane the Tartar. You may remember, Tamerlane surged out of Samarkand over this same pass with a thousand horsemen, two thousand years before Alexander the Great. Two waves of galloping, yelling, shooting riders; and here again in black breeches and boots but this time with flaming scarlet turbans. I was by now beyond being impressed or intimidated by these gangs of gypsy hoodlums. I drew Shopuni to a halt and raised my hand in international salute—palm open to show peace and no weapon. The lead horses were coming so fast they rode through us and slid to a dusty stop beyond, then returned and surrounded us.

I found myself fast-checking to see if I recognized any of the leadership. No dice. I shouted, "Shalom! Shalom Alaycum! General Talaboni's flank guard, I presume?" I had to repeat the question as the lead horse and its rider were having trouble deciding who was the boss. As I did so, I shifted from Arabic to the mountain tribal dialect. The leader saluted and responded immediately, "Of course! Of course! Shalom! General Talaboni sent us to invite the American

159

hero to camp with us up behind the wall." He pointed with his crop.

I glanced again at the sky and thought, *Hmm, mid-afternoon.* "Sir, please thank the General. But I need to press on across the border. I see the Talayot, yonder." I did not need further social delays, especially with freedom in sight. But the cavalry captain insisted, "Oh, but sir, you will want to rest before you cross into Persia tomorrow? It will be a busy time after." He posed it as a soft question; but knowing the culture, I knew it was a gentle command. By now I was totally surrounded, two deep. I thought, *General Talaboni is seeking to impress me. Why? Perhaps he is waiting lunch. I better go.*

The leader, who introduced himself as Captain Arak, reined his horse a little apart and shouted a command. "Scout Platoon, Escort Formation!" He rang it out into the afternoon air, and even in the mountain dialect, I was reminded of West Point Cavalry Summer at Fort Riley. "Column of twos, ho!" Shopuni and I found ourselves once again in the center of a friendly escort headed for someone's tribal camp.

The column followed a well-worn trail up, up, up into the shadow of the granite wall. We were about to enter under a high overhang when *KABOOOM,* a serious earthquake struck. Huge hunks of reddish-gray stone came tumbling off the wall. We all jumped to the ground beside our mounts. Some of the horses were having trouble standing. Others were snorting and pawing—seeming deeply disturbed by the irregular shaking of the turf beneath. I snatched Shopuni's reins close to his bit and began my best, soft, quieting speech. He was prancing as if on hot cinders. I found most of the troopers talking to their mounts, reassuring. Considering the routine nature of the quakes in this major fault mountain range, I would have expected the horses to be more used to the circumstance, but a nearby guard told me they never get used to the ground shaking. Then he added that this was an unusually strong quake.

Looking far up, I could see the wall shaking. Puffs of dust popped out here and there where the twisting stress vectors were causing heavy stone members to fail. Now a moderate slide broke loose. House-size hunks of the mountain led streams of gravel and dust down, down on all sides. Several full-size dead tree snags brought clouds of dust. Then the shaking stopped. Our little clutch of horsemen and our mounts were safe, but it took perhaps half an hour to reassure the animals and a couple of the men that life was back to normal and it was safe to proceed.

The quake had left before us a narrow passage between the main mountain wall and a massive granite slab standing vertically but leaning against the main mountain wall. It made a fifty-foot high tunnel that ran for perhaps a hundred meters along the mountainside. Without command, we all crowded into this tunnel. Most of the horsemen seemed to accept the tunnel as a proper passageway. All but two mounted—those two led their horses—and we rode along a quarter mile in the semi darkness then broke out into daylight. When my eyes accustomed, I found us in a football field-size grassy clearing. This was a classic stone fortress and a neat military camp. Vertical stonewalls rose above neat rows of green squad tents. Fresh horses were tied to a long rail. Soldiers were going about duties as though quakes were normal to life here. A sentry came forward to challenge us.

He and the captain exchanged words. Then our platoon rode on in along the main street, past a headquarters cabin with a flagpole flying colors I did not recognize. Long, empty, hitching rails guarded either side of the street. At the wall again, the leader held up his hand, "Halt!" We dismounted and immediately we were joined by a host of equerries who took the horses. The captain came directly to my side.

"Major, would you come into my tent and freshen up. I'm sorry about that tremor. We camp on a major fault here. We learn to expect."

I threw on my knapsack and followed him down a side path to his neat and trim officer's tent. His orderly came hustling out saluting as we approached. "Draw the Major a bath, Bandar. See to his needs." To me: "Sir Major, please excuse. I need to check in with the Sheikh. General Talboni is abroad. Likely the colonel will want us to dine with him and the high staff. So relax and enjoy."

The servant backed off toward the tent entrance giving me a series of bows and beckonings. I followed him inside.

It was just turning dusk when Captain Arak returned. I had been bathed, napped and fed some sort of mountain plum drink. I decided every fighter pilot major must have an orderly like Bandar. He didn't miss a trick. The captain too was very warm and cordial. "Sir Major, the Sheikh, Colonel Shazarak, is in charge here. He is thrilled that you have arrived safely. He has asked me to escort you to his headquarters office in the mountain. He wishes to personally escort the American hero to the Senior Officer Mess for dinner. Are you ready?"

I jumped up. I had heard of the legendary Colonel Shazarak. I did not know of his connection with General Talaboni. I had also heard scuttlebutt concerning his fabulous castle here in Kuh-el Tashin. It was known among all the mountain cadres as both luxurious and impregnable—mainly by reputation as few ordinary militia had ever been inside the stone bastion. The Sheikh himself was seen by the Islamic press and common Bedouins and Kurdish peasants and herdsmen as an independent Jihadist Wahhabi, warlord and beloved great grandson of Abd al-Wahhabi, beloved old great, great grandson of Mohammed, the Prophet.

Contrary to this respect and devotion, Shah Mohammed Reza in Iran had a standing offer of one million dollars gold for his head. This was because in 1923 when the old Shah died, Colonel Shazarack made a raid on Teheran from the Sunni north in an attempt to reassert the Safavids to power in Iran. Colonel Shazarack claimed Safavid bloodlines directly back to Mohammed.

I was eager to meet the old Hashimite. I had never met a man with common ancestry with the Prophet Mohammed. Plus I had never seen a castle or bastion cut directly into the side of a mountain. Most crusader castles I had visited were built with blocks of stone, but out in the open countryside surrounded by a moat.

I followed Captain Arak up the main trail leading toward the flagpole. Side by side we turned toward the mountain wall. As we reached the wall proper, I saw a series of steps had been cut into the stone. The steps led to a landing, thence through a short tunnel formed by slabs of granite leaning against the mountain proper, thence up to a six-foot-wide balcony or deck that ran horizontally along the entire mountain wall above the camp. This ledge or deck rose gradually as it proceeded west. I followed Arak up the steps. He was describing with colorful gestures a recent heroic in eastern Turkey on which he had accompanied the famous sheikh colonel as a captain-aide. We paused on reaching the ledge to catch our breaths and thrill at the view—the camp below and the countryside far out to a lake against another major mountain perhaps ten miles north. In a moment, we turned west and walked side by side along the six-foot-wide open stone ledge. The Captain had explained that this sloping ledge led from the steps to the hallway or cleft that formed the entryway or threshold where we would find Colonel Shazarak's crusader-type redoubt cut in Mount el Tashin. After a short climb, we saw it—about fifty yards further a deep dark cleft. The cleft must have been quake-cracked in the mountain and further eroded by ions of dripping water. The crack cut directly into the heart of el Tashin. I thought, *Wow! A perfect natural entrance.*

Captain Arak was explaining to me that Colonel Shazarack was one of the two independent regimental commanders under General Talaboni encamped in and around this fortress. The other commander and his regiment were out now with the general raiding Mosul on the Tigris to test the control of the new Iraqi revolution.

To my left a stone wall rose vertically perhaps 500 feet and then stepped back a few feet then rose a couple of thousand, stepped back, soared five thousand, stepped back, and so on. The mountain el Tashin appeared to be simply a massive lone slab of granite a mile and a half thick—one corner stuck straight in the earth, the opposite corner stuck straight in the sky. The colonel was obviously no geologist, but without hesitation he assured me that this mountain, el Tashin, stands starkly alone because it was born a million years ago of a massive quake, locally called a *karabaskat.*

To my right was open air. I could see far out over the valley to the northwest. Captain Arak pointed to the lake I had seen earlier and called its name: The Dokan Dam reservoir. It stood out like a flat blue sapphire. I wondered idly, "Good fishing?"

Arak pointed north, and named the two villages, Sar Dasht on the river and Zab-e Kuchek, fifteen miles or so northeast. I thought for a moment the villages looked like a dozen similar mountain villages I had visited around the world, clinging precariously to a tumbling mountain stream or astride a busy main road. We walked on.

Directly below me now, in a circle around what looked like a bale of some kind of hay, the platoon of my strangely uniformed cavalry escort, untacked and groomed our horses. They seemed to be talking and joking as troops at-ease do, waiting for the next adventure to develop. They appeared to be treating my faithful Shuponi with the same respect as their own. He was obviously enjoying the admiration and hand-currying of the troops.

The captain, walking beside me, was gesturing and talking enthusiastically in Arabic as we walked. "Isn't this a view! Up ahead, Major, at the cleft, there is a door into the colonel's headquarters. It's the check-in point. You'll be fascinated by his display of battle souvenirs—a bow reported dropped by Cleisthenes, cousin of Alcxander the Great, a bridle of Tamerlane's horse, *Dokuni, Genghis Khan's spear.* We are honored to be allowed." Here, with his long right index finger pointing, Captain Arak indicated a turn to the left into the sharp dark cleft. Then we cornered sharply left again, directly into the mountain. "The door is heavy. Takes a hard push to open. You must go first."

Arak gripped my right arm above the elbow and steered me ahead into the shadows. His voice was casual, confident. We took two steps into the darkness. I was beginning to feel uneasy, but the captain kept chatting away in comfortable Arabic. My left arm brushed against what felt like the edge of a table in the hallway. What sounded like a bucket rattled, I stopped. I could not see ahead.

Arak still held my arm tightly at the biceps and said quietly, "It's all right, Major, trust me. My eyes are accustomed. That's the door. Push hard with both hands. It will open." Here, the Captain released my arm, put his hand on my back and shoved me gently forward. I could not see the door, but I knew it must be directly ahead. I raised both hands and pushed forward hard, taking a step to add umph and keep my balance. I fully expected to feel a door and to step through into a lighted room.

I was wrong. I stepped into black open space. The captain chuckled softly somewhere behind. I felt myself free-falling. I involuntarily let out a long air-sucking. "Uu-uuhhh!"

I had stepped off a cliff into air. My hands snatched out to grab something. There was nothing! I flailed my arms frantically to grab something. There was nothing! Down, down, down! I yelled something that got half out, like "Waa-yaa-haa!" in rising pitch and volume—then, WHUUU-UMMMP! I landed flat on my stomach and face on solid rock.

A full-scale flash of red light exploded as my face banged the stone! The flash was followed by a swirl of lighted, pri-mary-colored tennis balls spinning wildly against a purple sky. After a moment the balls stopped spinning and started racing from far away directly in toward me. Each ball grew larger as it approached. Each exploded directly in front, BOOOM! Each was followed by another ball of different color. Each raced from far out, in, in, in, then BOOOM! This visual was accompanied by a loud nearby bugler blowing the emergency-command, "Charge!" Over and over and over!

I wanted to charge. I needed to obey. But I couldn't get up. Each time I bunched my muscles to charge, a giant ten-nis ball would explode directly in front, BOOOM! I don't know how long this went on. I had no control. I could nei-ther modify the pattern, slow it, quiet it or end it. I did notice that finally it began to change. First I began to feel an intense burning as if my face were on fire. Then the sound volume began to quiet some. Then the tennis balls colors paled to pastel. Finally, the booming stopped. My left knee pained acutely! It felt like I had struck it hard against something.

My eyes blinked involuntarily. "Where?" It was pitch dark. "I've been here before—not this again! I escaped this. Better just lie still—sort out, where, what, why." I raised my head a few inches. My mind began to grasp at passing fragments of thought. *I'm in a total black place—I am lying flat on my face. My nose and mouth are bleeding onto—tastes like stone. A dirty stone floor!* I pushed out with my arms. *Holy Schmoly! Buckets of room! God, my chest! My face! My knee!*

My mind was calm and catching up. *I fell, and I got knocked bonkers. I'm returning to consciousness—awakening and I hurt. I fell into a dark stone-bottomed hole. My head throbs a steady rhythm, but no sharp pain. My body tingles weirdly, but only my knee really hurts. Except my nose and mouth bleed and burn as if I've just been swatted in the face.*

I pushed up part way and tried to breathe—to taste the air. I could breathe only part way, then sharp pain. *Cracked ribs! I've been here before, too.* My mind rushed to answer questions: *I ain't dead. I know blood when I taste it. I hit on my face here—broke my nose and mouth. Need to get out of here, quick.*

WHOOPS!—Another presence! Something else was here. Right here, moving right beside me I felt something gently feel me down below, feel my ankle, take hold of my leg, whisper.

"Hey!" I tried to talk, but nothing came out but the "Hey!"

Someone beside me said, "Hey" back, softly and close to my ear. It was a man. Now he took my arms and gently rolled me over onto my back. "My knee!" I yelled it out. Fingers patted me. They moved along my legs and then my body, and then my head. Fingers—that's what it was. Fingers or fingertips. I recognized two sets of fingertips. These now moved gently, slowly over my face. What I was feeling or experiencing was neither shock nor fear. I felt slightly more comfortable somehow—more secure, knowing I was no longer alone. Another person, unhurt, was here apparently trying to help me.

Now I heard another sound. There were two men who were whispering an exchange. Next, I felt hands grip my shoulders. My daypack was removed, and I was pulled. I was slid along the stone floor. Not far. I was laid on my back now with my head a little higher than my body. This was comfort by comparison. I had been trying repeatedly to talk. I needed to know where I was. What was happening? Who this was? Nothing was coming out.

Something was put over me. I knew the smell. This was my wool blanket from my daypack. Something wet was put on and in my mouth and nose. My face stung badly, but cooled. Then I swam out into space. I went away again. I didn't go back to the tennis balls. I just passed out sort of swirling. After an unknown time, I felt someone patting me. I popped wide-awake in the pitch darkness. A hand was gently patting my chest. I now smelled a human odor, and a voice was whispering close to my ear. This time everything made sense. I knew where I was without knowing where I was. I remembered the lead-in circumstances, and I knew I had stepped wrong or had been pushed wrong in the dark and fell off a ledge into this dark hole between walls or behind something. I felt that wherever it was, I was not badly hurt, and I needed to get back with Captain Arak or we would miss dinner with Colonel Shazarack. I kept repeating over and over, "I'm an American fighting man. I will overcome. I'm an American . . ."

The whispering voice close to my ear addressed me in heavily accented Farsi-Arabic, "You are all right, Sir. You are not broken, and you are among friends. If you can speak Arabic tell me, are you English or French?"

"American." I spoke the word, but no sound came out—only air. I cleared my throat and tried it again, "American." I spoke the word, but I sounded very far away.

"Of course. I knew an American long ago in Karachi." The response was in the soft, gentle voice of a holy man, in a Pathan tribal, Farsi accent. My mind raced; I spoke: "I took a misstep back there up high. I fell into this dark pit. The fall knocked me out and apparently broke my nose, mouth and knee."

I reached out and took the gently patting hand by the wrist. "Can you help me find Captain Arak?" I asked.

The soft voice was near my ear. "My child, your captain has delivered you to us. You are in Mazid-Ghazu, the Pit-of-Forgotten Men. But, fear not—he will come."

With that rather enigmatic announcement, the owner of the gentle hand beside me picked up my hand as I released it. And I felt him put it against his bearded chin. "Mullah-Deen," he breathed the phrase. Again, "Mullah-Deen." He moved my hand slowly and carefully across his countenance, up over his closed eyes, back over his coarse, abundant hair and back across his soft-bearded face, "Mullah-Deen." He kept repeating.

I thought, *How weird! Some sort of religious ritual? I wonder how I am to respond.*

Now he put his hand in mine and closed my fingers around his wrist and moved his hand across my face just as he had done with my hand on his features, "Whooo?" He whispered in my ear. "Whooo?" It was clearly a question.

I got it. Not a litany at all. We were seeing each other, meeting each other in the pitch dark, with our fingertips. "Major," I said it again, I repeated my rank, "Major." I did not wish to produce name-type info when I was at near zero on knowing anything about the person or the place.

It came back, "Major," and was accompanied by a delightful laugh. "Ho, ho, ho—Major." A finger poked me. "Major—Major."

I poked him back. "Mullah-Deen—Mullah-Deen."

This man knew what Major meant. I felt warm all over. Here we were, primitive men in a primitive, blind environment introducing ourselves to each other and finding the simple joy—the instinctive warmth of making a new friend.

While this "getting to know you" activity was happening, my instinctive inner memory was settling a far off notion: I had heard the term "Mazjid Ghazu" before somewhere and it meant "Hopeless Prison." I flashed-back to my recent imprisonment in the culvert, and I immediately felt a deep quiet pass through me. *I have escaped the inescapable before; I will escape this one too. But I must relax. I need to forget Arak, forget Shazarak, forget Talaboni and focus on this "He" in this mullah's "He will come." That's got to be an American embassy man he knows about. He will come, he will get me out and he will take me back to school. My exhausting trip is over. I will be in class again by Monday.*

I tried my eyes again. Open—close. I touched them with my palm. Open or closed, it was the same. I felt so positive, I spoke out loud: "Alleluia! I am not blind; this is just another dark place. And by golly, Pit Gazu or whatever you call it, I can lick pits. I have escaped worse pits before, and I will escape again! I am an American Fighting Man. God is on my side, and I will not be intimidated or discouraged!"

The man was shouting. "Daoud!—Saradon!—Sufi—Countier!" The mullah called out into the darkness.

Names, I thought, I discovered later the third person nearby who had helped the mullah check me over and drag me from the crash-point to my slanted rest was named Amarillo.

In response to the call, came a general chorus of men's voices down a hollow hallway. "Whooo? Whooo? Whooo? Whooo? Whooo? Whooo?"

Next, I heard a soft shuffling sound approaching on the dusty stone floor. Immediately I smelled the bodies and felt the breaths of the men whose voices I had heard a moment earlier in the muffled, distant, owl-like response. "Beloved!" the mullah called. I found out very soon that the mullah always spoke to or of this flock, of which there were five plus himself. He called them collectively by this term of endearment, *Beloved*.

"Beloved, we are now complete. *Seven* has just arrived. Careful! Careful! He is bruised, but not broken. Number Seven is resting here." The mullah guarded me from the shuffling approach of the others. You can imagine the difficulty, in the pitch dark, a curious group of four men bent on "seeing" the new member without falling over him.

I should say here that although I introduced myself as *Major* to the mullah, he introduced me to the group as *Seven*—the seventh of them. The group immediately and until we separated a year and a few days later, addressed me only as *Seven*.

I learned later that it had been over a year since the last man had joined them, so of course, these permanent residents were very curious to "see" and meet a new addition. However, being a pitch-dark world, they could not just come, gather around and look, perhaps ask a few questions. But not surprisingly, the group of six, over the years, had adjusted to the total absence of light by substituting *tactile, audio* and *faith* cues for *visuals* in their life style. This "faith" cue was totally amazing. Under the mullah's guidance and continual encouragement, the group exercised a sixth sense that endeavored to see in the dark by focusing the mind. This paramystic effort he called *Blind Glory*.

So, now with this gathering around my resting place, the group of six introduced me to the most unusual caring, getting acquainted ceremony I had ever experienced. Of course, no one was in a hurry, so it went on for a couple of hours. Here's how it worked: Just as the mullah had done with me earlier, one after another, each man took my hand and moved it across his bearded countenance saying his own name again and again, Saradon, Saradon. And then, Daoud, Daoud. Then, Countier and finally, Sufi, Sufi.

After each such "feely-seeing," I was instructed to similarly take the hand of my new friend and place it on my face. He would then fingertip-explore my face, then my head and then my body, repeating my name, *"Seven—Beloved Seven—Welcome Seven"*—little introductory phrases, always ending with repeating my name which suddenly had become, *Seven*.

I was clearly named *Seven* whether I liked it or not, through the mullah's opening casual comment. The gang seemed to enjoy the name *Seven* partly because of the general felicity and good fortune traditionally connected worldwide and throughout time with the number seven.

During this little adventure in sociology, I learned a good deal about each of my companions, and a ton about our mutual circumstances. Each man told me a little about the pit or their activities or about one another. First, that this was an historic pit-prison and tomb in the Zab River Pass. The bones of Alexander the Great's Marshal Cleisthenes were reported here. I also relearned, or got Daoud's "take" on how The Pass is a cut through the narrow, craggy North Zagros Wall. The Wall is a veritable alligator's jagged, corrugated granite back which generally defines the Iran-Iraq border. From Saradon I reaffirmed that the whole Zagros mountain area is wracked by daily earthquakes because it represents the line where the southwest desert plate overrides the continental Asian shelf. This forms a classic fault of massive millennial instability.

Countier filled me in on history. I learned that this pit prison was traditionally used to do away with trouble-making political or religious figures when a trial was deemed inconvenient or inappropriate. My six companions had been pushed in for various political, social or religious insurgencies over a period of twenty years. Several Ottoman Empire prisoners had died in the pit over the years, and the most recent arrival, a brother-in-law of Sheik Shazarak, had come in wounded about a year before and died shortly.

The mullah, an Afghan Pushtu, was the senior prisoner and *pit boss*. He was a Sunni Moslem holy man who had come from the Dasht-e Khash of southwest Afghanistan. His mission or ministry had been to establish a cell of the Muslim Brotherhood or Mujaheddin in Baghdad during the early rein of King Faisal I. Almost immediately I discovered that the gentle and devout Amarillo, who had helped check me over upon arrival and helped the mullah slide me to my place, was our doctor. He had been a physician outside. He had apparently treated a plague-ridden Jewish community in Teheran during a sensitive time ten years ago and when ordered to desist, had continued his work. He had been an attending physician to the Shah's wife. So because of the royal connection, he was dropped in the pit by order of the Ayatollah Kumeini who, at the time, was in residence in Switzerland. Anyway, Dr. Amarillo, like me, had suddenly found himself shoved lovingly into the pit.

Amarillo, when his final turn came, without any direction, checked me over from head to foot for broken bones and other serious consequences of the fall. He found that my nose was broken, but it was straightened by feel with his fingers. Several ribs were cracked. My left knee was swollen and my left shoulder was wrenched. Nothing was broken and the concussion, no fracture, was healing normally. He washed my face with a damp cloth, and with that, held my arm up to point out a small spring that ran from somewhere above, down along the wall opposite. I could hear it trickling along. "It's our pure water supply." Now appropriately the doctor led an explanation of the health and sanitation rules of the pit.

"Five o'clock and all's well." Countier spoke this time-announcement quietly from somewhere close by in the dark. It was the second time I had heard him call out the hour. He had shared during our exchange of names, that he was the pit timer and so named (the French sound, Countiay). His function on the team was to keep track of time and keep the group generally aware of the time. I learned later at *group* that Countier had been a French petroleum engineer educated at the Sorbonne in Paris. In 1947 he had been drawn into a conspiracy of Jewish bankers bent on connecting oil-rich Kuwait to the new state of Israel.

Hourly, from morning prayers to vespers each evening, Countier announced the time by saying the hour quietly out loud. At the matin announcement, he called out the data also. With this amazing service, the group could stay abreast of the time and calendar. The pitch darkness forbade any normal time-of-day orientation and thus also day-of-the-week and so on. Without Countier's unusual service, *time,* one of the central facts of normal life, could have become meaningless. The absence of this one element, *time* would have rendered life in the pit, meaningless. I soon discovered that this single factor, more than any other, made it possible to organize and conduct a civilized and meaningful program of living with hope and motivation.

Le Countier, as he was called, kept the time of day by actually counting the seconds mentally, all day and all night. He did, however, have several time-check aids. Daily, after evening meal, the General Talaboni's military camp, through which we had all found our way in here, deposited its garbage into this pit. The KPs dumped the kitchen refuse from the very overhang where we had all jumped. It was accepted as the only opening into or out of the pit prison. This dumping was routinely done just before vespers. Le Countier often stood directly below the opening, which was roughly a hundred feet above our pit floor. This made it possible sometimes to hear the distant camp muezzin call the faithful to prayer. When this happened, Countier would quietly announce, "six o'clock" and reset his count system.

When this unusual introductory exercise (this touching and talking) began, I was still trying to get my bearings. My head was confused. It was pitch dark. I thought I had accidentally fallen. And I was still hoping to find a friendly Iranian border guard about. Sufi straightened me out. The Kurds in the camp outside were funded substantially by kidnapping revenues. It was Sufi's bet that I was jailed while the Sheik Shazarak checked out my going head-price on the Baghdad market or what the U.S. would pay to retrieve me. Sufi was physically a tiny man, and I should have deduced from his name, he was a *Sufi*—a cunning, ascetic mystic. He was in the pit for assassinating a notoriously bloody Kurdish nationalist on order of powerful Shiite Sheik Moqtada al-Sadr.

Let me finish discussing this unusual *touching practice.* I began this fingertip, touchy-thing to be a good sport, and because I was not sure of anything, and I needed some time to see if I were whole. As we continued the adventure, however, I caught the spirit. I noticed how warm and caring the men of the little group were at the very beginning. I felt all their presence on each of our original exchanges. No one lost interest or moved away after his turn. All made helpful, caring comments about the place, about one another and asked questions about me as the drama continued. And with this unusually caring beginning, as the days went by, I found this positive, encouraging, caring attitude had become the "way" in the pit.

175

And very often as the days went by, when conversation one-on-one took place, we would touch each other—sometimes faces—mainly because in my case, I wasn't sure who was who for a while. Then because there was no light—we couldn't see each other—the men would often touch one another gauzily, as you would look carefully into someone's face, to catch mood or emotion when a feelings issue was being discussed. So, this touching, along with smell and very careful listening, plus a sort of inner sense, was our substitute for vision.

As a consequence, something very profound—almost mystical—began happening to me. I found that I was learning to know people to a dimension I had never before known any fellow man. I began noticing differences in beard texture, chin shape, nose size, eye socket depth, different number of neck wrinkles, differences in smell, in tones of voice. But more significantly, I began to notice who was who inside. I found I was getting to know men to a more profound depth than I ever had before. I became aware of what each man stood for, held dear, believed in, as well as what each man disliked, was bugged by and felt guilty of. Under normal conditions, I would have never gotten around to developing this level of intimacy with any of my ordinary associates.

But let me go back to some of our early *get acquainted conversations.* I think it was Sufi I asked how big the Pit was. "The walls are straight up three sides." He took my arm and pointed, one, two, three. "Apparently long ago, slabs of granite either fell or slid or shifted during quakes to form this narrow cave. Our room here is about five meters wide by ten long. Three sides are smooth, dry, vertical." He pointed my index finger up. "That end where we all came in, we call *West End,* has high entrance bent. You understand, bent? No light come."

The mullah was listening. Actually, I found as time went by, the group normally all huddled around when any significant discussion was underway. Now, the mullah piped in, "Garbage dumped in there—our food supply."

Mullah-Din's thought here was broken by a fairly solid quake. It interrupted his communication, but no one moved or commented. He simply stopped talking, waited, then continued. I was more shaken than the others, of course, being new. I could taste the dust that filled the room.

Sufi, who was holding me by the hand, gripped me tight momentarily, then continued, "And sometimes can hear soldier shout. Maybe sentry post just outside. Can hear chair scrub stone deck." Now Sufi reached out and turned my head. "Over there." He pointed my index finger to the east. "Over there at other end is 'Edge.' "

I cut in, "A cliff?"

Sufi, who was holding my hand, put it against his cheek so I could feel him and nod his head. "Open chasm, very deep." Saradon whistled for emphasis and added, "Very, very deep! Sheer drop. Creek at bottom far below." Obviously, this end or aspect of the pit especially terrified Saradon.

Mullah-Din tried to soften it. "*The Edge* is very intimidating. No one has chosen to explore."

Saradon persisted, "Our water falls over *The Edge* and drops far down thousands of feet. When quakes, you can hear huge rock hunks fall and splash far below!"

Mullah-Din changed the subject to bring peace. "Saradon mentioned our water. Can you hear it?" He took my hand and pointed my index finger across the passageway and down. "It is a tiny spring. It runs along the base of the far wall from up high somewhere the west." He lifted my arm to point toward the entrance, then swung it across the room to point to the east end they called *The Edge*. "The water is our life. We guard it from source to edge. Only drink along wall. Bathe at edge only. Toilet at *Edge* only. I take you on tour later."

Daoud now moved in to take Saradon's place beside me as I lay reclined against the slanting south wall. Daoud wore no shirt, had a long, thick, bristly beard, was coarsely hairy on chest and back and smelled like a camel. I liked Daoud immediately because of his easy laugh. He opened bragging about his elite Wahhabi membership. Allah was between each phrase and his hands were together often in prayer and always when listening. He was ecstatic to learn I was a flier. He was sure I could teach him to fly, so he could go to heaven early. I had just completed my exchange with Daoud when there came the sound of scraping and bumping from up and back toward the west end entrance.

"Food!" several spoke the word at once. The mullah took my arm. "Let's all help Seven on his first dinner with us." Then came the sound, "Kersplash! Kerslump! Kerslump!" It was the exact sound one would expect upon hearing when a tub of barracks kitchen garbage is dumped on a stone floor having fallen a hundred feet.

"Before I pray, I want to say to you, Seven." The mullah with the help of Daoud lifted me to my feet. "I want to say to you, Seven, and I think all the beloved will agree: This eating activity, which comes only once a day, will be the real test of your will—especially this first one."

The five clustered behind allowing Mullah-Din and Daoud to guide me back toward the entrance end. "I warn you, Seven, this is the most ugly and animal aspect of this whole adventure. The reality of where you are will hit you now. Right, Beloveds? I hope you are not hungry."

The mullah and Daoud tucked their arms in mine, and we walked perhaps ten yards toward the splash sound at the west end. The mullah prayed as we walked along. He finished

178

his blessing as we neared the west end, and, as if on signal, at a certain unseen spot, everyone dropped to his knees.

I was from the beginning in awe of the way the other six seemed to know the direction and distance of everything in the pit down to the inch. Of course, with the pitch blackness of the entire venue, this was vital to safety, not only near the Edge, but also along the hallway with its sharp, steep walls, cracks and quake-dropped litter. Now listen carefully! This *distance and direction dimension* did not have to do totally with repetition or careful measurement, but rather had to do with a mystical belief which the mullah called, "Blind Glory." Because this idea was more than an *ordinary idea,* but carried a definite *spiritual* or *of God* aspect and power—and because its acceptance and practice was huge in the pit, I want to pause a moment here to address it directly.

First, I want to highlight: The Mullah-Din exercised total spiritual and political authority in the pit. This seemed to me to be the critical factor in the group's general day to day peace, buoyancy, positive approach and real victory over the dark adversity of imprisonment. The seven loved and respected the mullah and treated him as a true Servant of God. This dual authority is a fundamental of Islam. The world sees it practiced in some Middle East governments. I experienced it daily in the Mazjid Ghazu.

Further, our Mullah-Din exercised his moral-spiritual charisma and authority through a few cataclysmic rules or laws that were, as far as I could tell, totally accepted by all the Beloved. One of these principles was this notion he called "Blind Glory." Let me try to explain: Without making a huge issue of it, there was a powerfully concerted effort deep inside each man, gently, but intensely encouraged by the mullah, to "think-see," or put differently, to "will-sight." That is, we would try to see and expect to see and believe we could see what we *could not see.* Remember, there was absolutely no light, and being adaptive humans, we learned to fit into the pit environment by other means—hear, feel, smell, plus we all seemed to sort of subconsciously employ an "instinctive sense," particularly when we were near the Edge.

But this "God-Sight" was something more. Years ago I had been on the fringe of a para-mystical group who were exploring a similar notion in flying. So I picked up on the concept right away, and soon began to act like I was seeing places and things even though the place was, like I say, pitch black. I mean, there was absolutely no source of light of any kind anywhere. And yet we were all moving around people or things, reaching for and picking up things and reading expressions on faces and selecting or addressing individual items or persons precisely out of a group.

In explanation, the mullah would just keep saying, "Our mind, Beloved. We don't use half its potential. Make yours stretch, reach, work!" It was an especially gusty test when, in the beginning, after a few guided trips, I was cleared to walk free to the Edge to pee, bathe, meet, mill around or just sit and talk or think. Then after a few weeks, I found, like the others, I was living on the Edge, as well as in a narrow stone-walled hallway whose uneven floor was cluttered with large, sharp boulders daily changing location by moderate-to-severe quakes—and yet living and moving everywhere in the pitch dark with a relaxed ease and confidence of daylight.

Now back to our first supper. Mullah-Din, who was holding my biceps, restrained me. "You stay here. Just sit. I want to introduce you to this." He let go my arm and shuffled away on his knees. I leaned against the wall. I could hear several and feel others knee past me. Then, I could hear the men digging through the garbage. It was amusing talk. I could hear some eating. They were all together perhaps ten

180

feet from where I sat lotus fashion on the stone floor. My mind fled to McDonald's. As I say, the chat was amusing. Daoud described a food item. Sufi asked for a bite. Amarillo likened something he had found to an item on the menu at Maxime's left bank restaurant in Paris. Then I noticed from the undercurrent that Mullah-Din was kneeling beside Amarillo getting my stuff. I wondered why? Because he was a doctor?

While awaiting the return of the diners, I checked my place. I was right beside the tiny spring. I put my hand down and felt it flowing by. I judged the spring was maybe two inches deep and a foot wide. And it flowed along the angle where the wall met the floor. Over time, it had worn a slight gully in the stone floor and wall. My thought was, *This has been here a long, long time.* The water was very cold. I lifted my two cupped hands full and drank. It tasted very good. I thought, *Actually, this dungeon is full of blessings! I probably won't be here but a few days, but my role while I'm here is to join these men in accentuating the positive.*

Presently the mullah returned. "Here, Beloved." He took my hand and placed therein several strips of cold, wet stuff. "Eat this." I was hungry. I smelled it. It smelled spicy, but okay. I bit into it. It was meat with a kind of sauce one often finds accompanying the entrée in Middle East restaurants. "Here." Again, he reached into the dark and took my hand, turned it palm up. Again I felt some slimy pieces and something dry. This time it felt like and tasted like cabbage. The dry piece was plain bread. I was pleasantly surprised.

I leaned toward him and jested, "What, no coffee?" All laughed.

"Here, old boy. Will a glass of Chardonnay do?" Daoud jumped into the jest.

I ate the bread wondering who up there in freedom had smeared it with honey. Two of the others now crowded me with nearly whole pieces of meat and fragments of veggies. The first vegetable was slimy and felt like cauliflower. I hate cauliflower, so I thanked the hand by squeezing it—Saradon's, I think. Then I spit it quietly into my hand and chucked it into the creek. Instantly, a quiet voice was in my ear. "That is not allowed, Beloved. Pollutes the water."

The mullah and Amarillo sat close to me listening and sensing my reaction. I gave them a huge belch and "Exquisite!" Everyone laughed. "How did you find the good stuff in that random pile of garbage?" I was definitely curious, thinking of my future, regardless how brief.

Mullah-Din put my hand on Amarillo's shoulder. "Pat here." I patted. Amarillo chuckled. The mullah explained, "It took me half a year to find out why our doctor was gaining weight. The rest of us were barely holding our own eating random garbage. One day I kneeled beside Herr Doctor. I noticed he did not search for food at all. He went with his nose and found the flowers."

Saradon broke in to tell the story. "Amarillo has an unusual gift of smell. He would dig up the bouquet from the general's table."

The mullah continued, "Amarillo had reasoned that the only table in the officers' mess that always was adorned with flowers was the general's. It also was served the choice cuts of everything, including pastries. Doc would let the hungry paw and eat. He sniffed out the flowers and always found close by the filets."

Amarillo cut in, "I need to explain, I have noticed that the difference between surviving and enjoying in harsh, difficult places like this is very narrow. Usually it has to do with some aspect of *watching-the-money*." Everyone laughed in agreement.

"Eight o'clock . . . all's well." Countier was on duty.

Nine

I guess it was about a week later—again at dinner—I got to hear Daoud's version of *defeating-the-garbage*. Daoud was Egyptian. Very articulate, Daoud spoke British English with only a slight Arab accent. We were kneeling side by side at the garbage pile. I was conscientiously trying for the general's table bouquet. Daoud was watching me with his fingertips. I could feel them here and there just barely touch my outer movements. He leaned in close so that his comments would draw minimal kibitzing.

"Seven, I wouldn't spend too much good eating time fishing for the flowers. That's okay for the gourmets at heart, but you'll lose most of the good, solid life-food worrying about the filets. The reality? This is all too sickening and revolting to eat, right? That is because you are mentally picturing disgusting images of what you feel and smell. Leftover food. Bah! Some partially eaten and spit out, unidentified slime, cook's spit, KP's nose-blow, kitchen-dog poop and God knows what all."

I laughed and agreed. "It's largely either slippery, slimy and smelly or obviously chewed-on bones or joints."

Daoud, leaning closer, whispered, "You don't have to do that. You are choosing to let image rule. Take control. You have total power over your imagery. For my first month here, I found that I was starving. I allowed my mind to picture sewage-type stuff at every dining. I was sick before I began. Then one morning at Group I sat next to the mullah.

183

He opened with a brief bit on *Blind Glory.* He was encouraging us to think-see. As I listened I realized that I simply did not believe him. I had spent a year at Oxford. This childish psychology might intrigue some clods, but not me.

"That night Mullah knelt right next to me. Here—right here where we are. Mullah touched me. He said, 'Fix your mind on banquet table. Pick out specific items you like.' I laugh at him. I said, 'You fix, Mullah Beloved. I know garbage. I smell.' Two weeks and I'm down to seventy pounds of bones. Allah broke me through to the wedding feast."

Daoud was on a roll. "Praise Allah, I gave up on resenting the garbage. I saw salmon filet with sweet mustard. I smelled fresh homemade bread spread with honey. I began to smell and taste fried onions and goose liver. I shoveled the garbage away until I found what I virtually saw. I began to look forward to our evening repast. My health returned. My—what you say—buoyancy returned. I gained twenty pounds." Daoud slapped my shoulder and continued, "I began to see that this 'think-see' notion was a real power of vast, creative dimensions. Not just help me along the wall safely, but cover all aspects.

"So Seven, you see, you are now where we each was once. You don't believe that you can will reality, I know. Well, listen to me, Beloved Brother. Don't be stubborn-proud. Try it! Start little, where it can work. Think: 'This is Paris. I am escorting an elegant Dior fashion model to dinner at La Bougelaise. I have just paid 1000 francs for this buffet line. We are selecting poached quail under glass, green peas and Caesar salad prepared by the internationally famous chef, Francois d'Armand. The Cabernet Sauvignon will follow. Now, let's eat.' "

We ate. And I was thinking as we hunted for what we visualized, *This is a weird bunch! Where are the complaints?*

How can one man make a decent life happen under indecent conditions for all seven guys? It's largely by controlling their attitude. If I'm to get answers, I gotta get involved. This means a clear decision on my part to abjure my superiority complex and sincerely join in.

Amarillo sitting cross-legged on my right, touched my shoulder. "He's telling the truth, Beloved Seven. We almost lost him. Look at him now!"

A couple of week went by. I was working hard at fitting into the team and their amazing routine. My mind-set that someone was going to bail me out of this hole was slowly diluting. Still every time our collective sad plight somehow surfaced at "Group," the mullah would always turn our hopes back up by ending the conversation with his, "Fear not, Beloved, He will come!"

In a month or so, I knew our bunk area intimately. That is, I had been into everyone's place and had chatted with him, one on one, at length about who he was—his life, his dreams and hopes, his personal stuff. By "bunk area" I mean The Sacred Seven all lived together, side by side along the slanting wall opposite the stream. That is to say, we each had our own sleeping and personal place, side by side. Each man's place was the same, about six feet wide, perhaps two yards apart, one beside the other. This home area was where we slept and often lay or sat, sort of lounging, when we had Group in mid-morning or when some of us were just talking. The Sacred Seven would normally collect to talk or exchange views, or solve problems in one of two places: our "Home Area" or at the "Edge." We had no beds, of course. We slept in our clothes on the stone floor. I had the only blanket—my issue from the Taliboni Raiders.

This "Home Area" was made somewhat comfortable by its contour. The wall rose on about a thirty-degree angle for a yard before it tipped vertical. This formed a bevel along which we could all lie in a row with our feet toward the center of the hallway and our heads and shoulders raised, as if we were a row of hospital beds, one beside the other.

Of course no one had much stuff. I had my leather knapsack which carried a windbreaker, a number of Talaboni camp-issue odds and ends and in the bottom, my military emergency survival kit from Korea. My Talaboni issue blanket lay marking my bed place next to the mullah's. The mullah had some religious items including what he claimed to be a worn old Koran his mother had given him. Each of the others had a few personal items. Daoud had some books and oddly enough, a candle, no matches. Countier had two watches other members had given him when they arrived. One was a valuable Swiss wristwatch he kept wound. You could hear it ticking. Unfortunately it lacked a luminous dial or any kind of time-chime or alarm. Saradon had collected some rocks. The doctor had a few medical items: gauze, a bottle he claimed held iodine, but no scope.

We each had differing items of apparel, of course—mainly what was left of what each wore in. I was in military khaki knee-length shorts, my college T-shirt, and the mountain boots I got from the holy man on retreat. The mullah wore a rough wool chador and sandals. Daoud wore only pants that felt like the standard Milddle East black baggy pants, no shirt. Amarillo had a silky or satiny sari-sort-of-garment. Countier, a soft wool worsted shawl. Most were barefoot. I soon left my heavy boots beside my blanket. They represented my hope of early freedom.

In the beginning, I had been dragged to the place next to the mullah and laid down to recover there where I could be watched and cared for. His *residence* or place was closest to the western entry—maybe ten yards from the west end. Later, I found that each new man was always placed next to the mullah. This was important in a new arrivals quickly fitting into the unusually disciplined attitude and routine.

The doctor was in the center, and I remember Daoud was on the far end closest to the cliff. I can still hear his voice coming through the darkness from far away—often indistinct and always with a ripple of laughter braided in. Countier was next to Mullah-Din on the other side. Sometimes he whispered the hours at night in his sleep. If you have ever been locked-up, you know how rhythm becomes an all-consuming thing in prison.

Everyone seemed to sleep soundly. There was a certain amount of irregular sleep-talk. It often had to do with echoes from the pre-sleep discussion subject. This is common in or out of confinement, I suppose. Daoud was normally the last one to shut up at night. He always had something funny to comment on and often everyone would be chuckling and that would encourage him to add another one-liner until finally someone, usually the Qadi, would close in prayer, or the Countier would call the hour.

This living or sleeping area was about halfway between the dining area, which was directly under the entrance, and the bottomless cliff, the Edge.

About garbage disposal. Saradon and I were talking one night shortly after my arrival about *sanitation.* I was concerned about the leftover dumped garbage. He explained to me that the gang took turns cleaning up the dining area after the evening repast. A flat piece of stone was laid beside the water ditch and with that slab the duty man scraped up the leftover garbage and deposited it over the cliff. Then he splashed water and scrubbed the stone floor clean with a spongy kind of very light porous sandstone. Large hunks of this sandstone fell with each earthquake and littered the hallway floor.

As usual, Saradon explained how this cleanup duty worked by taking me with him on his duty tour. He first explained that I was next on the schedule. But let's let Saradon tell it: "Very early on, the discipline on this chore was encouraged by the erstwhile neglect of the duty by an unnamed culprit. That night the supper club was visited by a huge mountain rat the size of a raccoon. It may well have been a raccoon. Sufi claimed to have touched the animal. Or better put, the animal touched Sufi in its post-cleanup wanderings. We were all down for the night. Sufi let out a hoot you could hear in Baghdad. We all got up, of course, because of the disturbance. Daoud claimed the animal scooted for the Edge to escape or die. We made a search. Nothing, but it led immediately to the discovery that the garbage cleanup duty had not been performed." Saradon squeezed my arm knowingly and continued. "Sufi continued to describe the beast which, on first telling, had merely brushed him as he lay not quite asleep. With each new narration, the rat—or whatever it was—grew in size and ferocity. By dinnertime, it had become a small bear and had attacked Sufi as he slept.

"Upon hearing the story a morning later, the mullah acted like the whole thing was a conspiracy to embarrass the offender, which was the Mullah-Din himself! And I believe, it was his second offense! As the issue embarrassed the Sha'ir, it was quickly dropped. But these bursts of unexplained hilarity kept occurring during cleanup for a week or so."

I need to point out here that for about two weeks at the beginning, I had thought there might be eight of us, rather than seven. The Beloveds would talk about *Sufi* and flow right into *Zahir*—sometimes call him by one name, sometimes the other. My problem arose out of Zahir's strange way of sitting slightly apart whenever we gathered for Group.

His delicate, mystical Sufi belief system did not allow him to sit touching thighs with other men in the way the group had found comfortable when in serious discussion. When I would hear him talk in Group, I sometimes thought I was hearing another man. Here in Saradon's explanation of the duty delinquency of the mullah in "cleanup," I discovered that Zahir and Sufi were the same person. Also I noticed both men had the same voice, so I asked him about it. He told me the story. Like my being called "Seven," the mullah introduced him to the group as "Sufi" to let the others know they could expect him to be more sensitive and mystical about some aspects of Islam. But then he called himself "Zahir," so the double identity.

Almost every sort of routine, menial chore like this cleanup was handled by rotation, and when it was my turn next, the prior man would describe the duty to me, show me how it worked on his tour and then go through one duty-tour with me. I found out about the Edge's use as a burial site through Daoud's telling about the last man—the badly wounded commando-type nephew of Sheik Sazarack who died in here just over a year ago.

Daoud was impressed by the ceremony that preceded rolling the man's body over the Edge. Saradon, terrified by cliffs even in daylight, was, of course, powerfully impressed by the fact that it had been a very long clean drop before anyone had heard the body hit—first on the rocks, then, he, Saradon, said he heard it splash into the water far below. None of the others remembered having heard a splash at all. Sufi later told me that he had heard the mullah note at the time that it was his third funeral ceremony at the Edge.

No details, but one day I heard Daoud and the doctor discussing with great curiosity why Mullah-Din spent so much thought and energy guarding against loneliness and depression. The mullah had apparently been involved long ago as Qadi in a mosque where a close friend had been unjustly treated, became isolated and sick with depression and cut his own throat.

Dr. Amarillo stood peeing with me one day at the Edge and just out of the blue he observed, "It would be easy to draft a scenario for suicide, ya know. Especially if we didn't have such a brisk, challenging schedule, day in, day out."

I zipped up my pants. Then I stood pondering his notion while trying to hear something below. Nothing—just black velvet space. I could discern no sound of rocks falling or water cascading. Nothing. Not even a wind-song or a gurgle, gasp or howl. I said, "I thought Saradon told us that you could hear the water splash far below."

The doctor just stood silent. So I tried again, "Why would Saradon say he could hear . . ."

Amarillo cut in, "Saradon has never stood quietly at the Edge listening. He would not do that. He simply thinks that if it's very far, there must be water. The unknown width and length and depth terrify Saradon. There are a lot of unknowns in the dark."

At this point in this odd exchange came a scale three shake. An earthquake in the pitch dark can scare one to death if nothing else. You feel an urge to hold on to someone, but the rule is to be careful, for obvious reasons, not touch anyone while the shake continues. When the shake had shook, I realized that Amarillo had sounded very strange in this discussion of "suicide and unknowns," and I often wondered why he had surfaced this thought with me. Later I found out. Now, feeling I needed to make some response, I asked a dumb question, "Doc, do you think the bones of Callisthenes are down here?"

"Who on earth is Callisthenes?"

"I thought you knew. It's Daoud story. He told it at Group. Weren't you there?"

No response. I pursued, "Daoud says an historian at Baghdad University tells that in 331 B.C. Alexander the Great camped with his army of 30,000 Greeks in the pass right outside our pit prison here. He was pursuing the Emperor Darius who with his staff and major commanders was fleeing east following their decisive defeat down the hill at Gaugamela."

"Oh yes, I've heard this . . ." The doctor stood close now, listening.

I had always felt an urge to favorably impress Amarillo—probably because of his care-filled, healing ministering to me in the beginning. But beyond that, he was just a very good, kind, pleasant, likeable man. I storied on: "As often after a victory, the young Greeks got caught up in a series of wine-drinking victory celebrations. This one, in the camp clearing outside, culminated in a melee of sword fights between Alexander and his youthful, corps commanders. One named Callisthenes (Cleitus as he was affectionately called by his peers), happened also to be Alexander's cousin and boyhood chum. Cleitus happened also to be a God-son of Plato and nephew of Aristotle. History refers to the incident vaguely if at all, but generally reports that Alexander killed Cleitus accidentally in one of a dozen mock sword fights simultaneously taking place in the wild victory celebration."

The doctor had taken hold of my upper arm and was leaning gently against me indicating he was seriously interested in my recounting Daoud's story. So I took another breath and continued.

"Before I jumped in here, I had heard the same story with a different ending. The campfire legend among the mountain herdsmen and war bands comes down like this.

191

Toward the end of the duel, Callisthenes, cut-up and bleeding, ran a very clever and telling thrust to his leader's midsection and split. Took off and ran. A footrace ensued. Alexander chased Cleitus up along that mountain ledge right outside, familiar to all of us prisoners. Alexander carried his sword in one hand, a burning torch in the other. Cleitus ducked into the cleft and escaped by jumping down into this pit in the dark. Suddenly a major quake struck the mountain. Alexander, caught in the narrow, twisting entranceway, bleeding, weary and drunk, dropped his flare. Terrified by the quake in darkness, Alexander gave up the chase and groped his way back to camp. Cleitus, of course, was wounded and trapped forever in this pit.

"Young Alexander, twenty-eight, healed quickly and continued his amazing sweep beyond the Hindu Kush Mountains and south to the Indus River. Still, the mountain minstrels sing that he was ever mournful and lonely for his boyhood friend. Although he knew the God Apollo had snatched Cleitus up to heaven, Alexander died in Babylon at thirty-three—some say, of a broken heart."

Apparently this sad Alexander legend was news to Amarillo. Slowly, he reached down, lifted my hand to his head so I could feel him slowly shake his head for almost a minute, then he silently departed.

Nonetheless, his original concern about suicide was a logical one, especially for a doctor. As you can imagine, it was easy for depression to grip a hopelessly imprisoned group, and suicide. This disease is as contagious as smallpox and just as fatal. The hopelessness of our plight could sweep through the band with smoldering power. We saw it begin. Grown men would start crying quietly, stop eating and stay in bed. Others would quickly join. These tragic and debilitating storms were kept in check by the creative, demanding, disciplined firmness of our leader. The daily routine, the mullah's gentle but forceful leadership plus the unusual caring "team-sense" of our seven, kept pulling near train wrecks back on the track.

The mullah had us on a paramilitary schedule. I am convinced this routine was God-sent. It was absolutely essential to life. It kept the team physically, mentally and spiritually fit, healthy and free. We were not allowed to lie around in our place except during sleep time at night. Each day we had these mandatory attendance periods: (1) a morning period of wakeup songs, stretches and aerobic exercise, (2) Group which was a period of sitting or lounging usually in our Place or at the Edge to exercise our minds. (3) Meditation and prayer came in mid-afternoon. Then (4) after dinner in the evening, we would gather and listen to the mullah tell a Koran Story and then just talk at our Place or at the Edge.

I had never experienced anything like Group—ever. The mullah facilitated these sessions, and it was a most amazing experience. First, how he got away with making this sort of thing mandatory was a grace to behold. In fact, how he got total participation in almost everything the Seven did was a miracle—a classic lesson in deep moral leadership.

Let me try to describe Group: each mid-morning we would gather in a close circle and just sit together touching in silence for a while. Not just a few seconds. It was long enough to settle down, feel ourselves as One and appreciate the good we had here, then pray a little. Then one of the team would say, "Come with me to Tashkent." And he would take us on a journey to somewhere he had been or into a thought complex of unusual interest or controversy or into an accepted tradition or social behavior pattern.

We all went along. The idea was to think *free*, meaning, think *outside*. Part of the mullah's basic theme that *one's thoughts rule one's reality* was "We were only as imprisoned as we thought we were." When we visualized an adventure in a faraway place, we went there for a while. When we allowed ourselves to be caught up in Nietzsche, Karl Marx, St. Augustine, the Sunna, Guatama, Gauss or Jefferson we were set free in some far-off university or library for as long as the "thought journey" continued.

If it were to be a journey, the speaker would describe the journey as though we were all going along with him. For example, the mullah, one morning, took us on a walk through the streets of Kabul. His story was a major experience. He called us to see the sights, smell the smells, hear the sounds as we walked along the main street among fruit and vegetable stands, displays of crafts laid out on rugs on the street. We felt, smelled, and visited with kids, camels, donkeys, peasants, merchants, two spies and a robber.

We dickered with the merchants. We purchased items in the market. We listened to the muezzin call the faithful to prayer. We got involved in a small scuffle between some country herdsmen trying to push their goat flock through town. He watched a couple of Russian agents working their thing with a squad of Afghan soldiers in a sidewalk restaurant. And we helped the police catch a thief of a few potatoes from a poor old street vendor. It was fabulous because the mullah made it so real, used three languages in the telling and everyone got totally involved.

Daoud took us on a day at Oxford—including listening in art class to a Renaissance painter talk as he brushed a portrait of a huge-hatted merchant in Amsterdam. We toured the village on the Thames, and we found how the various colleges are embedded right in the city—Madeleine College, St. James, King's Cross, etc. Then we ate a picnic lunch on the riverbank watching the swans swim under the famous Bridge at Oxford on the London Road.

When it was my first turn, I decided to leave my flying days until later. I took the brothers on a day on the Tigris

River with my crafty family. Then we toured the archeological ruins of Nimrud with Dr. Max and Shaunelle, the beautiful Rhodes scholar from California. The gang was so caught up, I had to continue three days, then come back for more a few weeks later. Daoud told me I was stealing his place as the Storyteller. The experiential success actually established me as a legitimate "majnun," the Arabic slang which they call old established wizards. The word really means "possessed by spirits" but whatever, I achieved it here and actually moved up a notch in the pecking order.

Saradon, trying for a comeback, hired us to join his caravan from Karachi at the mouth of the Indus River, across the moonscape desert northwest to Safir, in what he still called Persia. You could feel your camel undulating under you across the sand dunes as you tried to keep in rhythm and not be jerked this way and that. We felt the scourge of hunger and thirst. Everyone kept visiting our nearby spring as we plodded the sand. We felt the magic of the desert night under the canopy of countless stars. He was good, Saradon.

The real value of these imaginary travels, of course, was the virtual freedom we felt. Every day we escaped the pit and virtually traveled afar. This was the heart of, but not the soul of, Mullah-Din's second Blind Glory law. Remember, I mentioned earlier that the Mullah-Din kept us together, bonded and healthy through his incredible moral-spiritual charisma. He exercised this power through a very few cataclysmic laws, rules and practices which for reasons known only to God, everyone accepted and, as far as I could tell, practiced. The first one was this *Think-See* or the persistent *Will-to-See* what we couldn't see.

The second one was *Think-Free*. In the same quiet, unintrusive way, the mullah kept urging each of us to think of ourselves as *free*. You can see how this attitude, so strong a force with Paul the Apostle in Scripture, encouraged each of us to refuse to permit the stone walls of the dungeon to confine us. As a result of this *Think-Free* attitude, the issue of confinement seldom arose. The talk, the thoughts, the imagery was always free and open and outside. We lived a lot trying to use the power of our minds. We were free because we thought free. I don't know about the others, of course, but for me this soul-releasing experience started me down a life-path practicing the notion: Thoughts lead directly to attitudes lead directly to behavior lead directly to habit patterns lead directly to character. I know my thoughts seed my reality, so generally speaking, I daily reaffirm that I am in control of what I say and do because I can control my thoughts. Thus, whenever I find my thoughts wandering sort of "downhill"—like critical or put-down or fault-finding—I can snatch them up and send them scrambling "uphill" in a sortie of approbation, respect, esteem, even reverence.

Thus, even when depression would strike, someone of the Beloveds would set us free with a creative, buoyant *freedom-thought.* Everyone felt it a solemn duty to the group to put a wrecked train back on the track. Or, more often, as I said earlier, catch a wrecking train weaving and faltering and lay a few healing rails to guide it back to honor and deference.

It was this prevailing unselfishness that urged me to write a story on the experience. I had never experienced this level of *Caring Goodness* actually practiced. Here in dark hopelessness, with circumstance made to order for complaining, bickering, jealousy and greed, a Heinz mix of spiritual pilgrims decided to rejoice in the light of one another, and with remarkably strong and creative leadership the seven worked hard to live it.

But let me not leave the impression that Group was limited to these fun and freedom-experiencing travelogues or mentalogues. They ran the gamut of geography, astronomy, art, music, dance, drama, theology, poetry, war and law. Many a day we spent with Kant, Goethe, Marx, Saint Paul, Gautama, Mohammed and Omar Khayam. As well as most of the contemporary political, economic and cultural actors alive or nearly alive and kicking such as Nehru, Stalin, Ibn Saud and Hassan II of Morocco.

I could never, and apparently neither could anyone else, anticipate the Imam's current area of interest. He would not telegraph it through casual conversation at the water cooler. He never talked in his sleep. He seemed to have an inexhaustible reservoir of curiosity. I say this because he never preached, so none of the rest did. He often gave his views usually after asking for yours. He found no such thing as inescapable right or wrong. It was always questions, questions, questions. What do you think of the Jewish tradition of Original Sin? Could you explain Mozart's aim in Concerto for Two Flutes? What modern composer has done similar work? Wherein lies the true beauty in Michelangelo's Pieta? Is it simply that it is religious? Will all civilizations rise, rule then decay and fall as Rome, Britain and Spain?

One day we got started on *Selfishness* as the root of "All Evil." For a random gathering of political religious prisoners stuck in a dark dungeon, by and large, we filled that cavern with the most creative and expansive discussion of ethics, virtue, evil and sin I had ever experienced. Days were spent openly and unemotionally reviewing Evolution—the change in the gene pool of a genus from generation to generation by such processes as mutation, natural selection and/or genetic drift. Oddly, at least to me, the authority in biology was not the doctor but Saradon, who was an Omayyad, he claimed to be related to Omayya, cousin of the grandfather of the prophet. Deism—belief in a creator and all-powerful

God on the evidence of reason and nature only, rejecting supernatural revelation. Theism—belief in one supernatural God creator and ruler of the universe who has disclosed Himself and His will to His creatures. Here, the mullah encouraged Daoud rather than himself to lead.

Fortunately we had a doctor. In one series Amarillo questioned all the great assumptions upon which Western medicine and all accepted traditional thought is based. He pressed his inquiry, questioning the basic assumptions of "Good" and "Evil" upon which our three major religions, the political theories, the economic notions, the philosophic ideas such as "Why we're here," God's mission statement, how did all start and why, what was going on before God. Amarillo was ruthless and fearless in inquiry, asking for free and open discussion on lifelong questions everyone had sometime wondered about but never had the nerve to ask.

To give our minds a rest, Countier opened the new year with the meaning and value of *Time*. And once again we dove into "How it all Began." The science vs. theology explanation brought the doctor and Saradon against Daoud and the mullah.

The miracle: I recall only a very few instances of superficiality in my year-plus or overemotional moments when a danger flag flashed. Of course we were human men, so hate and prejudice finally crept it. We'll come to that later. But for the main year, we each lived a miracle of free, caring exchange as if we each needed to do our best at this for the insight it would bring in living the rest of our lives.

It had just never occurred to me either at home, in school, college or in service officer bull sessions, how many of the fundamental assumptions in all of life we never question in respectable society because of either ignorance or fear of losing respect. I, at least, was always afraid I would appear stupid or disbelieving. Or I would lose respectability among my peers. Or I would call into question other dominos that would fall. Or I might find a compelling answer I didn't like. Or God would yell, "Bingo!" and it would all be over for me.

But really, can you imagine this scene? Seven men of all these various cultural backgrounds, religions, economics, geographics, seriously exchanging views and stretching our imaginations and souls for a couple of hours daily in the pitch dark? Why? Because it set us free, and kept us alive.

As well as I can piece the early days activities together, I initially jumped into the dungeon about the first of November, 1951. From my culvert experience in Mosul, I had been sure I would be back at school by Christmas. I am really surprised now, in retrospect, at how seldom the full career of events allowed me to dwell in depression, in broken morale and weeping sadness at missing Najua, my beloved Arab sweetheart. I sometimes wondered what she could be thinking happened to me, but it was, as I remember, always centered on the "mystery," never on the "tragedy."

In fact, the mystery arose in several forms. I wondered how the university authorities were coping with my sudden disappearance. Early on especially, I wondered what the U.S. government authorities were concluding had happened to me, and what they were doing about it. However, in every instance, I felt assured that the presence of Mr. William Colby in the Department of Economics at the university would cover most, if not all, of the AWOL problem. One of spymaster Colby's major responsibilities was "cover stories."

From a U.S. Government point of view, measuring Middle East airfield runways for post-strike atomic bomber recovery, was not a program needing wide examination in the press or public. Thus, I could just sort of disappear off the edge. After all, I was supposed to be hiding out anyway. How fortuitous can fortuitous get?

One of my major sources of depression lay in the fact that I am a member of the International Journalistic Society. Members of the IJS are under strong moral obligation to maintain a disciplined *daily journal.* Moreover, many of us in the service are additionally under commitment to the Pentagon and the American Archives in Washington to keep this daily journal for life.

Some history: I had started journaling at thirteen years of age with the encouragement of my mother, as a scouting requirement. Since that time in 1932, I had maintained my daily journal without serious break (and then only during two periods of hospital recovery from combat aircraft, crash-burns and breaks). Thus, journaling had become at age thirty, as much a part of my life as eating or sleeping. In this pit, I carried in my knapsack my Middle East Journal. This contained my daily unfolding story of the people, the places, the happenings of my Middle East adventure. The story was unfolding about school, about recreation, about espionage, about love—my Middle East life story up to the point of the step into darkness.

Here blind, I had ceased my journaling. Oh, I had made a couple of awkward efforts to write in the dark. But mainly I had been defeated in this singularly important aspect of my life. Like stopping eating or sleeping, it deeply and acutely hurt.

One day in the spring, I believe it was mid-April, 1952, I was lying on my blanket preparing for Group. It was my turn to define and lead the discussion. Suddenly, I heard a deep scratching sound down the passageway. I could not recall hearing this before. When it persisted, I called quietly to Mullah, "Mam." We often called Mullah-Din *Mam,* short for Imam—a sort of alternate word for mullah or emir, honorary as much as spiritual because we so loved and respected Mullah-Din.

No one answered. I moved and reached to see if the Imam was in residence. He was not. I reasoned he might be doing the scratching and wondered what and why he was scratching. I got up and walked slowly down toward the Edge. There, perhaps five feet beyond Daoud's place, I walked bodily into Mullah-Din on tiptoes scratching on the wall.

When I put my hand on his back he ceased his scratching and turned to me. Without a word, he took my hand and placed it flat on the wall near where he seemed to have been scratching. I could feel irregular angles and lines engraved into the flat, stone wall. As I felt the wall, I could only discern that the scratchings were in orderly columns and lines. I wondered a moment that I had not noticed this unusual aspect of this wall-portion before. But I hadn't. Of course I couldn't see it, but then I just never thought of feeling the surface of any wall except the walls at the west end where a couple of us had endeavored to climb.

Immediately the Imam turned me toward him, and opening my hand, placed there a flat, beveled slice of stone. I immediately put it in my mouth to test its texture with my teeth. It was flint. This was a flint stylus. Now the mullah pulled me down onto the floor and explained to me that he had been for several years and was now keeping a record of the salient happenings in the pit. Normally, he told me, he made an entry on the wall perhaps weekly. He took my hand as we sat against the wall, and with my index finger traced a reachable portion of his Arabic-shorthand—translating while tracing. He then narrated how he had found the piece of volcanic-hardened flint by accident. It had fallen from a crevice high in the ceiling. He had chipped it and whet-sharpented it to make it into an engraving tool. Being flint, it would cut into the ambient limestone of the inner pit wall.

201

He had over the years covered roughly the whole inner wall with journal.

When I explained to him that I was a journalist and needed to join him in this endeavor, he was so delighted he began to cry. This started a weekly conference between just him and me going over the happenings and discussions and picking out the central storyline. Then taking turns—he one week, me the next—in his shorthand code, which he taught me, we journalled our story on our wall.

I thought at first I would just get the Imam to help me find and craft a stylus then join him in keeping a separate journal of my own on a different wall. Still there was the matter of space and the scarcity of flint. And, perhaps, over-arching was the nature of our pit lifestyle. Although seven men, we were really one. Our geography was tight. Our activities were nearly identical. Our thoughts were controlled. In reality, our story was pretty much *one-story*. Thus, the notion of joining and keeping just one *family journal* was so convincing we started immediately. As I say, he taught me the code, and I found I could read back. He and I would stand together by the wall chatting about the issues past, while we both felt his journal of several previous weeks. Soon, knowing many of the issues he had recorded, I could read back his journals. This allowed my stepping right in as the pit co-journalist. It totally cleared my no-journal depression. I felt inside that I was alive again. I now had a significant, timeless purpose. And not surprisingly, this new role as co-recorder moved me up another step in the pecking order of the *Seven*.

Ten

On Friday, 10 October 1952, I took a major gamble. I had been thinking along the lines of "How can we reassert, here in the pit, a sense of individual achievement?" We are letting our circumstances rule. We have let the bleakness and darkness and hopelessness of the pit crush our normal practice of praise or saying "Well-Done!" I missed the warm compliments and stated heroics normal in my life outside. I felt, "We have accepted that we are criminals and unworthy. This is detrimental to men's morale and contributes to our spasms of depression. Our spiritual health depends on our stopping this character slide and begin a character climb." I had a plan. We needed to select a weekly "Best Something." We needed to pat someone on the back periodically.

I had chatted quietly with the mullah about this notion, Frankly, I got little encouragement. The Mullah was proud of our level-playing field. He loved our bonding and had a lifelong abhorrence of the "elite nature of man." In fact, he pointed with pride to the miracle that God had wrought here, out of seven completely diverse nationalities—completely different economically, religiously, culturally. Yet God had miraculously formed a warm, compatible, positive learning, caring, even "often happy" family. We should not tamper with it.

At Group that Friday morning, right or wrong, I went for it. I made a formal suggestion for adjusting our routine

203

and modifying our life style. I surfaced the idea of encouraging one another in a positive and personal way by instituting a weekly *Nobel Prize*.

Now, I didn't just pick this "award dynamic" out of the blue. I grew up in the middle of the Great Depression, in a family of seven boys. My Pop, a very smart lawyer and judge and an uncanny student of human nature, decided in an effort to break the depression of the Depression, to institute in our family a Pursuit-of-Excellence award.

At family dinner the first Sunday of September 1932 (hard times were at their hardest), with much drama, Pop announced the "Bottomly Nobel Prize for Excellence." The idea, of course, was to move our focus away from our hardships, shortages, misfortunes and complaints, and put our eyes instead on the "Joy of the Struggle." He and Mom had drafted the rules and procedures into an official-looking, stylish document. After his presentation, he tacked this parchment to the wall behind and above his place at the head of the table. It remained there all through the winter, '32–'33 as a sort of *Constitution* to be referred to in arbitration.

The idea of the Prize was each month to cite (with a suitable trophy, picture in the paper, and release from chores) that son who demonstrated the most Helpful, Unselfish, Caring Neighborhood Act. The heart of the program was the collection of inputs from every adult in our small town. Our whole town was to watch out for a noble, unselfish, helpful, caring, good-teamwork act on the part of one of the seven Bottomly boys. Each month, all these happenings, jotted on slips of paper—from phone calls, teacher or neighbor visits, word-of-mouth, direct observation or whatever—were collected by Mom. Then she and Pop would make a judgment. At the last Sunday dinner of each month, with increasing drama as the winter wore on, with about a dozen different invited guests each week—including the editor and photographer from the *Chinook Opinion*, our local weekly—the award would be presented. It came in the form of a two-and-a-half-inch shiny gold pendant on a long red, white and blue ribbon hung around the neck of the recipient by some local dignitary guest. It was awesome!

In our "Pit Nobel Award," I had thought along the lines of The Most Unselfish Act, The Most Group Caring Idea, The Most Honest Admission, The Kindest Compliment. The notion was to maintain a high level of caring, encouraging brotherhood in the face of some evidence of general deterioration—"Depression, Complaints, Fault-Finding, Etc."

I thought the person might be elected by some fair means, following discussion and voice-vote at a group meeting. We could celebrate the winner with some sort of royal treatment: a heroic news release, serve him a banquet dinner, you know, "King for a Day" sort of thing. We could think of something. The idea was to encourage "quality life," "noble thought," "civilized behavior"—"general Pursuit of Excellence."

Now you would think that this sort of initiative would be greeted with rousing approval—especially by a group of good-hearted, good-deed fellows who had been pursuing the same old, somewhat boring and hopeless routine for five to twenty-five years.

Wrong! My presentation was met with first, silence. In fact the silence was so edged that I felt like the idea had somehow leaked out and the blokes had discussed and rejected the idea en camera. I could not be sure because at this point in the moment of discussion there came a moderately severe, but extended tremor. As usual, the talking stopped for a time for the dust to settle. Then there always followed a quake psychology—a difficulty to focus seriously on anything profound. So, to keep the Friday meeting moving, when I tasted clean air, I just suggested that everyone think about the proposal and, when ready, someone might bring it up again for thoughtful discussion. From there, the meeting moved joyfully along as usual. As I recall, it was a fascinating discourse by Dr. Amarillo on the human fetus from egg through fertilization to birth. I remember hours of questions, mostly stuff every father wonders about but is not brave enough to ask someone who knows.

Sometime during the early fall of 1952, I think it was in September, Zahir, along with Daoud and Saradon, decided to try again to climb the very dangerous, but only possible escape route up the dark, slick concave wall to the west end entrance.

Zahir was a tiny man, so the others were employing him as the light, but tenacious rock climber. Daoud was a large, generally buoyant Arab, willing to try anything, but easily discouraged. I sat in on the planning session. Having gotten an okay from the mullah to try this, the three wannabe heroes sat down at the garbage landing spot, at least 100 feet directly below the opening, to work out their plan. First Daoud felt along and around in the blackness. He reached along the west wall and above the running spring on the south wall. He talked as he felt explaining what he was encountering. As I had tried this exploration alone several times and gotten nowhere, I could visualize exactly what Daoud was reporting. There was a moist, slick, smooth concavity that rose from our living level indefinitely and without indentures, or texture of any sort. I had found that all along and around the farthest end there was no way that a climber could get started, and without any sort of climbing tool, could not drill or cut any holds or starting points into the slimy, smooth, slick marble. Daoud and Saradon then decided to stand together and boost Sufi onto their shoulders.

From there, Sufi was to feel up the smooth concavity for texture of some sort upon which or into which a climbing start could be initiated.

We spectators were witness to an abundance of grunting and squealing. Apparently the concavity meant that the two base men had to stand well back in order to give Sufi room enough to maintain balance and feel along and up the wall. They seemed to be making some progress; at least it was all quiet with only brief, muttered audibles, when all of a sudden, WHUMP! Sufi came down in a violent and hurtful crash.

Dr. Amarillo had been napping and the mullah was at the Edge. We lay Sufi out flat. He had apparently landed on his shoulder and head. He was moaning incoherently, and I could feel some blood. As usual, Amarillo performed a caring miracle without medical supplies or equipment, and Sufi was on the mend in a day or two.

During the several days the Seven were sort of focused on the west end, Countier discovered that the camp muezzin's evening call-to-prayer came consistently immediately following the garbage drop. For several days in a row, Countier and I had found ourselves positioned so that we could just barely hear the "Call" from the camp minaret outside. The counter decided that he could safely establish that call as exactly 6 P.M. From this "time hack," he now endeavored to "count back" to the "strange ticking sound" of his expensive Swiss watch which, you remember, came in early afternoon and early morning. Although the mullah, supported by the other five, had made it clear to Countier that his rough time keeping was perfectly satisfactory for the group, Countier was a perfectionist when it came to time. He wanted an exact "hack." He worked and worried and worked and worried.

Finally, at a mid-October Group, Countier presented his mathematical triumph. He had "back-counted" the seconds from the evening 6 P.M. call-to-prayer. Checked it and double-checked it. Then he "forward-counted" from the early morning "ticking aberration" to the 6 A.M. camp reveille bugle call. Checked it and double-checked it. At the 17 October Group, Countier carefully explained how he now had established the exact time of the "strange ticking sound minute" of his expensive Swiss watch. There was strong applause and hearty thanks to Countier from all. Although I doubt if anyone understood how Countier arrived at his solution. I know I'm a college Math-Physics major, and I got totally lost about halfway through his explanation. Nevertheless, Countier was happy, and the pit had achieved a victory.

The major issue of my year and seven days broke the last week in October, 1952. Our doctor, Amarillo, had fallen ill. In fact several of us had developed a stomach cramp that the mullah said came often in the fall of the year. He and the doctor reasoned that it came when a certain pheasant was hunted by the local Bedouins and sold to the camp for food. The disorder passed through us all in about forty-eight hours except for the doctor.

As the days passed with no relief for Amarillo, we started taking turns sitting by him. He often got so sick to his stomach that he crawled to the Edge. Often he just slept there on the cold stone, close enough to throw-up, should the call come. Sometime in the second week—I think it was during the common lounge and chat time after dinner—Amarillo was audibly and rather constantly moaning in pain. He had stopped eating anything for a couple of days and was obviously in more serious trouble than our diarrhea and cramps. I decided to risk it. So I surfaced that I had hidden in my knapsack an emergency survival kit containing two vials of opium painkiller.

After listening to everyone's views, the Mullah-Din decided to break the glass of one vial and inject the doctor. I found my survival kit in my pack under the junk I had accumulated along my escape route. The emergency kit was still sealed, unused since Korea. I found the glass vial and cut across Mullah-Din's place to where he was kneeling beside Amarillo. The doctor was lying on his back, moaning softly and breathing heavily as one in pain. I leaned against the mullah and whispered, "We were taught to bite the capsule open and rub the liquid on the pain or push it gently into the jugular vein."

I handed the vial to Mullah-Din. He moved confidently toward Amarillo's upper body. I wondered momentarily at the mullah's equanimity. But only a moment, he returned forthwith and took my wrist. Opening my hand with the back of his, he deposited the thin glass vial onto my left palm. Then leaning his face against mine, he whispered, "You must do it."

I moved between the mullah and the doctor and with my right hand felt, first the bare stomach—which it seemed to me was quite puffed. Then I moved to his throat, put the vial between my eyeteeth and held it. Amarillo's pulse was strong, so I could identify the main artery, then the vein. I put two fingers on his jugular vein and simultaneously bit the vial. I gently but firmly lay the vial against the high side of the pulsing vein and pressed hard. Amarillo rolled half-a-turn away as I squeezed the vial dry.

"He will be in pleasure heaven in two minutes." I brushed by the mullah.

He patted my back in appreciation. "Thank you, I just couldn't do it."

We exchanged places. Mullah continued, "I must examine him to make sure he isn't cut or bruised or infected. He always takes such good care of us." Mullah felt out with his hands. Then, as I moved past him, I could hear him suddenly suck in air, indicating shocked surprise. I crouched close, thinking this sound might lead to a call for help.

"Seven—Seven!" Frantic, whispered shouts. Immediately, Mullah-Din's fingers raked my chest and grabbed my T-shirt front in a wodge. His mouth was close to my ear. "Don't go!" He pulled me by the fabric toward where Amarillo lay, now out cold—silent, happy.

Mullah breathed into my ear, "Look here!" We normally used the term *look* when we really meant *feel.* Mullah took my wrist in his grip. "Open!" He tore my palm open. "Feel!" Mullah was breathing hard and barely whispering to make sure only I heard his consternation. I felt Mullah take my right hand in his. He lifted it up over Amarillo's bare stomach. With my hand wide open, my fingertips were moved down over his lower torso. I expected to feel an open wound or the sticky presence of blood or a sharp break. I felt myself mentally readying for quick first aid. I was not ready for what I felt!

Mullah moved my open fingers down over Amarillo's pubic hair. I was suddenly very uncomfortable. I was thinking, *Mullah-Din, this is improper. Neither of us should have his hand here on Amarillo.* Then my mind caught up. I got it! There was nothing here. My immediate thought, *Wow! This man has been castrated!*

Mullah-Din's breath smelled of digesting food. He whispered right into my face, "You see? This is woman!"

The truth struck me like a sledge. Of course! I was so man-focused, no other possibility registered. I moved my hand up across the soft, puffed stomach again. At the navel I lowered my left ear and listened. I discerned a syncopation

210

and felt a number of definite thumps. Dr. Amarilla moaned and turned in her sleep. I completed my examination by checking for breasts. Definitely! I pulled Mullah close. "Mullah-Din, this dear lady is quite pregnant."

I don't know if you have ever been so totally and devastatingly surprised by something that you seem to function initially with cool instinct simply because the magnitude of the thing doesn't yet register? I was in an out-of-body experience here, totally swept away. So my actions and speech were low-key, cool and sensible. Mullah-Din had time to think. He grabbed me first by one arm. Then he faced me and held me by gripping both my biceps. I got a whiff of undigested supper again as he spit, "Are you sure?"

I hugged him to me. "Mullah. This is the most serious thing that could happen here. You can feel the heartbeat. I think I felt the baby kick. I would guess—totally from ignorance—that she is seven-plus months deep. I'm sure she knows she'll have to be her own doctor."

Mullah pushed me out to arms length. "Allah, oh, Allah, the Compassionate! We all have to get ready to take care of another prisoner, a special prisoner, a baby prisoner."

I felt the mullah's fingers close so tightly on my arms, it hurt. He leaned against me and barely whispered, "Can you imagine being born, living your whole life, then dying in the pitch dark in a one-room pit? You would only hear stories about the outside from elders whom you would never see—like we hear stories about heaven."

I felt Amarilla move and heard a low moan. I patted Mullah's back. "I suggest you call a special Group right now so we can all think about and talk about this while Dr. Amarilla is not a player."

Mullah moved quickly away from the still moaning doctor and whisper-shouted down the hall, "Beloved! Beloved!

211

All come to the Edge." In about a minute all the flock was assembled from far and near. We met at the Edge because Mullah knew that conversation at the Edge was inaudible at the dorm. The meeting was kept quiet and amazingly unemotional. In fact, quite subdued. The mullah opened with a narration of the discovery drama—the need for a pain reducer to help Amarilla through the night; my surfacing the opium shot; the sensible decision to physically examine for wounds, bleeding, infections; the discovery that Amarilla was a woman. There followed a sort of shocked, heavy-breathing stillness. No one even moved.

After perhaps a minute of heavily-charged quiet, Mullah-Din finished. "Now, gentlemen, we'll want to think about this. And rather than each of us brood alone over this shocking happening—or discovery—or situation, I think it's better that we think carefully together, out-loud, as a loving, caring Group. I pray to Allah that we can move this reality from the shock category to the caring-accepting category. We must begin our complex but very important task—accepting Doctor Amarillo, now Doctor Amarilla—for who she is and begin planning for lovingly handling the birth and care of our infant."

I thought, *Messiah!*

This gentle, loving approach to the shock brought another minute of dead silence. Then everyone wanted to talk at once. Everyone was commenting. Daoud was asking questions which no one was answering. I was surprised that no one seemed to question the fact of Amarilla's womanhood. No one suggested going personally to check. I had wondered earlier how we would all handle the question of: Who is the father? But the idea never surfaced. Both Daoud and Saradon seemed completely unable to believe a woman could or would pass herself off as a man. Daoud just kept deeply and audibly breathing with a strange "WHEEOO!—

212

WHEEOO!—WHEEOO!'' Sufi, on the other hand, seemed
deeply saddened and depressed that Amarilla, whom he had
trusted so totally as a godly, caring physician, would choose
this size and shape of lie. He moved away and would not sit
touching anyone.

I suppose we sat there in the dark threshing the various
aspects of this shocking new circumstance for maybe two
hours. I recall once Countier spoke out the hour. I didn't
notice which hour. Finally we all sort of drifted away, one
by one. All were emotionally exhausted by the shocking surprise and intellectually exhausted by the complexity of the
problem. No one went immediately to sleep. I could hear
one or two periodically verbalize out loud to himself, so totally upset, so broken, so emotionally destroyed were we all.

Two tense days passed, Group became suddenly a series
of very safe discussions. One day we talked about the Silk
Road to China, another, the New York Stock Exchange. Our
opinions were consistently brief, conservative and correct.
Our expressions were formally courteous and predictable.
Anything regarding the doctor was avoided. I checked her
every few hours, noting her breathing and heartbeat. Often
she would be softly sobbing or whispering to herself. I would
pat her shoulder and repeat Mullah Din's "Fear not, He will
come. It'll be all right. We all love you, Ami, and we'll take
care of you.''

Mullah surprised me one dinner by gripping my elbow
tightly with this: "Seven, listen carefully to the Wahhabis. I
tried to hug Doaud. He pushed me away. Something's going
on.'' I had long forgotten that Saradon and Doaud were
Islamic Puritans—formally titled Wahhabis or Fundamentals. For some reason our individual religious or spiritual
conditions had always been on the edges but never had surfaced as a prime subject of discussion. Long ago, however,

in one of our quiet personal discussions, Mullah-Din had gone over each man's spiritual dimension with me. He had noted Daoud's and Saradon's latent fundamental commitments as well as the sort of ascetic mystic sect of Islam that Sufi stood for. Mullah had always made this a character plus and never a threat.

I did not understand what this "fundamental Islamic commitment" had to do with the gender of one of the Sacred Seven. Being a nominal, church-going, American Christian and having only experienced Islam at AUB with my moderate schoolmates and here in the Mullah's loving, caring, creative leadership and the stern words but caring attitudes and unselfish deeds of the Seven. Plus I had daily joined the mullah-led prayers, Mullah-Din had early on chatted with me about my spiritual condition. In that conversation, he convinced me that our Higher Power was the same God. Arabs call Him Allah, Jews call Him Jehovah, Christians call him God.

Like most all Americans—but not true of the colonials, the British, French, Spanish—I was not intellectually or culturally mature enough to know the depth and power of the fundamentalist Islamic belief. I had not earlier encountered this total life or death opposition to all things not sanctioned by the Koran. I guess I had never before been around a declared Jihadist—certainly never seen one challenged.

I tried to be attentive to this new spiritual aspect on the part of the *Wahhabis,* as Mullah-Din had called them. I was not really sure what this strict Koran adherence meant or who was included. I sort of passed it off as part of the mullah's responsibility. He was our Imam. He always had and would surely now rule on any spiritual or religious aspect of this issue.

As I listened carefully in each discussion, I noticed that Amarilla's pregnancy did not seem to concern the three Jihadist Brothers. The other three of us seemed to be trying hard to work the "pregnant mother and child" problem. Contrarily, the three brothers were focused on the "female-living-a-lie" and tempting-six-innocent-men issue. I kept hearing the word "betrayal." And when that term or thought was applied to Dr. Amarilla, to me it was just very depressing. I could not believe that these caring men would turn so abruptly.

Day 3—Suddenly at Group, someone suggested an "All-of-Us'" physical exam. I guess we were beginning to wonder how far this deception may have gone. This notion led to the question of how do you physically examine people in the pitch dark? Daoud suggested an immediate circle-sex-check of all of us by all of us. I thought, *This is a new low for the curse of darkness. In any kind of daylight, we could have just stood in a circle, dropped our drawers and looked.* Here, actual touching was insisted upon. I was sure the mullah would draw a line. He did not. But he was right on his suspicion. Something was definitely going on with the fundamentals. We were definitely not approaching this adversity with our normal, thoughtful, circumspect togetherness.

One thing had become patently clear in three brief days. Three of us wanted to take up the central issue that we would soon have a baby on our hands. The discussion issue of the day was three-fold: How to safely deliver a baby. How to care for him or her as a baby in the dark. And then we talked at length about the long-term problem of raising a child through his or her teens in this pit. The three others were contrarily caught up in the ethical or moral issue: Someone had taken advantage of the dark and lived a lie. A woman pretended to be a man. What penalty should the group impose for this moral violation?

Day 4—Group starting right after our opening prayers. Here, all of our open, trusting rules came under question

215

by the Wahhabis. New Rules were suggested. Daoud asked whether free peeing at the Edge would now be possible. Saradon suggested that our caring, *touchy-freely intimacy* when someone was depressed or hurting was no longer appropriate. He also asked whether sleeping in a row was proper? Sufi suggested we always have at least three people together, and that we arrange for guard-posts for collective security. I was having trouble keeping up. For the first time in nearly a year's intimate contact, I was not proud of our team of normally dependably caring, empathetic men. Some of my cellmates, from whom I would have expected the most loyal and loving response to this emergency, were turning. And the central factor was this religious thing. Our Islamic spiritual connection and the presence of the mullah had always brought a softer more circumspect approach by the group to any *victim* issue in any of our previous theoretical discussions.

Today the conversations went something like this: Saradon observed that it was impossible for him to sleep soundly in the arrangement we now had. Sufi was amazed that no one had heard anything going on at night over the years. Now that he was listening, he imagined lots of things. Daoud suggested we permanently move Amarilla's place to the Edge. This suggestion caused Sufi to notice that this was impossible. That would mean we would have to move the toilet. Countier retorted that it was too dark to worry. Frankly, I was beginning to feel the cold fingers of terror creeping in. I always sat close to the mullah now. Still, I was afraid if I took too strong a stand in opposition to the growing jihadist stand, I might get included as a traitor against God.

Saradon pointed out that now, with a woman aboard, we could no longer just go to the Edge whenever we chose, even just to talk. Sufi suggested a schedule be arranged. His and Hers signs were mentioned. For the first time everyone laughed. The mullah finally ended the meeting by opening our prayer around the circle. We had not done this since once in May when no garbage was dumped for several days. Hunger had struck. Now something even more painful had struck. Hate was creeping into our pitch dark midst, and curiously, it was creeping in through the door of religion.

Eleven

Day 5—It was Mullah's turn to journal, and I noticed he spent more than the usual amount of time. He had to be careful how he coded the turn of events for posterity. He also had to be careful how he handled his moral leadership of the group. I desperately wanted to help him, but I was uncomfortable with the split in our attitudes toward what I saw as a pregnant mother-new baby problem and to others there was blood in the water and sharks were gathering.

This "divisive edge" to our conversations was not restricted to these initial meetings. The "sharp edge" had become evident in every discussion and conversation on every subject toward the end of October. I was not helpful here. I became quiet and depressed. The smooth bonding of our Special Seven was becoming morbid. Serious cracks, painful blisters, dangerous infection was beginning to show. This was bringing an electric tension into current daily living; but more troubling, it signaled dark clouds for our future. Of course, we could not see each other. Therefore one would expect we had a built-in privacy. Wrong! In reality, because of our longtime, loving, trusting, sharing life style, we could not now get away from each other. Besides we had grown together physically. We could constantly hear, smell and feel each other's presence and state of mind.

Amarilla slept peacefully and stayed in her place for four days. When she rejoined Group on the afternoon of the fifth day, the mullah, in a very nice way, disclosed how he and I had in good faith discovered her gender and the cause of her difficult morning sickness. I was sitting next to her, and I heard Amarilla heave a ten-ton sigh of relief. An eight-year burden had just been lifted. Countier, sitting next to me, leaned across my leg to pat her shoulder. I had not fully put Countier on either team. Now I chalked him up as one of the moderates—one of the "Let's Forgive and Get on with Life."

As Mullah spoke, Amarilla had begun to cry softly and silently. I reached out to support Countier's effort. When the mullah closed, there was a long silence. Then Amarilla cleared her throat and very softly spoke.

"I am terribly, terribly sorry, Beloved. I know I have lived a lie among you for more than eight years. The darkness protected my secret. I am a woman. I could only pray. For three years I asked Allah to change me into a man—not because I dislike being a woman, but simply because of the inherent tragedy in my difference. As a known female among males, I would immediately cause evil. Contrarily, if I hid in the darkness, every day the lie's inherent evil would corrode my goodness, and finally, another's. And sure enough.

"Allah wouldn't help me. Although I know he could. He has done it before. For some reason, he wanted me here, and He wanted me a woman. I'm terribly sorry. I really never said I was a man. You assumed I was, and I simply failed to correct you." Amarilla paused here as if allowing for a comment. None came. She continued, "Almost every day I would decide, I must just go." Her voice told me she had turned to look toward the Edge. "But we badly needed a medic. Then, there came a child to consider. I could no longer just go, alone."

That was all she said. We—the whole group—must have sat there in our lotus circle for half-an-hour in silence. I must tell you that as we sat quietly letting the magnitude of this new circumstance filter through our individual and collective depths, I could feel in the sound of the sighs, the breathing, the shifts of body positions as well as just hunch—I could feel the once and former solidarity of our family breaking down in a strangely complex but profound way along these new, curious, fundamental religious lines. Whatever it was—right there—without moving, six men, in total darkness, and without any signals whatsoever, took sides. The blood was in the water and there was no turning back. That night two moved their places down to the west end.

If you call Halloween a holiday, Halloween is one of my favorite holidays. The mystic, the legendary, the imagined, the not-quite-real, the ghostly, the scary, the dramatic! I love this atmosphere. The little child in me reaches out for this exciting ambiance. Nonetheless, Halloween, 1952 was my worst day, ever.

Day 6—Halloween, Mullah and I arrived for Group early to chat discretely about counter-measures or projects to initiate that might convert the *Amarilla Challenge* into an interesting challenge with major positive aspects. We were hellbent for solving the problem rather than finding fault with its creation. And neither of us was prepared to accept that the Group had slid beyond the point of no return. Anyway we had surfaced several approaches, but had not agreed on what to propose to the others by mid-morning.

Sufi was sitting with the "Tough-Two" down at the West End. Sufi whispered to me as Mullah and I joined, "Relax, Yank, the guys just want to have a fair trial."

I thought, *Good God! Trial? Trial for what? I could observe that Middle Eastern women were a century slow at achieving social equality. But could being a woman be illegal?*

Soon we were all in a circle sitting in our standard lotus fashion. We had stopped meeting in the bunk area. Now we gathered down close to our dinner-place and instead of lounging, we now sat in a lotus circle. Group, once a fun, relaxed and very creative and free-open time, had recently acquired an edge. And I could feel that our lotus circle had divided into two half-circles. I noticed the Wahhabis positioned themselves side by side. I felt like going over and sitting between them, but Mullah-Din, reading my mind, pulled me down beside him, and held me there.

Group traditionally opened with Mullah-Din sort of starting things with a prayer, then a warm, encouraging comment or challenging question. The idea was to start everyone off in a trusting, open, reflective mood. Contrarily, today Daoud led right out with a prepared statement: "The Koran, Sura XXVII—and I believe also your Bible, Seven—in Exodus 20, tells us that it is sin to lie, cheat or steal. We are commanded to speak and live truthfully and not hide anything from our brother. Beloved Doctor Amarilla has betrayed us by hiding her gender except for one of us who sleeps with her. Although unknown, he is one of our Holy Seven, now despised by all."

Daoud paused as though to allow for a challenge. Then when none came, "This is hateful and divisive to the brotherhood. Now that all know Amarillo's sex, lust is already entering. Murder will surely follow. To enjoy or be refused her favors is certain to cause despicable hatred and division. We are certain to be confined here for many years together. The space is small. We must maintain our oneness of spirit as well as body. Until this, it has been a God-miracle that we have lived in harmony. Now suspicion, distrust—already you can feel it growing daily. This woman, by her lie, has destroyed our dark paradise."

Silence followed this heavy judgment. When no one spoke, Daoud pushed on. "Last night in the early hours

221

Saradon had to get up to go. While at the edge, some unknown one pushed or nudged him hard in an effort to accidentally push him off."

Mullah-Din broke in. "Beloved Daoud, all this is not necessary. We can live in peace and love. We need but to work out a caring program. When did you lads suddenly . . ."

Saradon broke in to support his fellow Wahhabi. "Beloved Mullah and Brothers—we have the Koran. All know Allah's Word says, Amarilla has, by her action against Allah and against us, chosen for herself death. It is not our solution; it is the only solution. There is no other way to return peace and trust. If she lives, we will all die, one by one." There was a vocal rumble around the circle, then just heavy breathing.

Perhaps a minute, then Mullah-Din responded, quietly and with excellent composure, but in deadly earnest. "No, Beloved! No, no, no, please! After all the years we have been building agreement to practice, to live out the noble way, the caring, forgiving way. No, no, no! We discuss issues openly and at length, with everyone listening, everyone speaking his heart. Then we give a little, take a little and care a lot."

By the quality of velvet in his voice, you could tell that this old saint and mentor was disappointed, but not judgmental of his flock. The essence of patience, he would go to the well once more. I felt the old man reach across Amarilla and squeeze my leg to reassure me.

"I blame this sort of aggressive problem solving on my American friend, Seven. We didn't have any of these power caucuses before. This is the way they go off in special interest cells in America. But America is very big. The great nation is made up of thousands of tiny building stones. These building stones no longer trust and care for one another. Too bad. The birthplace of freedom and trust is washing away, declining. We, on the other hand, are very small, but strong and dependable. We can do these things together, out in the open, no surprises. We are one family."

There followed an uncomfortable silence for perhaps a minute. Then the Mullah-Din continued. "What you say—Daoud, Saradon—is legally correct, of course. But I wonder if Allah is not more a lover than a lawyer? And speaking of Allah, have we all prayed over this complex problem? And while we are on prayer, while I love you both as all of us love one another, and while I respect your spiritual connections, still I am curious why you two have gone directly to Allah in his ancient word without consulting me, your Imam. Most of the Word of Allah I have in my heart, memorized. But let's see, we have, what, three Angels of God trying a capital case without consulting the Allah's Man-in-Residence." He paused to sense the group.

Then—"And what did Allah say while you were holding this special court-martial? Is this death sentence you are announcing the words Allah whispered in your ears? Is this true, Sufi?"

Here the mullah paused. I heard and felt the mullah move from one to another of the heavies who were side by side. He paused several seconds with each man hugging or leaning or somehow expressing love and close personal brotherhood. Then he spoke again.

"Who prayed? Not you, Daoud, I'm sure. You don't believe you can talk to God and be heard. Right, Daoud? It has all been said. Right? Surely not Sufi. Sufi would tell Allah to call this 'shadow' away. Claim we have a virtual baby here. Not real. Right, Sufi? It must have been Saradon who prayed for guidance—or Countier. Countier, is Allah French? Did he say Mort? That's death in French, right? I didn't hear. Did you, Seven? Did you hear any God-voices calling through the hollow caverns? Mort! Mort! Mort-a-Amarilla!?"

The mullah halted here. He was being sarcastic, critical, and this was not his way. He was very uncomfortable, but I quickly reflected on how I, as leader, would handle these terrorists suddenly in our midst. I came up empty. I would simply support the mullah.

Mullah-Din's voice was almost a whisper and almost a weep now. "I think we better spend a little more time in prayer. Surely no one can object to prayer. Eh? Let's take a little time. Let's be a little patient, and let's try to put aside our personal conclusions. Let's see if we Beloveds can discern Allah's will in this." He paused again. Silence reigned again except for the sound of very heavy breathing and the soft sound of the running water very close at hand.

Then Mullah-Din again—"Beloved, we go back too far. We've been through too much together. And we have too far ahead to walk together on this journey. You know? To jump at a judgment. A judgment that could mean losing two of our Sacred Seven. Two, because it is not only Amarilla whom we choose to judge. It takes two to tango, Eh? What do you think, Beloveds? Patience?"

Daoud was sitting lotus-fashion on my left. I heard him crawl over to the waterway and drink. I tried to pick up Saradon's smell, but lost it in the movement. I thought, *Those two usually sit together at everything—same age and same general way of approaching things.* Now Sufi whispered something indiscernible to Saradon and immediately I pictured their relative locations in the circle. I wondered if there was any historic connection between the Sufis and the Wahhabis. I listened carefully to each man separately, thinking, *The Father of Amarilla's baby should be giving himself away by his breathing.*

Sufi was my first guess as father. More than a guess. Although we all were breathing heavily, but with the same degree of tension, Sufi kept nervously whispering brief sentences to either Saradon or Daoud or Mullah-Din. He was in trouble. Moreover, I selected him additionally on my sense that he was the quiet, meditative, poetic type that could ease his way into an intimate relationship anywhere. Further, he would not be shocked to discover a woman among us. He would simply, quietly and gently make the most of it.

I decided the mullah's rebuff of the Wahhabis' impetuous judgment would carry more weight if I put my small reputation behind it. I wanted everyone to know that I supported the mullah. Further, I wanted to establish that the Bible, which I sort of represented, and the Koran, which Mullah-Din represented, were strong allies on this sort of moral issue. Although I was a very liberal Christian in the strict sense of the term, I had read the Bible through in my American university days. Then at AUB we were in the process of studying and comparing the Koran with the Jewish Old Testament. From these two bits of heart-knowledge, I knew that regardless of specific passages in either, both spoke strongly and basically about love and forgiveness. And finally, I wanted to make a point about Dr. Amarilla's incredible caring service to the Seven.

So, I took a deep breath and after a reasonable pause, "Dr. Amarilla has been a kind and wise counselor through tons of depressing troubles for all of us. I don't know if you have ever needed healing. I was smashed and broken just flying in here, a year ago. For nothing in return, Amarilla set my bones and stabilized my concussion. Then again in the spring, pneumonia. We all . . ."

Countier broke in, "Excuse me, it's ten o'clock, and may I support Seven? True, Brothers, this is a complex agenda. Ya know, protecting a lady doctor and raising up a baby in a dark world. But for what have we been training through all this caring prison patience? Why are we so un-selfishly bonded? Is it all so we can now split in anger and hatred over our physician whom Allah made a woman? As I remember, when she was thrown in here with us eight years ago, she had been in uniform and working as a fighting medic and just kept on being a fighting medic. We accepted her in the dark. Next to the mullah, she has been the most useful of us. And I doubt she would have stayed alive among six virile men if she had revealed her sex anymore than if she had revealed her sex earlier in the militia. Allah spoke to her as a child encouraging her to become a healer. As an open Arab woman, she could not have been obedient to Him."

Countier reached over and held my wrist. "Let me fin-ish. Think about it. What would have happened if when she first joined us, she had sat up, cleaned up her bruises and joined the group with, 'Hello boys. This is your lucky day. I'm a woman?' "

Again, silence overlaid with heavy breathing and the ripple of running water. Mullah-Din reached across me and patted Countier's shoulder. I decided I didn't need to finish my speech. Countier had said it all.

Day 7—Group. The dust has settled some. Now, the Mullah opened with a "call-for help" prayer. Then he gave everyone a chance to say anything he or she had left on his or her heart. I think he wanted to see who had changed his mind, if any. He was disappointed. The Islamic puritans stood on the law—execute the apostate. The rest stood for a kinder, gentler solution—forgive both the man and the woman and protect the woman in our midst and raise the child as a loving, caring "Eight."

When a lull came, the "Old One" asked everyone to pull in close so that our knees could touch one another.

"Beloved, I am your spiritual leader. I have never pushed spiritual things upon you because I know we each see Allah differently. That is good because He lives with each of us in a unique and personal way. I have done my best to fulfill my duty by setting aside times for thought, prayer, meditation, even awareness. Now, Beloved, our world has suddenly changed. We must seek power or we all perish." There was the sound of deep breathing and of water running softly by.

After, I suppose, five minutes of this, Mullah-Din continued, "Here some of us are asking that we snuff the life of one or two. This is really reaching up and taking Allah's work upon ourselves. If we choose to do His work, we need His help. So I'm going to charge you each to spend some time thinking about and praying about this.

"On the one hand, I want you each seriously to consider in prayer the value of our doctor alive, serving us as she has been for what, eight years? A healer. A caregiver. I want you to remember the dreadful fortnight we were all twisted in pain and calling out to Allah? No, we were calling out to Amarillo!

"At the same time, I want you seriously to think of how, or whether, after forgiving, we can all live together in peace and harmony—all seven. And finally, I want you to think whether we can live in peace as five or six after sentencing one or two of us to die and then executing them. Can we do this and live with ourselves and with each other—some knowing that others are murderers? And if we feel right in executing one or two of our own, how do we do it? Push them off the Edge? Cut their throats with a sharp stone? Smash their skulls with a stone hammer? What? And are we physically strong enough to carry out a death penalty? Suppose, just for discussion, the guilty man were to be Daoud. Suppose his strong Jihadist Islamic Law position has been defensive—to cover his guilt. Which of you is going to execute Daoud? Not me, I'll tell you."

The mullah stopped to give us time to think. I could hear and feel Mullah-Din's right arm moving past my chest to reach Daoud. He wanted to caress him somehow to release any angst.

Thirty seconds of only breathing, then the mullah charged on, "Now, regardless of what you call your God, or what he looks like, or where he lives, I beseech you, Beloved, pray! Call upon him for wisdom and peace of heart. We shall meet again to discuss and decide in three days—not before. I will not meet with angry men planning hate. No Group will meet in this mosque until—Countier, what is this, Tuesday? Well, no matter. You will call us back into session seventy-two hours hence. During those three days, we will live our normal routine as though this issue had not arisen, except, no Group. Pray! Now, Go with Allah."

I felt his hand leave Daould's shoulder where it had rested during this little discourse. When I reached for him, he was gone. I felt beside me and found Amarilla's hand, squeezed it and whispered "Fear Not, Beloved, He will come."

Seventy-two hours passed. No Group. In fact, four days, five days, six days—still no Group. It must have been about noon on Day six. I sat down beside Mullah-Din. He took it as a question. "Not yet, Seven Beloved. We are not ready yet. Allah will call us when."

Twelve

Day 8—Our caring prison family had clearly separated into two segments. Toward six in the evening, when the familiar sound came, the Islamic puritans, the Wahhabis along with the counter, Countier, went to eat first. I had been sitting beside Mullah. When we heard Countier leave, talking earnestly with Daoud, Mullah nudged me with his elbow. I turned to him and taking his wrist, whispered, "No, no—fear not. We can feel very warm and confident about Countier. He is not only supporting our cause. He is bolder than either of us. He is our active missionary."

The Mullah was in deep prayer all night long at the Edge. I would go periodically and just sit beside him—to be there for him, but he didn't seem to notice. I had saved him some food. I was on cleanup. I took it to him on a flat stone tray. I don't know what time. I found him on his prayer rug flat on his face pointed to the southwest crying out to Allah like a broken-hearted child. I put my hand on his back and patted him like you would a little child. I didn't know what else to do. He sat up then. His legs hung over the Edge. He didn't seem to care that he was toying with horror in the dark.

"Has she eaten something?" His first thought was of Dr. Amarilla. I set the food down beside him. "I have not seen her. The men went to eat when it came down. I don't know about her." I was really at a loss as to how to handle the now private aspects of this problem. It had occurred so suddenly, and had exploded in such an unexpected way. I asked, "Should I take her something?"

The Imam leaned back against my knees. "Take this to her, Seven Beloved. I'm not hungry." I felt the stone plate graze my leg as the mullah handed it up.

Although I felt it was the middle of the night, we had all pretty much lost track of time. Countier, as sort of pivotal man in our troubles, was becoming intermittent in his duties as "Town Crier." Anyway, as I headed down the stone passageway from the Edge toward where four of us still called home, I could hear loud talking from the dining area. Catching a word here and there, I knew the Amarilla judgment was under debate. I turned in to Amarilla's place. She was lying flat on her stomach facing south. That told me she was facing Mecca and thus in painful prayer. I laid the food down beside her, patted her gently on the back and just stood there. I didn't know what to do. I didn't know where to go. I wasn't sleepy and my mind was stuck. I could not reason a solution to our fix that had any chance of success. Birth and raise a child here in the dark? Wheeeooo!

After standing there in hopeless quandary for maybe ten minutes, it occurred to me that my only good would be in the discussion with Countier and the three Wahhabis. If I were really to be on the side of right, I needed to understand how the opposition had got where they had gotten. As I turned to go, I realized I was very thirsty, so I knelt down, drank, then crawled on toward the voices. I touched a foot. I recognized Countier's. I needed to make a verbal join, so I waited until Daoud finished rephrasing his monologue on honor among men. Then I spoke: "Daoud, Beloved, how did this *terrorist* idea of a trial get started, anyway?" I immediately wanted to unsay the word *terrorist* and substitute the word, *imperious,* but realized even that was an emotionally loaded term. I couldn't come up with any neutral Arabic. Anyhow it was too late.

Daoud responded quietly, without anger or resentment. "Tell me, Major Seven, is everything traditional Moslem, terrorist to you Americans? I'm sorry, we Arabs see this as a matter of reality and honor among men. This is subject of long tradition among Arabs. Actually, all Semites—older than Mohammed—back to Abraham. But you are not Semitic. You could not possibly understand."

Daoud grunted his final words here as he got up. He stepped over Sufi, and pushed gently between Countier and me. I had been watching the guy's breathing for indicators of tension. Here I noticed that Daoud was very relaxed. I remember thinking, *This man is not at all angry with me.* He put his hand against my chest to find me. Then he grasped my shoulder like a good friend. "Seven Beloved, we hope, being an American man, you will try to empathize, try to feel as we Arab men do, try to visualize how impossible it would be to expect long-term peace, trust, brotherly love among six virile men with one known woman, eh? Ha, ha, ha. When we could not even trust ourselves when only one knew there was a woman here."

Saradon cut in. "For a woman to hide her central truth—live a lie and serve only one of six male comrades until carelessness caught her, we have a verdict directed by Allah. Written in his word." Saradon paused for support, then continued. "We hope, Brother Seven. But if you can't, perhaps you will stay out of a local cultural issue. You know what I mean?"

Daoud returned, "Yes, Seven, we love and respect you. Still, this is a family thing. We would not interfere if we were in America and you were lynching a black or locking down a Mexican, a Japanese or an Arab."

Day 9—There was a long series of heavy mountain tremors interrupted by stretches of tense quiet. The dust was choking. Everyone lay close to the water, wearing a wet cloth mask. Daoud complained that he needed to remove his tattered shirt to wet it, breathe through it. Amarilla was up and about now, performing her usual role, medic and encourager. She lay a patch of bandage on Daoud's head and patted his cheek as he lay choking beside the waterway. He wet it and breathed again.

The isolated group discussions continued during the quiet breaks. I could not figure out Mullah-Din. He would not enter into any of the angry fights except in a whisper with me, away from the others. He acknowledged that he would make the final judgment, but he refused to influence the discourse. He had made his position known. Ask Allah, then follow His direction, I got the clear feeling that he trusted Allah would rule from within hearts, and this role as Allah's man on the site was to exercise patience and put no spin on the process.

Countier was recovering and sounding most hours now. The day dragged painfully. In mid-afternoon, Mullah found me reasoning with Sufi. He touched my shoulder, dragging his fingers toward him, which signed *Come*. I followed him to his place.

"We need to journal this event, Seven. And we need to do the story objectively, expressing the problem as a news item. No bias. Let's go out and talk it through and then chisel it in." We did. It took about four hours as we talked then cut—then talked some more, then cut some more.

I was unable, nor was Mullah, to recall the Koran verse that commanded the believers to capital action, so I crawled along the passageway to Daoud's new place where a chat was underway. Daoud immediately cited Suras XXVII. I returned and Mullah-Din cut in. We took Daoud's word for it.

Toward evening, I listened from a distance as Countier encouraged Dr. Amarilla. It was after dinner. Amarilla had not eaten, but it was her turn to clean up. She was on duty scraping. Countier joined her, helping and trying to keep her spirits up. I made it three. We were centering our encouragement on the mathematics of three-to-three. With this equation, no judgment could be rendered. Time, we felt, would heal over the jihadists, caring reason would then surely return. Although we never got together and voiced it, I'm sure the three friends of the doctor felt that God would prevail, and we would find a way to birth and raise a child. The near impossibility of the thing made the idea addictive. We three were constantly surfacing some new notion—some fascinating new aspect of "Child Raising in Mazjid-Ghazu."

Day 10—My habit was to awaken just a few minutes before Countier called out "Seven!" He usually did not call out six in order not to awaken the sleepers, which was most of us, but to make a kind of reveille out of seven. The routine called for exercises and joyful songs at roughly seven-thirty. Of course, no one really blew a bugle or called *Assembly* to start the event, and recently the joyful songs had been replaced by Islamic chants from the Hijrah Days and stories of the Muhajirun.

Probably an hour before seven, Countier and Daoud shook my blanket. "Have you seen Amarilla? Sufi is sick again with the runs."—a fairly often occurrence recently. Amarilla normally administered some chalky stuff she made by grinding a certain clay-like rock and adding water. It worked like a charm. As soon as I heard the question, I was violently struck by a thousand-volt, dark, dark, premonition! I jumped up from my blanket and sprang over to Mullah. "The Doctor is missing!"

Mullah also took on an immediate emergency mode. He grabbed a handful of my shirt front. "Go to the entrance and search back. I go to Edge." He was gone!

I knew where a small pile of the clay-dust was in Amarillo's place. In feeling around, I noticed by feel that the doctor's place was very normal. I found the chalk-pile undisturbed and in a skin, mixed some into a drinkable milk. I took it in to Sufi who was in pain from gas, but drank the medicine and lay back down moaning softly. I gave him a pep talk but did not mention the absence of Amarilla. Countier joined me to search the west end of the tunnel. He counted out loud seven o'clock just as we left the barracks area. The others were surfacing from the night.

Though rarely visited by anyone until the recent team effort and only attempted to climb twice to my knowledge—both futilely—the west end was a steep, almost vertical concave rise directly from the floor. I started my search there. Countier came beside me double-checking my search. Being totally dark, we felt with our hands and whispered out her name. Then I climbed up on the narrow ledge opposite the dining area and felt as high as I could feel. I noticed there was some caked food splatter that over the years had hardened into cement. I looked far, far up, but could not see any light at all emerging from the entry hole. I called out her name, "Amarilla! Amarilla!" No response. I listened in deadly stillness. Nothing.

Then I heard the hollow, far-off call, "Am . . . ar . . . illa!" as the mullah called her name down the hallway from near the Edge. I now felt along the wall, first on the dry side, then along the waterway. I walked back and forth across the passageway, with Countier following. We could both make a very thorough, feeling search. I kept softly calling her name as I progressed. Periodically we could hear Mullah-Din doing the same. To be sure, we rechecked the dining area. Then we worked our way toward the sleeping area or barracks as I humorously called our old place. The Wahhabis now slept together near the dining area.

I met the mullah, and we touched hands at Amarilla's place in our normal sleeping row. It was very nearly the exact center of the long pit-prison hallway. The mullah spoke first, "She has gone over." He glanced toward the Edge. His voice tailed off signaling his resignation. Mullah-Din cleared his throat and called everyone to his place.

We all gathered in a tight circle on our knees. "Brethern, Beloved Amarilla has sacrificed herself for our peace. She has stepped off the Edge into eternity."

I cannot describe the deep sorrow and brokenness in Mullah-Din's voice. Fighting tears, he spoke so softly one could barely hear him. His announcement was followed by absolute stillness for a very long time. No one moved. I could not hear the deep, heavy breathing so apparent before. Now only the soft ripple of passing water along the wall. I suspect we were all in shock, regardless of which side of the issue we held.

Finally, Mullah reached out and touched each of us. And I need to note here, Mullah-Din spoke and touched and dealt with each of us with the same total, loving care as before the Amarilla problem had surfaced. He was absolutely blameless. He patted, squeezed, rubbed and scratched each of us the same—Wahhabi, Sufi, Yankee, Afghan, whatever. Finally, he spoke, now clearly and without emotion.

"It is still early, and I know that many of you have been in prayer about our Beloved Am . . .a . . ." At her name, Mullah lost it. He could not say the name. He crumpled. I reached across and put my arm around his shoulder. I found another arm coming from the other way. It was Daoud's.

After perhaps a minute, Mullah continued. "I am going to declare this day Amarilla's final day of prayer. I suggest you all join me in thanking Allah for her. She was an angel of healing and care. Only God knows what pain she suffered from her first day with us. She hid her sex because she didn't know how else to survive, provide medical care and allow us to live in peace. What would you do if you suddenly dropped into a pitch-black cave full of only women?" The circle buzzed with scrambled thoughts and readjusting attitudes. Mullah-Din continued, "Some of us questioned her choice. It was not a choice, Beloved. The only choice was to serve Allah here or go. She has done both. No one is to blame. Let's take this day to pray. Rejoice that we had her for a time, then put it behind us and go on."

Saradon and Daoud, thinking me the logical substitute medic, pulled me over to where Sufi was still down. Sufi had heard everything. He took my wrist in a firm grip. "Seven, thank you for the drink. Nothing seems to work. I think Allah will take us all for what we have done. I know you believe we drove Amarilla off . . ."

I covered his mouth with my palm. "I believe Allah rules with huge forgiveness in these trials. He has simply taken her out of our jurisdiction—Shalom."

A major earthquake, called a Karabaskat in the Azerbaijan, comes suddenly—BAAAMMM! The mountain gypsies say an angry god strikes the earth with his hammer and splits it open. There follows a five-second gap, then—BAAAMMM! The whole segment of the earth suddenly drops again. Three times spaced, I counted them. BAAAMMM!—BAAAMMM!—BAAAMMM!

In the Zagros, Karabaskat speaks with the authority of a major Tsunami in the Orient! A Karabaskat is a geological phenomenon of the same order as a major typhoon at sea that flips ships end-over-end and flattens islands—the same order as a tornado that pushes a wave of water ashore and destroys a city. A Karabaskat earthquake has the same sort of terrible, destruction power of a major thousand-acre Western forest fire that jumps canyons and turns mountain ranges to ashes.

Technically, here is the way a Karabaskat happens—the desert plate of the earth's surface, which millennia past pushed up onto and barely caught on the Asian Continent Shelf, spills. That is, the massive desert plate of the earth's surface breaks loose and drops suddenly a hundred vertical feet. Then it holds for a few seconds, then drops another hundred feet. Then it holds another few seconds, drops again and finally holds fast for a few more hundred years until it works loose again.

Karabaskat Eighteen (Mullah-Din told us these destroyers are numbered from Mohammed's death) came to us imprisoned in the *Mazjid-Ghazu* on my three hundred and seventieth prison-day. It came seventy-four days after Amarilla's suicide, and it came at night, so the Sacred Six were all asleep. The mountain suddenly cracked with an ear-slitting BAAAMMM! and fell one hundred feet. No one among us mistakenly took it for one of our daily normal earthquakes.

It opened with the power of God—KER-BAAAMMM! I jumped to my feet, stood for five seconds as the mountain shuddered up and down and laterally—then, KER-BAAAMMM! I was down flat. I clutched the stone floor, I guess to hold it still, or perhaps just to hang on. I knew immediately and instinctively the mountain was coming down. I thought, *Pray man! We'll be buried alive for sure.* Then again, KER-BAAAMMM! I felt a human body push past me.

The mullah shouted, "To the dining place!" He had Sufi and Daoud in tow. Saradon was now down with diarrhea. The air was dry powder. It caught in my throat as I tried to shout something. Nothing came out. I began to cough. I snatched my knapsack and immediately ran—BAMB!—into the opposite wall of rock. It had moved. It was coming down now. That wall normally rose vertically from the watercourse. Not now. The vertical wall slanted about forty-five degrees, and it was moving steadily down, down. Stones that sounded like army tanks rumbled and bounded down into the open vault of our passageway and bounced and slid down into the bottomless chasm, our Edge.

I ducked low, pushed off and KERBOOM! An airborne granite basketball hit me like a cannon ball and smashed my left shoulder. I went down again. I could not find yelling for help appropriate, so I rolled to my feet, grabbed my wounded shoulder with my free hand, and scuttled west toward the dining place and the sound of the others' shouts. Countier, behind me, yelled something inarticulate and pushed me along. We both had to crouch down to stay under the angled wall. We both coughed constantly because the air was thick with dust.

One of the violent twists had opened a fissure across our walkway. The water normally running at the base of the south wall was now falling into the fissure. Luckily, I heard this falls and thus avoided following it several thousand feet to hell below. I measured across, then jumped and slid in the muddy dust. Down again, guarding my left side. Countier jumped, fell, hit my wounded shoulder. I screamed, cussed, grabbed my arm and pushed on.

I'm not in any way describing the terror, the mortal fear that ruled here. I had won two war medals for valor in combat, but here in this dark quake, I was scared to death. I'm sure all of us were on pure survival instinct—barely short of panic. Countier and I found the fleet four huddled together at the west end. Why the west end? Simply because there at the west end was, although it was 100 feet straight up, the only opening we knew of—thus, our only hope out.

As we joined, the mullah chanted a prayer. The other three clutched one another and howled like terror-crazed animals. I physically ran into the group in mid-passage. Daoud felt my push and responded, "Pray to Allah, Yank! Pray!"

Mullah-Din, his mouth in my ear, a horror-tone in his voice, shouted a whisper. "You got Countier and Saradon?"

I flailed behind me with my good arm. Countier was there somewhere. Saradon was still in bed, sick. I tried to sound cool, and lied, "Yes, Sir."

At that moment—perhaps a minute after the third and final shock—the most astonishing miracle occurred. The dusty air of our vault was suddenly filled with a dim golden glow. It seemed to come from above but was everywhere. We all looked up toward from where the garbage-food fell—toward the opening by which we all had entered. In slow motion, as we watched, a tiny gold light came tumbling down through the dust. It bounced off a high stone ledge, flared, died, burned again and tumbled on down and came to rest on our flat granite floor nearby.

It flickered once, died out, then flickered to life! We six men stood frozen—staring. There on the stone floor of the prison lay a candle-stub perhaps an inch in diameter, two inches tall, brownish wax, tiny wick, golden flame.

As you can probably guess, none of us could keep our eyes from the tiny light. Suddenly, just beyond the flickering point of light, I saw two shining eye-slits in a mass of curly black beard. And I heard Mullah-Din's awe-filled voice whisper-shout, "Hal-le-lu-ia! He has come!" A brisk after-shake answered him.

Though the shaking died out, periodically huge hunks of stone, accompanied by brief rivers of gravel, continued to plunge down. The loudest of the violence seemed to come from the direction of the Edge. The mullah knelt down beside the candle, and straightened it. "Close your eyes, Beloved. Just peak. Don't stare at the light! And don't get too close! It's hot."

Now we could all see the pit was dense with heavy airdust painted gold by the tiny candle's flame. There was a shuffle of bodies to get close. In a very few moments, all circled perhaps a yard back from the flame. I could see high and low eye-slits shining out of bearded faces—faces no one knew. Some stood, some were on our knees, one on his belly, hypnotically staring through tiny eye-slits at the now steady half-inch gold flame. It was a strange mystic scene.

The mullah spoke again. "Beloved! I said, 'Don't stare at the light!' Daoud, go quickly! Fetch your candle." One pair of eyes, above a reddish-brown bearded face, withdrew from the circle.

I now knew the mullah and Daoud! Who were these other squinters? I took the initiative. "I'm Seven, Beloved." I waved both hands beside my head. Oddly, in the midst of loud, storm-like thunder, thick choking dust and hellish, crushing danger, howling laughter broke out as we once again held each other, one by one and once again felt each other's bearded faces with our hands while repeating each name—Mullah-Din, Daoud, then Major.

We all huddled around the tiny candlelight staring at the tiny golden blaze, rubbing our eyes and complaining while hugging one another at the miracle of light and repeating each name just as we had done long ago in the pitch dark. This strange ceremony was accompanied by unbelievable joy, and it seemed to occupy our total attention while the world was literally coming down around us.

With this inch of brownish wax came a whole new world of hope. Mullah-Din, our leader, who should have been pressing us on to some critical survival activity, instead stood in the laughing, hugging circle shouting over and over again, "Halleluja! He is here! Halleluja! He is here! Halleluja! He is here!"

Daoud's candle, which he lit from the miracle-candle and held up between his thumb and index finger, provided a slightly larger flame. Now, Mullah-Din quickly took charge. "We must be extremely careful of the lights. We are not used to light. We must stay together. This violent shake is called a *Karabaskat.*" He gave the r a long roll. "That means a major shock. A quake of huge magnitude. None has come here before." He pointed, "Look! Even by candlelight, you can see." He held up Daoud's arm so the candlelight showed down our now devastated pathway. "This end is closing down. Our sleeping area will go down next. We must work quickly to the Edge and pray.

"Trust me, Beloved, He has come, and He will open this mountain, wide!" The old man carefully scooped up the brown wudge of wax with its tiny precious flicker. He turned and moved east along the wall, his arms extended, his palms open against the stone wall.

"Daoud, hold your candle high." Mullah beckoned us. "See! The passage wall above the waterway is buckling. Climb over and around." We crowded after him in a bunch, hunched over to accommodate the lowered ceiling, crawling at times.

The fissure I had jumped earlier in the dark, now in the shadowy light, showed as a twenty-four inch black seam diagonally across the floor. Our spring water poured down it in a shouting waterfall. All six of us hunched cautiously along, arms wide, hands on the wall or crawled over piles of stone and gravel under the sharply angled, crumbling overhead. All were talking and making suggestions—but no one was listening.

Beside our sleeping place, we found the final convulsion had closed the passageway down. It was now only a ragged crawl-space. We paused here a moment to collect things. Each man, by dim candlelight, quickly sorted through, then picked an item or two from his ageless, precious collection. Saradon, sitting among his belongings, had missed the west end drama, but now appeared barely able to crawl.

Mullah-Din asked me about the arm I was holding in pain. While Mullah supervised, Saradon and Countier worked to set my shoulder. Although I screamed in pain as they pulled and twisted, I felt it snap into place. Immediately, I noticed some freedom of movement of my left arm. We were stopped just below our barracks area by three gigantic boulders fallen from somewhere above and wedged in together. There was an eighteen-inch space below. I volunteered to go under first. The offer was not heroic. I was really in deep fear that my handicap might force me to drop out of the group. I scrunched flat, rolled slightly and Eureka! I made it under. As soon as I slipped through, I was in pitch darkness except, of course, for the dim, dusty-gold air and a dim gold patch painted on the floor by the candlelight behind me.

Under normal conditions, I knew the passageway in the dark like the back of my hand, but now, in this new half-light my *think-see* sense was totally destroyed. I was badly disoriented. I quickly understood the urge to grab the wall. I stood up with arms wide and hands flat on the stone. Every few minutes came a brief after-crash—a settling—with the sound of gravel rumbling down. Countier came under next. I leaned down and called to Mullah-Din. "Please send a light. Everything has changed."

"You take the larger light," I heard the mullah tell Daoud. Immediately, a candle appeared under, then Daoud's head and arms. I took the light. Daoud scrunched under on his belly. I noticed now he was heavier or thicker than I had thought him. He was built like a line-backer. He took the candle back. We could hear the others grunting under. Daoud and I crawled on down the passageway.

I noticed as we came abreast our journal wall on the left, the cuneiform code lettering that Mullah had developed shadowed clearly. I snatched up the flint stylus (always placed exactly ready at the base of the wall, now just beyond the dry, sandy creek-bed) and, while the others moved along by, I incised the date and a brief note describing the cataclysm. I ended our wall journal with a phrase of hope. "He has come and we are set free." My thought was, *We're outa here, but I have no idea how.* Strangely, though the mountain was clearly coming down on us, dying under there was not my focus. Mentally, I simply would not *go there.* I signed the entry with both our signs and put the flint dutifully in its place.

I crawled along quickly following the dim glow beyond and caught up with the huddle clustered at the very Edge. The dim candlelight through the dust showed the awesome, terrifying abyss. The half-light showed the far side—the wall across the chasm—coming slowly down as we watched. The roof or ceiling, too high for our light to reach, was falling, then holding, then falling, then holding. Half-ton hunks of granite and accompanying gravel rumbling down into the sharp, deep precipice. We could hear the splashings far, far below, but no one looked down.

I had just rejoined the clutch when I heard Daoud yelp a profanity. Then I saw. His tiny light went flying through space—out, out, out and then down, down, down into the dark. There was a momentary violent tussle as his neighbors shouted and tried to catch the light. Then, still shouting, Countier and I grabbed and caught the reaching, teetering, falling Daoud. The moment was monumental. For the first time, as the candlelight fell, we could all see down into the depths of the awful Edge.

Daoud was hurt! He had apparently been struck hard in the face by something flying as he held his candle aloft. Now he went down hard on the stone floor. There was a scramble to keep him from rolling over the edge. I joined, tugging violently. Then I realized his chador or shirt was very rotten. It tore away. Mullah and Countier finally pulled and twisted him back onto the stone floor. I carefully felt his head while someone—Countier, I believe—was checking his lowers. The single dim candle in Mullah's hand allowed me to see the scarlet flow, plus I could feel the sticky fluid on my hands. A major gash above his left eye cut three inches straight back into his hair.

"I've got it! Mullah, get the flint!" I spoke quietly but earnestly. We needed our journal stylus to stop the bleeding. We were at a signal disadvantage to pressure-stop bleeding without any spare fabric to wad or fold. "Check his pulse," I whispered. Mullah was down on his knees straightening Daoud's body. He had fallen in an awkward heap. Louder now, I took charge, "Tear my T-shirt off, Countier. Just rip it down the back." The pain of my shoulder made it impossible for me to tear it myself.

"He's very strong—just knocked out." Mullah-Din spoke loud so everyone including Saradon, who was lagging behind, could hear. Then he addressed the latter specifically, "Saradon, Beloved, you must stay with us. Take up your bed and walk!" He paraphrased Jesus at the Pool of Bethesda. "We can't leave you here to die. He is here, and He will open this mountain! We must be ready to escape!"

Countier and I bound Daoud's head. I felt in my knapsack and from my survival kit pulled a vial of pain pills I had been using to pull Amarilla through her tough times. Two pills remained. I put one in Daoud's mouth and said, "Swallow." He did. I took the other one myself.

It's a strange characteristic of human nature—while expecting to die shortly, one keeps on struggling to overcome the adversity, and at the same time, plan for the future. I sat there in the dim light, having fully faced the reality of life expectance a matter of minutes; and yet I kept note of how Mullah-Din's encouraging aphorism was a strong positive input to our team's maintaining unity and buoyancy in the clear face of death. I made a note to remember this paradigm when I might be the team leader similarly facing death.

Contrarily, considering the reality of the saying, "Fear Not, He has come" and particularly its personification in the *Coming-of-the-Light,* this was a tad too mystical for my military mind and heart. My West Point background, coupled with the high action of two wars, led me to note that good leadership must keep up a run of encouraging confidence-building, assured victory sayings. I gave the mullah full leadership marks, but as for anyone's actually coming—don't hold your breath.

At this point I was exhausted. I dropped my legs over the Edge to relieve my shoulder pain. Immediately I felt Mullah drop beside me. Through the dim flicker, I watched him reach over to comfort Saradon who was lying on the cool stone floor of the Edge nearby. Suddenly, he leaned hard against me. I expected him to admonish me to keep praying. He did not. Instead, "Did you hear that?" Mullah-Din whispered. He was holding the candlelight high. Although very tiring for him, it gave courage and hope to the group. I sucked in a ton of air as the light came close above. I was even closer now than earlier. The sheer awfulness of the Edge was apparent in the shadowy candlelight. No one else was eager to gaze over and down. It was obvious we were all in a last resort, survival mode, hanging in a close huddle, totally terrified, barely holding on to a thread of hope. All stuck with the same question: So, here we are at the Edge. What do we do now? Along that wall opposite, the peak above and the whole mountain, we are going down that chasm.

When I didn't respond, once again my friend leaned hard against me with the intense whisper into my ear, "Did you hear that?" There was clamor and chaos—stones falling and gravel rumbling down on all sides like the destruction of the world in the last days, and this guy was asking if I heard something.

My immediate thought, *Mullah, my beloved buddy, time is too short! Let's don't waste it playing games. In a matter of minutes, that crumbling ceiling is taking us all to the bottom of this abyss; and like Callisthenes' bones, we will belong to the ages.* Out loud, "Shouldn't you be conducting some Islamic Last Rites of some sort?"

Mullah-Din apparently didn't hear my question, so I pulled his head over and spoke close to his ear. "No, Sir, I hear noth . . ." I cut off my own response. I now, in fact, heard—though very, very faintly—against the crashing, rumbling background, a definite faraway cry-sound trailing off into the ambient din.

"There! Hear that?" Mullah grabbed my arm above the elbow, as he often did when he wanted my individual attention.

I flinched, "Ow! Not there! Mullah, for God Sake!"

Again, beyond the dimmest distance of our candle's mini-beam—in fact, from the deep, velvet blackness, down to the right along the extended Edge where none of us had ever explored—the cry came again! This time it seemed closer—or at least, clearer—helped by a brief pause in the ambient tumult. Now Countier joined us with a sort of frantic shout, "Hey, hear that? Sounds like a howl. An animal is dying—a wolf!" Countier had exceptional senses. I watched him, hand cupped to his ear, leaning down toward the south. There the Edge chasm had always felt too black, too steep, too dangerous, too terrifying to explore. Now, we all sat or stood in a clutch, frozen on the stone ledge. But at Coutier's shout, everyone turned.

Now again. It sounded much closer now, an intentionally elongated call, sort of a "Yoooo, Hoooo." It echoed and reechoed from far down the long cavern. Simultaneously, Mullah and I answered with the same kind of call, "YOOOO, HOOOO!" Then the five of us who were up, bellowed together, "YOOOO, HOOOO!" We were so loud we drew sand and gravel from the roof. Now Saradon, who seemed to be only barely alive and was apparently hearing the call for the first time, sat up against the nearby back wall and whisper-shouted, "Allah, Be Praised! He is coming—in person!"

The group was now leaning over one another toward the south darkness in a tight clutch, totally focused. The Edge was much more dangerous a killer now because we had a dim light which gave the false impression we could see. And when taken together with the overriding reality that death was very near, we were caught in a uniquely dangerous, easy-to-panic, group-psychology."

The call or sound had suddenly brought the danger very local. We were all sitting or kneeling, with one standing, on the very edge of the precipice. The dim light, which the mullah still held high overhead, was worse than none. It made us think we could see in the flickering weird shadows. And now came the heart-stopping addition of an alien voice—a person or animal coming toward us. You can imagine the race of thoughts running through our minds. The group was alternately dead silent, in frozen tension—then all shouting at once! Mainly hopeful suggestions concerning miracle-rescue or wounded-animal theories, only to fall deathly silent again, trying to bear against the pulsing uproar. The mullah, leaning against me toward the sound, whisper-prayed, "Thank you, Allah! You have come."

Now the call came clear "Mu—llah—Deen!" A pause, then, "YOOO, HOOO!" A pause, then again, "Mu—llah—Deen!" About three of us shouted at once, "He's calling you! He's calling you, Mullah!"

Again and not far now, the call was coming from down and along the Edge where the chasm, now dimly lit a few yards, extended as a tunnel off to our right. We had never explored, nor even looked down there, as it was all black, deadly-dangerous chasm.

"Mu—llah—Dee . . ." The mullah cut off the call with a shout, "That's Amarilla! That's our doctor! I would know that voice anywhere! Praise Allah—the Only High God! Praise Allah, the Compassionate One! Amarilla! Amarilla!" Two of us were physically holding the mullah by his chador to keep him from falling into the abyss.

The next voice was clearly Amarilla's. "Look—over—the—edge. Look—down—here! Here to the right, Beloved! It's me—It's your doctor—It's Amarilla."

Mullah held his light high. We all leaned out looking down along the cliff edge, clutching one another to keep from falling in.

I saw it first. Down the cliff wall, perhaps ten feet down and a hundred feet away into the tunnel to our right, was another light! This one was huge! A burning torch and as we watched, it approached slowly along the face of the cliff.

Mullah-Din called, "We see you, Amarilla! But, you are down the cliff—how . . . ?"

"There is a ledge! Wait, Beloveds! Don't try to come. I will show you."

Closer and closer the flare crept. We huddled now in tense silence. The mountain kept coughing and grumbling. Huge chunks of granite and tons of gravel kept crashing and rumbling and sliding down. Finally Amarilla stood directly below our shadowy huddle on the Edge.

Mullah handed me his candle. I held it high. We all held the mullah somewhere—head, shoulder, chador. He reached down, stretched and grunted. "I can only touch your fingers, Amarilla!"

She responded in surprise, "You have a light? Where did you . . . ?"

She cut off, cautioning us, "Mullah—all, listen. Don't look at my torch. It will blind you. This is death-dangerous! We will all escape. But we must be very careful. We don't need to lose one, after all this."

Mullah asked, "What holds you there?"

Amarilla said, "There is a meter-wide ledge of stone—apparently a paleolithic extruded strata. It goes all the way around the corner and out a cave-mouth onto the hillside."

Countier, Daoud and I spoke as one: "How shall we . . . ?"

Amarilla cut in: "I think one at a time. We must help one another down. I will catch the first. Then each man down must catch the next. When down, crawl along the ledge out just as I came in."

Mullah spoke to us gathered on the Edge. "Beloved, we must take out the wounded first." Then to Amarilla: "We have three sick and wounded, doctor. Can we let them down first?"

There was a long pause. I suppose half-a-minute, then Amarilla said, "No, that will be too slow. The mountain may not wait for us to be noble. How sick? How wounded?"

Daoud spoke up immediately, "I'm okay now. Just a headache. Count me whole."

I came in then. "I would like to go last. My shoulder hurts, but I can crawl."

Amarilla closed out the talk. "We must get out the healthy first, and we must do it now." The doctor sounded like a doctor giving sensible medical emergency instructions. No one argued.

Mullah took charge above, like a military captain. "Countier first, then Daoud, then you, Sufi, then me." He punched my good arm. "Seven, you and Saradon will come last. Daoud, listen—you and I will first lower Countier, Amarilla!" He called down. "You will catch the first one and lead us out. Everyone up here will help lower each next man. When you reach the ledge, turn and catch the next one before you crawl away. Got it?"

Amarilla called from down below: "Good! Listen to me, boys! You must sit on the Edge up there, roll to your belly, slide slowly down here. As the mullah says, I will catch Countier. Notice, it's only about two meters." Now she repeated the mullah's instructions, "When you reach the ledge, each must catch and steady the next one. I have secured my torch here in a cleft in the wall, so there will be some light. As soon as you help the next down, you crouch and crawl away. See there—"she pointed. "Along the ledge to the right. It'll get dark. Just keep crawling. We'll escape just as I did on my first trip out. If I can do it pregnant, any man can do it. Ha, ha, ha. Now, let's go."

Countier asked, "Doctor, can't we walk?"

Amarilla answered, "No. The mountain is shaking, the ledge is narrow, it's pitch dark and it's not that far. Crawl."

Countier sat, rolled, slid away and was gone. There were sounds including a ruffle of laughter below. Then "Next!" Daoud gripped my hand meaningfully, sat, rolled to his belly, slid out of sight. Then, Sufi, whimpering with terror, sat, rolled, slid a little and began to weep, "It's too far!" Daoud spoke to him from below, and Sufi disappeared. I turned and the mullah was already over the side. He had handed his candle to Saradon as he slid over. I noticed as Saradon passed the candle to me, it was almost gone. Saradon was lying down already, so I rolled him with my foot. He bent and disappeared.

I was the last to leave. I glanced over the side and saw Amarilla's torch flooding the landing area in dusty gold. Down to the right separated by ten yards on what appeared to be a clear, flat ledge, two butts were visible crawling away from the shadowy flicker. On the ledge below stood Saradon looking up at me. I yelled, "Go, man, go!" then I kissed the tiny wad of burning wax and tossed it into eternity.

In a moment I found I was too cavalier in sending Saradon on his way. I crouched, rolled and slid over. But, my feet did not touch anything. This was no problem for those ahead as someone would hold their legs and steady the short drop. With no one there, I felt a moment of panic. How far? Though there was flare light, I had no idea how far I would fall. Worse, any stagger or step-back to gain balance meant disaster. At that moment the mountain shook a final good one.

I yelled, "Saradon, Wait! Help!" By the grace of God, he had only crawled about six feet. Upon hearing my plea, he backed up along the ledge and brushed my dangling feet with his back. I called, "Hold still, just hold still." I stepped down onto his flat back then onto the ledge. "Thanks, Brother. Now go." Saradon shuffled away.

I decided to leave the torch burning. It gave all us crawlers some dim illumination. I could just see Saradon up ahead crawling, and I could hear him join those ahead. They were all chanting *Ghanna Ibada,* an Islamic Thank God spiritual I had learned the words on our muhelah on the Tigris.

The original Sacred Seven were on their way to freedom. As Mullah-Din had always promised, He Had Come—only, He was a She.

The ledge wound around a sweeping curve perhaps two hundred yards. Parts of the "paleolithic extrusion," as Amarilla had termed it, were scary narrow. Parts were comfortably wide, much was strewn with gravel from the quake. Some was banked with sand. All the way along I could hear, far below, a rushing cascade of mighty water plunging on down from somewhere—to somewhere.

Where the chasm became wall, the ledge followed a crack through the mountain. I was expecting daylight ahead and thought about our eyes. But when we finally slipped through a narrow opening hidden by a cluster of low mountain chaparral and stood up in freedom . . . Wow!

Thirteen

We found ourselves on a grassy hillside under a moonless sky, a million stars in the dead of night. Each man, as he came out, stood up whispering, through heavy puffs of breathing, a prayer of thanks to Allah. And each of us—Amarilla too—joined, one by one, into a hug-circle. Arms around shoulders. All were crying.

When I came out last, the circle was chanting together this Love Allah song, "Ghanna Ibada." Mullah-Din prayed thanks for us all, aloud. Then Daoud held up his hand and started to speak.

Amarilla cut in to explain her disappearance. "No, No, Daoud, Beloved. I know you are going to say you are sorry for judging me. Let me tell you—in the name of Allah, I forgive you, all of you. Listen, I came awake that night, remember? The Angel Gabriel who, long ago sat by Mohammed, sat by me in there, near my blanket.

"He say nothing, but beckon me. I follow. I thought, *He knows I will cause all these men to die, one by one.* Angel led me to the Edge—sat, roll, slide down. I follow. Angel hands guard my belly, protect my baby. On ledge, he point—whisper, 'Go!' He vanish. I crawl out."

Her long arm and index finger pointed north down the mile slope to where several dim campfires showed the village of Sar Dasht. "My baby, Gabriel and I wait with friends in village until mountain open. You are free. Good-bye, Beloved."

The night swallowed her. Now the hugging ring of the Sacred Seven sprang apart. A dash, wild and free, down the grassy slope.

Somewhere a sentinel yelled, "Waqafa!" A rocket swooshed! High up, a white flare popped! I ducked low and dashed east among the chaparral. Up ahead, I caught the shadowy silhouette of Alexander's "Talayot" marking the border. Down behind, only the dying flare and the fading sound of running feet. I never saw one of the Sacred Seven again.

If you happen to be somewhere near the massive west windows at Gate 77C, Beirut International Airport, you can't help staring out at the magnificent sea. The vast, deep blue Mediterranean stretches far, far out to the west, to the north, to the south! It begs you to find Gilbraltar, 5000 miles to the west. I involuntarily stand on my tiptoes and, without thinking, my eyes sweep from the west to the north along the beach, past the low cliffs, past the white scar where the Coast Highway cuts into the city, over the scrubby pine and the sandstone ledges that mark probably the worst golf course on Earth, to the tall Engineering & Architecture School and the Main Gate of the American University.

I feel a sharp pain in my heart as my vision picks up. Yes, there it is!—"The lone cypress tree a thousand years old." Remember? It marks the crest of the cliff—the top of the path down to the water where my beloved Najua and I so often stood together and watched the sunset into the sea.

Two years and three months, yet it seems like yesterday. I have not been back to the university. First of all, none of my classmates are there anymore. They have all graduated, scattered back to their homelands—Syria, Iraq, Kuwait, Saudi and Egypt. Secondly, I knew when I originally was set free from Mazjid-Ghazu that I needed to stay away. Any story

I told here about where I had been for over a year would have to be a lie. I couldn't do that to Dr. Kurani, my faculty advisor or Najua, my beloved, who must have found a more reliable escort—or any of my professors, counselors or fellow students, most of whom had finished and gone home.

Next my mind reviews my year with the Mixed Armistice Commission at Amman, Jordan. I know the Air Force stuck me there for a year to sort of "use-up-time." Still, it was a godsend for me. It got me back into flying at an interesting job without tension. Plus, it was cover. I could now go home to family and service friends without fear of embarrassing questions.

But my beloved Najua! I simply had no idea how to face her. The unbelievable complex of adventures and fascinating adversities that bloomed out of my busting my assignment at Mosul had sort of scabbed over my heart. Whenever the vision came of Najua's soft, brown eyes, the wind in her hair, the sound of her laughter, I would have to force in a "covering thought." Usually I would need to sit down and deliberately choke back a storm of violent emotion. I was simply unable, during the whole year at Amman, to visualize how a "first meeting" with Najua would play out.

Well, how would you explain your disappearance to a girl you loved, whom you were planning to wed? Why you suddenly just dropped out. How?

Then there was always the shadow of fear. I knew if I saw her again, I would surely have to tell her the truth—a clear violation of my national trust. As a life professional, American fighting man, I flat could not risk that at any price.

Besides, the two years plus that have passed under the bridge were not just *two years*. I am no longer the same person who had so often stood under that cyprus tree holding Najua in my arms. I am no longer the serious, focused student that had studied so diligently in that quiet, old college library. The student that once sat in seminar with those serious, focused twenty-something Arab kids and dispassionately pondered creative options for solving the Arab-Jew charade, the Kashmir conundrum and the Kurdish claim to nation-state. I am not the same American who had paced off the length of this very airdrome where I stand and called in the coded numbers to VOA Vienna. And certainly the year-and-a-week in brotherhood with the "Sacred Seven" at the feet of Mullah-Din in the pitch darkness of the Mazjid-Ghazu has disqualified me from any normal, intimate relationship during this stretch of my journey on earth.

All things considered, I have to go home now. I've got to start over. I've got to redefine myself and reconstruct some life goals—and get back on the standard respectable climb. I'm thirty-something, and right now I feel like I've wasted a huge hunk of the peak of my ultimate manhood.

One last glance north at that incredible campus, one last memory-thought of my beloved Najua. She had whispered that funny story on our final watch together: "Honey, they say on a clear day at sunset, you can see Gibraltar—if you stand on your tiptoes." She giggled. I cried. We held each other close and watched the sun die, both on our tiptoes. Then we laughed and fled down the zig-zag trail to join schoolmates in the park. It was Friday.

I stuffed my handkerchief back into my rear pocket. To myself, out loud, "Get over it! Put it away!"

Something brushed my sleeve. "Strange, there is no crowd." Someone was standing very close beside me. Thin, rimless glasses, gray hair, gray suit, perhaps five-nine and smelling of Old Spice. He stared straight ahead, toward Gibraltar.

"Colby."

"I know."

There was an awkward pause. People were milling behind us at the gate creating busy airport noises in five languages. The TWA man called: "Flight 74 to Frankfort—all aboard, please."

Still staring west through the huge window, the gray suit spoke, "You're going home. Well, you got all but one—good job!"

People now begin shoving past the ticket girl—down the passageway toward the waiting 747.

Suddenly, Colby turned, gripped my hand, looked straight into my eyes. This was exactly as I remembered him behind the consulate when he had commissioned me to measure and report. His voice is low, now—barely audible—but the same steel-intense. "Don't forget—you are a national trust." He was gone.

My seat by the window was next to a huge, cigar-puffing Bavarian beer-belly. He spent the entire flight across Greece, across the Dolomites and across Austria describing—in German—his vital part as a *starter* in the coming Munich Olympics.